C++ Gotchas

Addison-Wesley Professional Computing Series

Brian W. Kernighan, Consulting Editor

Matthew H. Austern, *Generic Programming and the STL: Using and Extending the C++ Standard Template Library*

David R. Butenhof, *Programming with POSIX® Threads*

Brent Callaghan, *NFS Illustrated*

Tom Cargill, *C++ Programming Style*

William R. Cheswick/Steven M. Bellovin/Aviel D. Rubin, *Firewalls and Internet Security, Second Edition: Repelling the Wily Hacker*

David A. Curry, *UNIX® System Security: A Guide for Users and System Administrators*

Stephen C. Dewhurst, *C++ Gotchas: Avoiding Common Problems in Coding and Design*

Erich Gamma/Richard Helm/Ralph Johnson/John Vlissides, *Design Patterns: Elements of Reusable Object-Oriented Software*

Erich Gamma/Richard Helm/Ralph Johnson/John Vlissides, *Design Patterns CD: Elements of Reusable Object-Oriented Software*

Peter Haggar, *Practical Java™ Programming Language Guide*

David R. Hanson, *C Interfaces and Implementations: Techniques for Creating Reusable Software*

Mark Harrison/Michael McLennan, *Effective Tcl/Tk Programming: Writing Better Programs with Tcl and Tk*

Michi Henning/Steve Vinoski, *Advanced CORBA® Programming with C++*

Brian W. Kernighan/Rob Pike, *The Practice of Programming*

S. Keshav, *An Engineering Approach to Computer Networking: ATM Networks, the Internet, and the Telephone Network*

John Lakos, *Large-Scale C++ Software Design*

Scott Meyers, *Effective C++ CD: 85 Specific Ways to Improve Your Programs and Designs*

Scott Meyers, *Effective C++, Second Edition: 50 Specific Ways to Improve Your Programs and Designs*

Scott Meyers, *More Effective C++: 35 New Ways to Improve Your Programs and Designs*

Scott Meyers, *Effective STL: 50 Specific Ways to Improve Your Use of the Standard Template Library*

Robert B. Murray, *C++ Strategies and Tactics*

David R. Musser/Gillmer J. Derge/Atul Saini, *STL Tutorial and Reference Guide, Second Edition: C++ Programming with the Standard Template Library*

John K. Ousterhout, *Tcl and the Tk Toolkit*

Craig Partridge, *Gigabit Networking*

Radia Perlman, *Interconnections, Second Edition: Bridges, Routers, Switches, and Internetworking Protocols*

Stephen A. Rago, *UNIX® System V Network Programming*

Eric S. Raymond, *The Art of UNIX Programming*

Curt Schimmel, *UNIX® Systems for Modern Architectures: Symmetric Multiprocessing and Caching for Kernel Programmers*

W. Richard Stevens/Bill Fenner/Andrew M. Rudoff, *UNIX Network Programming Volume 1, Third Edition: The Sockets Networking API*

W. Richard Stevens, *Advanced Programming in the UNIX® Environment*

W. Richard Stevens, *TCP/IP Illustrated, Volume 1: The Protocols*

W. Richard Stevens, *TCP/IP Illustrated, Volume 3: TCP for Transactions, HTTP, NNTP, and the UNIX® Domain Protocols*

W. Richard Stevens/Gary R. Wright, *TCP/IP Illustrated Volumes 1-3 Boxed Set*

John Viega/Gary McGraw, *Building Secure Software: How to Avoid Security Problems the Right Way*

Gary R. Wright/W. Richard Stevens, *TCP/IP Illustrated, Volume 2: The Implementation*

Ruixi Yuan/ W. Timothy Strayer, *Virtual Private Networks: Technologies and Solutions*

Visit www.awprofessional.com/series/professionalcomputing for more information about these titles.

C++ Gotchas

Avoiding Common Problems
in Coding and Design

Stephen C. Dewhurst

⋏⋎ Addison-Wesley

Boston • San Francisco • New York • Toronto • Montreal
London • Munich • Paris • Madrid
Capetown • Sydney • Tokyo • Singapore • Mexico City

Many of the designations used by manufacturers and sellers to distinguish their products are claimed as trademarks. Where those designations appear in this book, and Addison-Wesley was aware of a trademark claim, the designations have been printed with initial capital letters or in all capitals.

The author and publisher have taken care in the preparation of this book, but make no expressed or implied warranty of any kind and assume no responsibility for errors or omissions. No liability is assumed for incidental or consequential damages in connection with or arising out of the use of the information or programs contained herein.

The publisher offers discounts on this book when ordered in quantity for bulk purchases and special sales. For more information, please contact:

U.S. Corporate and Government Sales
(800) 382-3419
corpsales@pearsontechgroup.com

For sales outside of the U.S., please contact:

International Sales
(317) 581-3793
international@pearsontechgroup.com

Visit Addison-Wesley on the Web: www.awprofessional.com

Library of Congress Cataloging-in-Publication Data
Dewhurst, Stephen C.
  C++ gotchas : avoiding common problems in coding and design / Stephen C. Dewhurst.
    p. cm—(Addison-Wesley professional computing series)
  Includes bibliographical references and index.
  ISBN 0-321-12518-5 (alk. paper)
  1. C++ (Computer program language) I. Title. II. Series.

QA76.73.C153 D488 2002
005.13'3—dc21

2002028191

ISBN 0-321-12518-5
Text printed on recycled paper
2 3 4 5 6 7 8 9 10—CRS—0807060504
Second printing, January 2004

To John Carolan

Contents

Preface   xi
Acknowledgments   xv

Chapter 1   Basics   1

Gotcha #1:   Excessive Commenting   1
Gotcha #2:   Magic Numbers   4
Gotcha #3:   Global Variables   6
Gotcha #4:   Failure to Distinguish Overloading from Default Initialization   8
Gotcha #5:   Misunderstanding References   10
Gotcha #6:   Misunderstanding Const   13
Gotcha #7:   Ignorance of Base Language Subtleties   14
Gotcha #8:   Failure to Distinguish Access and Visibility   19
Gotcha #9:   Using Bad Language   24
Gotcha #10:   Ignorance of Idiom   26
Gotcha #11:   Unnecessary Cleverness   29
Gotcha #12:   Adolescent Behavior   31

Chapter 2   Syntax   35

Gotcha #13:   Array/Initializer Confusion   35
Gotcha #14:   Evaluation Order Indecision   36
Gotcha #15:   Precedence Problems   42
Gotcha #16:   for Statement Debacle   45
Gotcha #17:   Maximal Munch Problems   48
Gotcha #18:   Creative Declaration-Specifier Ordering   50
Gotcha #19:   Function/Object Ambiguity   51
Gotcha #20:   Migrating Type-Qualifiers   52
Gotcha #21:   Self-Initialization   53
Gotcha #22:   Static and Extern Types   55
Gotcha #23:   Operator Function Lookup Anomaly   56
Gotcha #24:   Operator -> Subtleties   58

Chapter 3   The Preprocessor   61

Gotcha #25: `#define` Literals   61

Gotcha #26: `#define` Pseudofunctions   64

Gotcha #27: Overuse of `#if`   66

Gotcha #28: Side Effects in Assertions   72

Chapter 4   Conversions   75

Gotcha #29: Converting through `void *`   75

Gotcha #30: Slicing   79

Gotcha #31: Misunderstanding Pointer-to-Const Conversion   81

Gotcha #32: Misunderstanding Pointer-to-Pointer-to-Const Conversion   82

Gotcha #33: Misunderstanding Pointer-to-Pointer-to-Base Conversion   86

Gotcha #34: Pointer-to-Multidimensional-Array Problems   87

Gotcha #35: Unchecked Downcasting   89

Gotcha #36: Misusing Conversion Operators   90

Gotcha #37: Unintended Constructor Conversion   95

Gotcha #38: Casting under Multiple Inheritance   98

Gotcha #39: Casting Incomplete Types   100

Gotcha #40: Old-Style Casts   102

Gotcha #41: Static Casts   103

Gotcha #42: Temporary Initialization of Formal Arguments   106

Gotcha #43: Temporary Lifetime   110

Gotcha #44: References and Temporaries   112

Gotcha #45: Ambiguity Failure of `dynamic_cast`   116

Gotcha #46: Misunderstanding Contravariance   120

Chapter 5   Initialization   125

Gotcha #47: Assignment/Initialization Confusion   125

Gotcha #48: Improperly Scoped Variables   129

Gotcha #49: Failure to Appreciate C++'s Fixation on Copy Operations   132

Gotcha #50: Bitwise Copy of Class Objects   136

Gotcha #51: Confusing Initialization and Assignment in Constructors   139

Gotcha #52: Inconsistent Ordering of the Member Initialization List   141

Gotcha #53: Virtual Base Default Initialization   142

Gotcha #54: Copy Constructor Base Initialization   147

Gotcha #55: Runtime Static Initialization Order   150

Gotcha #56: Direct versus Copy Initialization   153

Gotcha #57: Direct Argument Initialization   156

Gotcha #58: Ignorance of the Return Value Optimizations   158

Gotcha #59: Initializing a Static Member in a Constructor   163

Chapter 6   **Memory and Resource Management**   **167**

Gotcha #60: Failure to Distinguish Scalar and Array Allocation   167

Gotcha #61: Checking for Allocation Failure   171

Gotcha #62: Replacing Global New and Delete   173

Gotcha #63: Confusing Scope and Activation of Member `new` and `delete`   176

Gotcha #64: Throwing String Literals   177

Gotcha #65: Improper Exception Mechanics   180

Gotcha #66: Abusing Local Addresses   185

Gotcha #67: Failure to Employ Resource Acquisition Is Initialization   190

Gotcha #68: Improper Use of `auto_ptr`   195

Chapter 7   **Polymorphism**   **199**

Gotcha #69: Type Codes   199

Gotcha #70: Nonvirtual Base Class Destructor   204

Gotcha #71: Hiding Nonvirtual Functions   209

Gotcha #72: Making Template Methods Too Flexible   212

Gotcha #73: Overloading Virtual Functions   214

Gotcha #74: Virtual Functions with Default Argument Initializers   216

Gotcha #75: Calling Virtual Functions in Constructors and Destructors   218

Gotcha #76: Virtual Assignment   220

Gotcha #77: Failure to Distinguish among Overloading, Overriding,
             and Hiding   224

Gotcha #78: Failure to Grok Virtual Functions and Overriding   230

Gotcha #79: Dominance Issues   236

Chapter 8   **Class Design**   **241**

Gotcha #80: Get/Set Interfaces   241

Gotcha #81: Const and Reference Data Members   245

Gotcha #82: Not Understanding the Meaning of Const Member Functions   248

Gotcha #83: Failure to Distinguish Aggregation and Acquaintance   253

Gotcha #84: Improper Operator Overloading   258

Gotcha #85: Precedence and Overloading   261

Gotcha #86: Friend versus Member Operators   262

Gotcha #87: Problems with Increment and Decrement   264

Gotcha #88: Misunderstanding Templated Copy Operations   268

Chapter 9   **Hierarchy Design**   **271**

Gotcha #89: Arrays of Class Objects   271

Gotcha #90: Improper Container Substitutability   273

Gotcha #91: Failure to Understand Protected Access   277

Gotcha #92: Public Inheritance for Code Reuse   281
Gotcha #93: Concrete Public Base Classes   285
Gotcha #94: Failure to Employ Degenerate Hierarchies   286
Gotcha #95: Overuse of Inheritance   287
Gotcha #96: Type-Based Control Structures   292
Gotcha #97: Cosmic Hierarchies   295
Gotcha #98: Asking Personal Questions of an Object   299
Gotcha #99: Capability Queries   302

Bibliography   307
Index   309

Preface

This book is the result of nearly two decades of minor frustrations, serious bugs, late nights, and weekends spent involuntarily at the keyboard. This collection consists of 99 of some of the more common, severe, or interesting C++ gotchas, most of which I have (I'm sorry to say) experienced personally.

The term "gotcha" has a cloudy history and a variety of definitions. For purposes of this book, we'll define C++ gotchas as common and preventable problems in C++ programming and design. The gotchas described here run the gamut from minor syntactic annoyances to basic design flaws to full-blown sociopathic behavior.

Almost ten years ago, I started including notes about individual gotchas in my C++ course material. My feeling was that pointing out these common misconceptions and misapplications in apposition to correct use would inoculate the student against them and help prevent new generations of C++ programmers from repeating the gotchas of the past. By and large, the approach worked, and I was induced to collect sets of related gotchas for presentation at conferences. These presentations proved to be popular (misery loves company?), and I was encouraged to write a "gotcha" book.

Any discussion of avoiding or recovering from C++ gotchas involves other subjects, most commonly design patterns, idioms, and technical details of C++ language features.

This is not a book about design patterns, but we often find ourselves referring to patterns as a means of avoiding or recovering from a particular gotcha. Conventionally, the pattern name is capitalized, as in "Template Method" pattern or "Bridge" pattern. When we mention a pattern, we describe its mechanics briefly if they're simple but delegate detailed discussion of patterns to works devoted to them. Unless otherwise noted, a fuller description of a pattern, as well as a richer discussion of patterns in general, may be found in Erich Gamma et al.'s *Design Patterns*. Descriptions of the Acyclic Visitor, Monostate, and Null Object patterns may be found in Robert Martin's *Agile Software Development*.

From the perspective of gotchas, design patterns have two important properties. First, they describe proven, successful design techniques that can be customized in a context-dependent way to new design situations. Second, and perhaps more important, mentioning the application of a particular pattern serves to document not only the technique applied but also the reasons for its application and the effect of having applied it.

For example, when we see that the Bridge pattern has been applied to a design, we know at a mechanical level that an abstract data type implementation has been separated into an interface class and an implementation class. Additionally, we know this was done to separate strongly the interface from the implementation, so changes to the implementation won't affect users of the interface. We also know this separation entails a runtime cost, how the source code for the abstract data type should be arranged, and many other details.

A pattern name is an efficient, unambiguous handle to a wealth of information and experience about a technique. Careful, accurate use of patterns and pattern terminology in design and documentation clarifies code and helps prevent gotchas from occurring.

C++ is a complex programming language, and the more complex a language, the more important is the use of idiom in programming. For a programming language, an idiom is a commonly used and generally understood combination of lower-level language features that produces a higher-level construct, in much the same way patterns do at higher levels of design. Therefore, in C++ we can discuss copy operations, function objects, smart pointers, and throwing an exception without having to specify these concepts at their lowest level of implementation.

It's important to emphasize that an idiom is not only a common combination of language features but also a common set of expectations about how these combined features should behave. What do copy operations mean? What can we expect to happen when an exception is thrown? Much of the advice found in this book involves being aware of and employing idioms in C++ coding and design. Many of the gotchas listed here could be described simply as departing from a particular C++ idiom, and the accompanying solution to the problem could often be described simply as following the appropriate idiom (see Gotcha #10).

A significant portion of this book is spent describing the nuances of certain areas of the C++ language that are commonly misunderstood and frequently lead to gotchas. While some of this material may have an esoteric feel to it, unfamiliarity with these areas is a source of problems and a barrier to expert use of C++. These "dark corners" also make an interesting and profitable study in themselves. They are in C++ for a reason, and expert C++ programmers often find use for them in advanced programming and design.

Another area of connection between gotchas and design patterns is the similar importance of describing relatively simple instances. Simple patterns are important. In some respects, they may be more important than technically difficult patterns, because they're likely to be more commonly employed. The benefits obtained from the pattern description will, therefore, be leveraged over a larger body of code and design.

In much the same way, the gotchas described in this book cover a wide range of difficulty, from a simple exhortation to act like a responsible professional (Gotcha #12) to warnings to avoid misunderstanding the dominance rule under virtual inheritance (Gotcha #79). But, as in the analogous case with patterns, acting responsibly is probably more commonly applicable on a day-to-day basis than is the dominance rule.

Two common themes run through the presentation. The first is the overriding importance of convention. This is especially important in a complex language like C++. Adherence to established convention allows us to communicate efficiently and accurately with others. The second theme is the recognition that others will maintain the code we write. The maintenance may be direct, so that our code must be readily and generally understood by competent maintainers, or it may be indirect, in which case we must ensure that our code remains correct even as its behavior is modified by remote changes.

The gotchas in this book are presented as a collection of short essays, each of which describes a gotcha or set of related gotchas, along with suggestions for avoiding or correcting them. I'm not sure any book about gotchas can be entirely cohesive, due to the anarchistic nature of the subject. However, the gotchas are grouped into chapters according to their general nature or area of (mis)applicability.

Additionally, discussion of one gotcha inevitably touches on others. Where it makes sense to do so—and it generally does—I've made these links explicit. Cohesion within each item is sometimes at risk as well. Often it's necessary, before getting to the description of a gotcha, to describe the context in which it appears. That description, in turn, may require discussion of a technique, idiom, pattern, or language nuance that may lead us even further afield before we return to the advertised gotcha. I've tried to keep this meandering to a minimum, but it would have been dishonest, I think, to attempt to avoid it entirely. Effective programming in C++ involves intelligent coordination of so many disparate areas that it's impractical to imagine one can examine its etiology effectively without involving a similar eclectic collection of topics.

It's certainly not necessary—and possibly inadvisable—to read this book straight through, from Gotcha #1 to Gotcha #99. Such a concentrated dose of mayhem may put you off programming in C++ altogether. A better approach may be to start with a gotcha you've experienced or that sounds interesting and follow links to related gotchas. Alternatively, you may sample the gotchas at random.

The text employs a number of devices intended to clarify the presentation. First, incorrect or inadvisable code is indicated by a gray background, whereas correct and proper code is presented with no background. Second, code that appears in the text has been edited for brevity and clarity. As a result, the examples as presented often won't compile without additional, supporting code. The source code for nontrivial examples is available from the author's Web site: www.semantics.org. All such code is indicated in the text by an abbreviated pathname near the code example, as in ➤➤ gotcha00/somecode.cpp.

Finally, a warning: the one thing you should not do with gotchas is elevate them to the same status as idioms or patterns. One of the signs that you're using patterns and idioms properly is that the pattern or idiom appropriate to the design or coding context will arise "spontaneously" from your subconscious just when you need it.

Recognition of a gotcha is analogous to a conditioned response to danger: once burned, twice shy. However, as with matches and firearms, it's not necessary to suffer a burn or a gunshot wound to the head personally to learn how to recognize and avoid a dangerous situation; generally, all that's necessary is advance warning. Consider this collection a means to keep your head in the face of C++ gotchas.

Stephen C. Dewhurst
Carver, Massachusetts
July 2002

Acknowledgments

Editors often get short shrift in a book's acknowledgments, sometimes receiving only a token ". . . and I also thank my editor, who surely must have been doing something while I was slaving over the manuscript." Debbie Lafferty, my editor, is responsible for the existence of this book. When I came to her with a mediocre proposal for a mediocre introductory programming text, she instead suggested expanding a section on gotchas into a book. I refused. She persisted. She won. Fortunately, Debbie is gracious in victory, and she has yet to utter an editorial "We told you so." Additionally, she surely must have been doing something while I slaved over the manuscript.

I would also like to thank the reviewers who lent their time and expertise to help make this a better book. Reviewing an unpolished manuscript is a time-consuming, often tedious, sometimes irritating, and nearly thankless task of professional courtesy (see Gotcha #12), and the reviewers' insightful and incisive comments were much appreciated. Steve Clamage, Thomas Gschwind, Brian Kernighan, Patrick McKillen, Jeffrey Oldham, Dan Saks, Matthew Wilson, and Leor Zolman contributed advice on technical issues and social propriety, corrections, code snippets, and an occasional snide remark.

Leor started review long before the manuscript was written, by sending me barbed comments on Web postings that were early versions of some of the gotchas appearing in this book. Sarah Hewins, my best friend and severest critic, earned both titles while reviewing various versions of the manuscript. David R. Dewhurst frequently put the entire project into perspective. Greg Comeau lent use of his marvelously standard C++ compiler for checking the code.

Like any nontrivial work about C++, this book is an amalgam of the work of many people. Over the years, many of my students, clients, and colleagues have augmented my unhappy facility for stumbling across C++ gotchas, and many of them have helped find solutions for them. While most of these contributions can no longer be acknowledged explicitly, it is possible to acknowledge more direct contributions:

The `Select` template of Gotcha #11 and the `OpNewCreator` policy of Gotcha #70 appear in Andrei Alexandrescu's *Modern C++ Design*.

I first encountered the problem of returning a reference to constant argument, described in Gotcha #44, in Cline et al.'s *C++ FAQs* (it began to appear in my clients' code immediately thereafter). Cline et al. also describe the technique mentioned in Gotcha #73 for circumventing overloaded virtual functions.

The `Cptr` template of Gotcha #83 is a modified version of the `CountedPtr` template that appeared in Nicolai Josuttis's *The C++ Standard Library*.

Scott Meyers has more to say about the improper overloading of operators `&&`, `||`, and `,`, described in Gotcha #14, in his *More Effective C++*. He describes in more detail the necessity of value return from a binary operator, as discussed in Gotcha #58, in *Effective C++* and describes the improper use of `auto_ptr`, treated in Gotcha #68, in *Effective STL*. The technique, mentioned in Gotcha #87, of returning a const from postfix increment and decrement operators is described in his *More Effective C++*.

Dan Saks presented the first cogent arguments I had heard for the forward declaration file approach described in Gotcha #8; he was also the first to identify the "Sergeant operator" of Gotcha #17, and he convinced me not to range-check increment and decrement on enum types, mentioned in Gotcha #87.

Herb Sutter's *More Exceptional C++*, Item 36, caused me to reread section 8.5 of the standard and update my understanding of formal argument initialization (see Gotcha #57).

Some of the material of Gotchas #10, #27, #32, #33, #38–#41, #70, #72–#74, #89, #90, #98, and #99 appeared in my "Common Knowledge" column that ran initially in *C++ Report* and later in *The C/C++ Users Journal*.

1 | Basics

That a problem is basic does not mean it isn't severe or common. In fact, the common presence of the basic problems discussed in this chapter is perhaps more cause for alarm than the more technically advanced problems we discuss in later chapters. The basic nature of the problems discussed here implies that they may be present, to some extent, in almost all C++ code.

Gotcha #1: Excessive Commenting

Many comments are unnecessary. They generally make source code hard to read and maintain, and frequently lead maintainers astray. Consider the following simple statement:

```
a = b;  // assign b to a
```

The comment cannot communicate the meaning of the statement more clearly than the code itself, and so is useless. Actually, it's worse than useless. It's deadly. First, the comment distracts the reader from the code, increasing the volume of text the reader has to wade through in order to extract its meaning. Second, there is more source text to maintain, since comments must be maintained as the program text they describe is modified. Third, this necessary maintenance is often not performed.

```
c = b; // assign b to a
```

A careful maintainer cannot simply assume the comment is in error and is obliged to trace through the program to determine whether the comment is erroneous, officious (c is a reference to a), or subtle (assigning to c will later cause the same assignment to be propagated to a somehow). The line should originally have been written without a comment:

```
a = b;
```

The code is maximally clear as it stands, with no comment to be incorrectly maintained. This is similar in spirit to the well-worn observation that the most efficient code is code that doesn't exist. The same applies to comments: the best comment is one that didn't have to be written, because the code it would otherwise have described is self-documenting.

Other common examples of unnecessary comments frequently occur in class definitions, either as the result of an ill-conceived coding standard or as the work of a C++ novice:

```
class C {
  // Public Interface
  public:
    C(); // default constructor
    ~C(); // destructor
    // . . .
};
```

You get the feeling you're reading someone's crib notes. If a maintainer has to be reminded of the meaning of the `public:` label, you don't want that person maintaining your code. None of these comments does anything for an experienced C++ programmer except clutter the code and provide more source text to be improperly maintained.

```
class C {
  // Public Interface
  protected:
    C( int ); // default constructor
  public:
    virtual ~C(); // destructor
    // . . .
};
```

Programmers also have a strong incentive not to "waste" lines of source text. Anecdotally, if a construct (function, public interface of a class, and so on) can be presented in a conventional and rational format on a single "page" of about 30–40 lines, it will be easy to understand. If it goes on to a second page, it will be about twice as hard to understand. If it goes onto a third page, it will be approximately four times as hard to understand.

A particularly odious practice is that of inserting change logs as comments at the head or tail of source code files:

```
/* 6/17/02 SCD fixed the gaforniflat bug */
```

Is this useful information, or is the maintainer just bragging? This comment is unlikely to be of any use whatever within a week or two of its insertion, but it will hang on grimly for years, distracting generations of maintainers. A much better alternative is to cede these commenting tasks to your version control software; a C++ source code file is no place to leave a laundry list.

One of the best ways to avoid comments and make code clear and maintainable is to follow a simple, well-defined naming convention and choose clear names that reflect the abstract meaning of the entity (function, class, variable, and so on) you're naming. Formal argument names in declarations are particularly important. Consider a function that takes three arguments of identical type:

```
/*
  Perform the action from the source to the destination.
  Arg1 is action code, arg2 is source, and arg3 is destination.
*/
void perform( int, int, int );
```

Not too terrible, but think what it would look like with seven or eight arguments instead of three. We can do better:

```
void perform( int actionCode, int source, int destination );
```

Better, though we should probably still have a one-liner that tells us what the function does (though not how it does it). One of the most attractive things about formal argument names in declarations is that they, unlike comments, are generally maintained along with the rest of the code, even though they have no effect on the code's meaning. I can't think of a single programmer who would switch the meanings of the second and third arguments of the `perform` function without also changing their names, but I can identify legions of programmers who would make the change without maintaining the comment.

Kathy Stark may have said it best in *Programming in C++*: "If meaningful and mnemonic names are used in a program, there is often only occasional need for additional comments. If meaningful names are not used, it is unlikely that any added comments will make the code easy to understand."

Another way to minimize comments is to employ standard or well-known components:

```
printf( "Hello, World!" ); // print "Hello, World" to the screen
```

This comment is both useless and only occasionally correct. It's not that standard components are necessarily self-documenting; it's that they're already well documented and well known.

```
swap( a, a+1 );
sort( a, a+max );
copy( a, a+max, ostream_iterator<T>(cout,"\n") );
```

Because `swap`, `sort`, and `copy` are standard components, additional comments inserted above can only clutter the source and introduce imprecision in the description of the standard operations.

Comments are not inherently harmful—and are often necessary—but they must be maintained, and they're typically harder to maintain than the code they document. Comments should not state the obvious or provide information better maintained elsewhere. The goal is not to eliminate comments at any cost but to employ the minimal volume of comments that permits the code to be readily understood and maintained.

Gotcha #2: Magic Numbers

Magic numbers, in the sense used here, are raw numeric literals used in contexts where named constants should be used instead:

```
class Portfolio {
    // . . .
    Contract *contracts_[10];
    char id_[10];
};
```

The main problem with magic numbers is that they have no semantic content to speak of; they are what they are. A `10` is a `10`, not a maximum number of contracts or the length of an identifier. Therefore we're obliged, when reading or maintaining code that employs magic numbers, to determine the intended meaning of each raw literal. That's work, and it's unnecessary and often inaccurate work.

For example, our poorly designed portfolio above can manage a maximum of ten contracts. That's not a lot of contracts, so we may decide to increase it to 32. (If we had any concern about safety and correctness, we'd use a standard `vector`.) The trouble is that we're now obliged to examine every source file that uses `Portfolio` for each occurrence of the literal `10`, to decide if that `10` means maximum number of contracts.

Actually, the situation can be worse. In large and long-lived projects, sometimes word gets out that the maximum number of contracts is ten, and this knowledge becomes embedded in code that doesn't even indirectly include the Portfolio header file:

```
for( int i = 0; i < 10; ++i )
    // . . .
```

Does this literal 10 refer to the maximum number of contracts? The length of an identifier? Something unrelated?

The chance confluence of raw literals can sometimes bring out the worst coding tendencies in programmers:

```
if( Portfolio *p = getPortfolio() )
    for( int i = 0; i < 10; ++i )
        p->contracts_[i] = 0, p->id_[i] = '\0';
```

Now the maintainer has to somehow tease apart the initializations of the different components of a Portfolio that would not have been combined but for the chance coincidence of the values of two distinct concepts. There is really no excuse for provoking all this complexity when the solution is so simple:

```
class Portfolio {
    // . . .
    enum { maxContracts = 10, idlen = 10 };
    Contract *contracts_[maxContracts];
    char id_[idlen];
};
```

Enumerators consume no space and cost nothing in runtime while providing clear, properly scoped names of the concepts for which they stand.

Less obvious disadvantages of magic numbers include the potential for imprecision in their types and the lack of associated storage. The type of the literal 40000, for instance, is platform dependent. If the value 40000 can fit into an integer, its type is int. Otherwise, it's a long. If we don't want to leave ourselves open to obscure problems (like overload resolution ambiguities) when porting from platform to platform, it's probably best to say precisely what we mean rather than letting the compiler/platform combination decide for us:

```
const long patienceLimit = 40000;
```

Another potential problem with literals is that they have no address. This is not a common problem, but it is nevertheless occasionally useful to be able to point to or bind a reference to a constant:

```
const long *p1 = &40000; // error!
const long *p2 = &patienceLimit; // OK.
const long &r1 = 40000; // legal, but see Gotcha #44
const long &r2 = patienceLimit; // OK.
```

Magic numbers offer no advantage and many disadvantages. Use enumerators or initialized constants instead.

Gotcha #3:   Global Variables

There is rarely an excuse for declaring a "raw" global variable. Global variables impede code reuse and make code hard to maintain. They impede reuse because any code that refers to a global variable is coupled to it and may not be reused without being accompanied by the global variable. They make code hard to maintain because it's difficult to determine what code is using a particular global variable, since any code at all has access to it.

Global variables increase coupling among components, because they often end up as a kind of primitive message-passing mechanism. Even if global variables work, it's often a practical impossibility to remove them from a large piece of software. If they work. Because global variables are essentially unprotected, any novice maintainer can trash the behavior of your global-dependent software at any time.

Users of global variables often cite convenience as a reason for using them. This is a fallacious or self-serving argument, because maintenance typically consumes more time than initial development, and use of global variables impedes maintenance. Suppose we have a system that requires access to a globally accessible "environment," of which (we're promised by our requirements) there is always exactly one. Unfortunately, we choose to use a global variable:

```
extern Environment * const theEnv;
```

Requirements live but to lie. Shortly before delivery, we'll find that the number of possible, simultaneous environments has increased to two. Or maybe three. Or maybe the number is set on startup. Or is totally dynamic. The usual last-minute change. In a large project with meticulous source-control procedures in place, it can be a time-consuming process to change every file, even in a minimal and straightforward manner. It could take days or weeks. If we had avoided the use of a global variable, it would take five minutes:

```
Environment *theEnv();
```

Simply wrapping access in a function permits extension through the use of over-loading or default argument initialization without the necessity of significant change to source code:

```
Environment *theEnv( EnvCode whichEnv = OFFICIAL );
```

Another, less obvious, problem with global variables is that they often require runtime static initialization. If a static variable's initial value can't be calculated at compile time, the initialization will take place at runtime, often with disastrous consequences (see Gotcha #55):

```
extern Environment * const theEnv = new OfficialEnv;
```

If a function or class guards access to the global information, the setting of the initial value can be delayed until it's safe to do so:

➤➤ gotcha03/environment.h

```
class Environment {
 public:
    static Environment &instance();
    virtual void op1() = 0;
    // . . .
 protected:
    Environment();
    virtual ~Environment();
 private:
    static Environment *instance_;
    // . . .
};
```

➤➤ gotcha03/environment.cpp

```
// . . .
Environment *Environment::instance_ = 0;

Environment &Environment::instance() {
    if( !instance_ )
        instance_ = new OfficialEnv;
    return *instance_;
}
```

In this case, we've employed a simple implementation of the Singleton pattern to perform lazy "initialization" (actually, to be technically precise, it's assignment) of the static environment pointer and thereby ensure that there is never more than a single Environment object. Note that Environment has no public constructor, so users of Environment must go through the instance member to gain access to the static pointer, allowing us to delay creation of the Environment object until the first request for access:

```
Environment::instance().op1();
```

More important, this controlled access provides flexibility to adapt the Singleton to future requirements without affecting existing source code. Later, if we go to a multithreaded design or decide to permit multiple environments, or whatever, we can modify the implementation of the Singleton, just as we modified the wrapper function earlier.

Avoid global variables. Safer and more flexible mechanisms are available to achieve the same results.

Gotcha #4: Failure to Distinguish Overloading from Default Initialization

Function overloading has little to do with default argument initialization. However, these two distinct language features are sometimes confused, because they can be used to produce interfaces whose syntax of use is similar. Nevertheless, the meanings of the interfaces are quite different:

➤➤ gotcha04/c12.h

```
class C1 {
  public:
    void f1( int arg = 0 );
    // . . .
};
```

➤➤ gotcha04/c12.cpp

```
// . . .
C1 a;
a.f1(0);
a.f1();
```

The designer of class C1 has decided to employ a default argument initializer in the declaration of the operation f1. Therefore the user of C1 has the option of invoking the member function f1 with an explicit single argument or with an implicit single argument of 0. In the two calls to C1::f1 above, the calling sequences produced are identical.

➤➤ gotcha04/c12.h

```
class C2 {
 public:
    void f2();
    void f2( int );
    // . . .
};
```

➤➤ gotcha04/c12.cpp

```
// . . .
C2 a;
a.f2(0);
a.f2();
```

The implementation of C2 is quite different. The user has the choice of invoking two entirely different functions named f2, depending on the number of arguments passed. In our earlier example, the meanings of the two calls were identical. Here they're completely different, because they invoke different functions.

An even greater difference between the two interfaces is evident if we try to take the address of the class members C1::f1 and C2::f2:

➤➤ gotcha04/c12.cpp

```
void (C1::*pmf)() = &C1::f1; //error!
void (C2::*pmf)() = &C2::f2;
```

With our implementation of class C2, the pointer to member pmf will refer to the f2 that takes no argument. The variable pmf is a pointer to member function that takes no argument, so the compiler will correctly choose the first member f2 as the initializer. With class C1, we'll get a compile-time error, because only one member function is named f1, and that function takes an integer argument.

Overloading is generally used to indicate that a set of functions has common abstract meaning but different implementations. Default initialization is generally used for convenience, to provide a simplified interface to a function. Overloading and default argument initializers are distinct language features with different intended purposes and behavior. Distinguish them carefully. (See also Gotchas #73 and #74.)

Gotcha #5: Misunderstanding References

There are two common problems with references. First, they're often confused with pointers. Second, they're underused. Many current uses of pointers in C++ are really C holdovers that should be ceded to references.

A reference is not a pointer. A reference is an alias for its initializer. Essentially, the only thing one can do with a reference is initialize it. After that, it's simply another way of referring to its initializer. (But see Gotcha #44.) A reference doesn't have an address, and it's even possible that it might not occupy any storage:

```
int a = 12;
int &ra = a;
int *ip = &ra; // ip refers to a
a = 42; // ra == 42
```

For this reason, it's illegal to attempt to declare a reference to a reference, a pointer to a reference, or an array of references. (Though the C++ standards committee has discussed allowing references to references in the future, at least in some contexts.)

```
int &&rri = ra; // error!
int &*pri; // error!
int &ar[3]; // error!
```

References can't be `const` or `volatile`, because aliases can't be `const` or `volatile`, though a reference can refer to an entity that is const or volatile. An attempt to declare a reference `const` or `volatile` directly is an error:

```
int &const cri = a; // should be an error . . .
const int &rci = a; // OK
```

Strangely, it's not illegal to apply a `const` or `volatile` qualifier to a type name that is of reference type. Rather than cause an error, in this case the qualifier is ignored:

```
typedef int *PI;
typedef int &RI;
const PI p = 0; // const pointer
const RI r = a; // just a reference!
```

There are no null references, and there are no references to void:

```
C *p = 0; // a null pointer
C &rC = *p; // undefined behavior
extern void &rv; // error!
```

A reference is an alias, and an alias has to refer to something.

Note, however, that a reference does not have to refer to a simple variable name. It's sometimes convenient to bind a reference to an lvalue (see Gotcha #6) resulting from a more complex expression:

```
int &el = array[n-6][m-2];
el = el*n-3;
string &name = p->info[n].name;
if( name == "Joe" )
    process( name );
```

A reference return from a function allows assignment to the result of a call. The canonical example of this is an index function for an abstract array:

➤➤ gotcha05/array.h

```
template <typename T, int n>
class Array {
 public:
    T &operator [](int i)
        { return a_[i]; }
    const T &operator [](int i) const
        { return a_[i]; }
    // . . .
 private:
    T a_[n];
};
```

The reference return permits a natural syntax for assignment to an array element:

```
Array<int,12> ia;
ia[3] = ia[0];
```

References may also be used to provide additional return values for functions:

```
Name *lookup( const string &id, Failure &reason );
// . . .
string ident;
// . . .
Failure reasonForFailure;
if( Name *n = lookup( ident, reasonForFailure ) ) {
    // lookup succeeded . . .
}
else {
    // lookup failed. check reason . . .
}
```

Casting an object to a reference type has a very different effect from the same cast to the nonreference version of the type:

```
char *cp = reinterpret_cast<char *>(a);
reinterpret_cast<char *&>(a) = cp;
```

In the first case, we're converting an integer into a pointer. (We're using `reinterpret_cast` in preference to an old-style cast, like `(char *)a`. See Gotcha #40.) The result is a copy of the integer's value, interpreted as a pointer.

The second cast is very different. The result of the cast to reference type is a reinterpretation of the integer object itself as a pointer. It's an lvalue, and we can assign to it. (Whether we will then dump core is another story. Use of `reinterpret_cast` generally implies "not portable.") An analogous attempt with a cast to nonreference will fail, because the result of the cast is an rvalue, not an lvalue:

```
reinterpret_cast<char *>(a) = 0; // error!
```

A reference to an array preserves the array bound. A pointer to an array does not:

```
int ary[12];
int *pary = ary; // point to first element
int (&rary)[12] = ary; // refer to whole array
int ary2[3][4];
int (*pary2)[4] = ary2; // point to first element
int (&rary2)[3][4] = ary2; // refer to whole array
```

This property can be of occasional use when passing arrays to functions. (See Gotcha #34.)

It's also possible to bind a reference to a function:

```
int f( double );
int (* const pf)(double) = f; // const pointer to function
int (&rf)(double) = f; // reference to function
```

There's not much practical difference between a constant pointer to function and a reference to function, except that the pointer can be explicitly dereferenced. As an alias, the reference cannot, although it can be converted implicitly into a pointer to function and then dereferenced:

```
a = pf( 12.3 ); // use pointer
a = (*pf)(12.3); // use pointer
a = rf( 12.3 ); // use reference
a = f( 12.3 ); // use function
a = (*rf)(12.3); // convert ref to pointer and deref
a = (*f)(12.3); // convert func to pointer and deref
```

Distinguish references and pointers.

Gotcha #6: Misunderstanding Const

The concept of constness in C++ is simple, but it doesn't necessarily correspond to our preconceived notions of a constant.

First, note the difference between a variable declared const and a literal:

```
int i = 12;
const int ci = 12;
```

The integer literal 12 is not a const. It's a literal. It has no address, and its value never changes. The integer i is an object. It has an address, and its value is variable. The const integer ci is also an object. It has an address, though (in this case) its value may not vary.

We say that i and ci may be used as lvalues, whereas the literal 12 may only be an rvalue. This terminology comes from the pseudoexpression $L = R$, indicating that an lvalue may appear as the left argument of an assignment and an rvalue may appear only as the right argument of an assignment. However, this definition is not perfectly applicable in the case of C++ or standard C, where ci is an lvalue but may not be assigned to because it's a nonmodifiable lvalue. Consider lvalues as locations that may hold values, and rvalues as simple values with no associated address:

```
int *ip1 = &12; // error!
12 = 13; // error!
const int *ip2 = &ci; // OK
ci = 13; // error!
```

It's best to consider const, in the declaration of ip2 above, a restriction on how we may manipulate ci through ip2 rather than on how ci may be manipulated in general. Consider declaring a pointer to a const:

```
const int *ip3 = &i;
i = 10; // OK
*ip3 = 10; // error!
```

Here, we have a pointer to a constant integer that refers to a non-constant integer. The use of const in this case is simply a restriction on how ip3 may be used. It doesn't imply that i won't change, only that we may not change it through ip3. Even subtler are combinations of const and volatile:

```
extern const volatile time_t clock;
```

The presence of the const qualifier indicates that we're not allowed to modify the variable clock, but the presence of the volatile qualifier indicates that the value of clock may (that is, will) change nonetheless.

Gotcha #7: Ignorance of Base Language Subtleties

Most C++ programmers are confident that they're fully familiar with what might be considered the C++ "base language": that part of C++ inherited from C. However, even experienced C++ programmers are sometimes ignorant of the more abstruse details of these basic C/C++ statements and operators.

The logical operators are not what one would ordinarily consider abstruse, but they seem to be increasingly underutilized by new C++ programmers. Isn't it irritating to see code like this?

```
bool r = false;
if( a < b )
   r = true;
```

Instead of this?

```
bool r = a<b;
```

Do you have to count to eight when presented with the following?

➤➤ gotcha07/bool.cpp

```
int ctr = 0;
for( int i = 0; i < 8; ++i )
   if( options & 1<<(8+i) )
       if( ctr++ ) {
           cerr << "Too many options selected";
           break;
       }
```

Instead of this?

➤➤ gotcha07/bool.cpp

```
typedef unsigned short Bits;
inline Bits repeated( Bits b, Bits m )
   { return b & m & (b & m)-1; }
// . . .
if( repeated( options, 0XFF00 ) )
   cerr << "Too many options selected";
```

What ever happened to Boolean logic?

Likewise, many programmers are ignorant of the fact that the result of a conditional operator is an lvalue (see Gotcha #6) if both its potential results are lvalues. This ignorance necessitates code like the following:

```
// version #1
if( a < b )
   a = val();
else if( b < c )
   b = val();
else
   c = val();
```

```
// version #2
a<b ? (a = val()) : b<c ? (b = val()) : (c = val());
```

An alternative solution with an lvalue conditional is definitely shorter and undeniably cooler:

```
// version #3
(a<b?a:b<c?b:c) = val();
```

While this piece of esoteric knowledge may not seem as immediately relevant as a sound appreciation of Boolean logic, many contexts in C++ allow only expressions (constructor member-initialization-lists, throw-expressions, and so on).

Additionally, note that the call to the entity val occurs multiple times in versions #1 and #2, whereas it appears only once in version #3. If val is a function, this is of little importance. However, if val is a preprocessor macro, the presence of multiple expansions may produce incorrect side effects (see Gotcha #26). In these contexts, the availability of an effective conditional operator as a substitute for an if-statement can be essential. Effectively, while I do not recommend that this construct be commonly used, I do recommend that it be commonly known. It should be available to the expert C++ programmer for those rare occasions when its use is required or preferable to other constructs. It's part of the C++ language for a reason.

Surprisingly, even the predefined index operator is often misunderstood. We all know that both array names and pointers may be indexed:

```
int ary[12];
int *p = &ary[5];
p[2] = 7;
```

The predefined index operator is just a shorthand for some pointer arithmetic and a dereference. The expression p[2] above is entirely equivalent to *(p+2). Most C++ programmers with a C background are also aware that it's legal to use negative indexes, so the expression p[-2] is well defined and equivalent to *(p-2) or, if you prefer, *(p+-2). However, it doesn't seem to be common knowledge that addition is commutative, since most C++ programmers are surprised to find that it's legal to index an integer with a pointer:

```
(-2)[p] = 6;
```

It's a simple transformation: p[-2] is equivalent to *(p+-2), which is equivalent to *(-2+p), which is equivalent to (-2)[p] (we need the parentheses because [] has higher precedence than unary minus).

What's the use of this bit of trivia? Well, for one thing, note that this commutativity of the index operator applies only to its predefined use with pointers. That is, if we see an expression like 6[p], we know we're dealing with the predefined index operator rather than with an overloaded member operator [] (though p is not necessarily a pointer or array). It's also terrific when conversation lags at cocktail parties. However, before employing this syntax in production code, review Gotcha #11.

Most C++ programmers know that a switch-statement is pretty basic. They just don't know how basic. The abstract syntax of the switch-statement is simple:

```
switch( expression ) statement
```

The implications of this simple syntax are sometimes surprising.

Typically, the substatement that follows the switch expression is a block. Within the block is a set of case labels that implement basically a computed goto to a statement within the block. The first subtlety that new C and C++ programmers face is the concept of "fallthrough." That is, unlike many other modern programming languages, after a switch branches to the proper case label, its work is done. Where execution leads after that is totally up to the programmer:

```
switch( e ) {
default:
theDefault:
    cout << "default" << endl;
    // fallthrough . . .
case 'a':
case 0:
    cout << "group 1" << endl;
    break;
case max-15:
case Select<(MAX>12),A,B>::Result::value:
    cout << "group 2" << endl;
    goto theDefault;
}
```

Conventionally, whenever fallthrough is used on purpose—as opposed to its more typical inadvertent use—we insert a comment to indicate to future maintainers that we actually intended the fallthrough. Otherwise, maintainers have a tendency to insert inappropriate breaks.

Note that the case labels must be integer constant-expressions. In other words, the compiler must be able to determine their values at compile time. However, as the somewhat flaky example above shows, there is quite a lot of leeway in how constant expressions may be defined. The case expression itself must be integral, or it may be an object with a conversion to an integral type. For example, e could be the name of a class object that declares a conversion operator to an integral type.

Note that the abstract syntax of the switch implies that it's even less structured than our example above implies. In particular, the case labels may appear anywhere within the switch-statement, and not necessarily at the same level:

```
switch( expr )
   default:
   if( cond1 ) {
        case 1: stmt1;
        case 2: stmt2;
   }
   else {
        if( cond2 )
            case 3:stmt2;
        else
            case 0: ;
   }
```

This may look a bit silly (it is, actually), but these more esoteric aspects of the base language can be useful on occasion. The above property of the switch, for instance, has been used to implement efficient external iteration of a complex data structure for a C++ compiler:

➤➤ gotcha07/iter.cpp

```
bool Postorder::next() {
   switch( pc )
   case START:
   while( true )
       if( !lchild() ) {
           pc = LEAF;
           return true;
```

```
    case LEAF:
          while( true )
            if( sibling() )
                break;
            else
                if( parent() ) {
                    pc = INNER;
                    return true;
    case INNER:   ;
                }
                else {
                    pc = DONE;
    case DONE:    return false;
                }
        }
    }
```

In the above code, we were able to use the esoteric semantics of the lowly switch-statement to implement coroutine semantics for the next tree traversal operation.

I've received strong, negative, and sometimes abusive reactions to my use of every one of the constructs above. I do agree this is not necessarily the kind of code you'd want to unleash on a novice maintainer, but such constructs—suitably encapsulated and with accompanying documentation—do have an occasional place in highly tuned or highly specialized code. Familiarity with the esoterica of the base language can be useful.

Gotcha #8:   Failure to Distinguish Access and Visibility

The C++ language does not implement data hiding; it implements access protection. Private and protected members of a class are not invisible, just inaccessible. Like many other visible but inaccessible objects (managers come to mind), they can cause problems.

The most obvious problem is the need to recompile code that uses a class even though only an "invisible" aspect of its implementation has changed. Consider a simple class that has added a new data member:

```
class C {
  public:
    C( int val ) : a_( val ),
```

```
                b_( a_ ) // new
   {}
   int get_a() const { return a_; }
   int get_b() const { return b_; } // new
 private:
   int b_; // new
   int a_;
};
```

In this case, a number of aspects of the class have changed, some of which are visible and some of which are not.

Visibly, the size of the class has changed, due to the addition of the new data member. This will affect all code that uses an object of the class, dereferences or performs arithmetic on a pointer to the class, or in some way references the size of the class or the names of its members. Notice also that the placement of the new data member will affect the offset of a_ within the class, invalidating all existing references to the a_ member and any pointer to members that refer to it. Additionally, the behavior of the constructor's member initialization list is now incorrect, because b_ is initialized to an undefined value (see Gotcha #52).

The major invisible changes concern the meanings of the implicit copy constructor and copy assignment operator supplied by the compiler for class C. By default, these were defined as inline functions and, therefore, were inserted into any code that initialized or assigned one C with another (see Gotcha #49).

The major effect of the modification of C (aside from the bug mentioned above) is the need to recompile nearly all uses of C. In large projects, such recompilation can be time-consuming. If C is defined in a header file, all code that (transitively) includes that header file must be recompiled. One way to improve this situation is to "forward declare" the class C by using an incomplete class declaration in contexts where more information about the class is not required:

```
class C;
```

Such an incomplete declaration will still allow us to declare pointers and references to a C as long as we perform no operations that require the knowledge of C's size or members, including base class subobjects (but see Gotcha #39).

This approach can be effective, but to avoid maintenance problems, it's important to pick up the incomplete class declaration from the same source that supplies the class definition. That is, the provider of a facility of significant complexity used in this way should provide a "forward declaration" header file that supplies an appropriate set of forward declarations.

For example, if the full definition of class C is presented in the header file c.h, we might consider providing a file called cfwd.h that contains the incomplete class declaration. Uses that didn't require the full definition of C would include cfwd.h rather than c.h. The reason for providing the forward declaration file is that the definition of C may change in the future to a form incompatible with a simple forward declaration. For example, C may be reimplemented as a typedef name:

```
template <typename T>
class Cbase {
    // . . .
};
typedef Cbase<int> C;
```

Clearly, the provider of the c.h header file is trying to avoid forcing source code changes on the present users of class C, but any code that contains an incomplete declaration of class C will now be in error:

```
#include "c.h"
// . . .
class C; // error! C is a typedef-name
```

The availability of a cfwd.h file would circumvent these problems. This approach is used in the implementation of the iostream standard library in the header iosfwd that corresponds to the header iostream.

More commonly, the need for recompilation of code that uses C makes it difficult to patch updates (bug fixes, typically) into installed software. Probably the most effective way of separating the interface of a class from its implementation, and thereby achieving true data hiding, is to employ the Bridge pattern.

Applying the Bridge pattern to a class involves separating the class into two parts, an interface and an implementation:

➤➤ gotcha08/cbridge.h

```
class C {
  public:
    C( int val );
    ~C();
    int get_a() const;
    int get_b() const;
```

```
   private:
      Cimpl *impl_;
};
```

➤➤ gotcha08/cbridge.cpp

```
class Cimpl {
 public:
    Cimpl( int val ) : a_( val ), b_( a_ ) {}
    ~Cimpl() {}
    int get_a() const { return a_; }
    int get_b() const { return b_; }
 private:
    int a_;
    int b_;
};
C::C( int val )
    : impl_( new Cimpl( val ) ) {}
C::~C()
    { delete impl_; }
int C::get_a() const
    { return impl_->get_a(); }
int C::get_b() const
    { return impl_->get_b(); }
```

The interface contains the original interface of class C, but the implementation of the class has been moved to an implementation class hidden from general use. The new version of C contains just a pointer to the implementation, and the entire implementation—including the member functions of C—is hidden from client code. Any change to the implementation of C that doesn't affect the class's interface will now be restricted to a single implementation file.

Employing a Bridge incurs a clear runtime cost, in that a C now requires two objects for its representation rather than one, and each member function call is both indirect and non-inline. However, the advantages of massively reduced compile times and the ability to update client code without recompilation often outweigh the additional runtime cost. This technique has been used extensively for many years and goes by a number of amusing names, including the "pimpl idiom" and the "Cheshire Cat technique."

Inaccessible members can also affect the meanings of derived classes and base classes when accessed through a derived class interface. For example, consider the following base and derived class:

```
class B {
  public:
    void g();
  private:
    virtual void f(); // new
};
class D : public B {
  public:
    void f();
  private:
    double g; // new
};
```

The addition of a private virtual function in the base class B has made a formerly nonvirtual derived class function virtual. The addition of a private data member in D has hidden a function inherited from B. Inheritance is often known as "white-box" reuse, since changes to classes affect the meaning of base and derived classes in a fundamental way.

One way to mitigate these problems is to employ a simple naming convention that partitions names by their general function. Typically, it's best to have different conventions for type names, private data members, and all other names. In this book, our convention is to capitalize type names, append an underscore to class data members (all of which are private!), and (with few exceptions) start other names with a lowercase letter. Following this convention would have prevented our hiding the base class member function g in D, above. Above all, resist the temptation to establish a complex naming convention, because such a convention is unlikely to be followed.

Additionally, never attempt to encode a variable's type in its name. For instance, calling an integer index iIndex is actively damaging to understanding and maintaining the code. First, a name should describe a program entity's abstract meaning, not how it's implemented (data abstraction can apply even to predefined types). Second, in the common case that the variable's type changes, just as common is that its name doesn't change in sync. The variable's name then becomes an effective source of misinformation about its type.

Other approaches are discussed elsewhere, especially in Gotchas #70, #73, #74, and #77.

Gotcha #9:   Using Bad Language

When the wider world invaded the comfortably cliquish C++ world some years ago, they brought with them some reprehensible language and coding practices. This item is an attempt to tutor proper, idiomatic C++ diction and behavior.

Diction

Table 1–1 lists the most common diction errors and their correct equivalents.

There is no such thing as a "pure virtual" base class. There are pure virtual functions, and a class that contains or fails to override such a function is abstract.

C++ has no "methods." Java and Smalltalk have methods. When you talk about an object-oriented design and are feeling particularly pretentious, you may use the terms "message" and "method," but when you get down to discussing a C++ implementation of your design, use the terms "function call" and "member function."

Some otherwise reliable C++ experts (you know who you are) use the term "destructed" as an orthogonal analog to "constructed." That's just bad English. The term is "destroyed."

C++ does indeed have cast (or type conversion) operators—four of them, in fact: (`static_cast`, `dynamic_cast`, `const_cast`, and `reinterpret_cast`). However, the term "cast operator" is often incorrectly used to refer to a member conversion operator that specifies how a class object may be implicitly converted to another type:

```
class C {
    operator int *()const; // a conversion operator
    // . . .
};
```

Table 1–1 | Common diction errors and their correct equivalents

Wrong	Right
Pure virtual base class	Abstract class
Method	Member function
Virtual method	???
Destructed	Destroyed
Cast operator	Conversion operator

Of course, it's also permissible to invoke a conversion operator explicitly with a cast operator, provided you know which is which.

See also Gotcha #31 for a discussion of const pointer versus pointer-to-const sloppiness.

Null Pointers

Once upon a time, there was potential for disaster in C++ programs if the preprocessor symbol NULL was used to represent the null pointer:

```
void doIt( char * );
void doIt( void * );
C *cp = NULL;
```

The trouble was that NULL would be defined in various ways on different platforms:

```
#define NULL ((char *)0)
#define NULL ((void *)0)
#define NULL 0
```

These various definitions wreaked havoc with portability of C++ programs:

```
doIt( NULL ); // platform-dependent or ambiguous
C *cp = NULL; // error?
```

In fact, there is no way to represent a null pointer directly in C++, but we're guaranteed that the numeric literal 0 is convertible to a null pointer value for any pointer type. That is what C++ programmers traditionally used to ensure the portability and correctness of their code. Now the standard indicates that definitions like (void *)0 are not allowed, so this isn't so much a technical issue with the use of NULL (except that it's a preprocessor symbol and is therefore looked on askance). However, real C++ programmers still use 0 to represent the null pointer value. Any other usage will mark you as hopelessly démodé.

Acronyms

C++ programmers have the acronym disease, though perhaps not to the extent managers do. Table 1–2 may be of use the next time one of your colleagues tells you that the RVO won't be applied to a POD, so you'd better define a copy ctor.

Table 1–2 | Meanings of common acronyms

Acronym	Meaning
POD	Plain old data, a C struct
POF	Plain old function, a C function
RVO	Return value optimization
NRV	Named RVO
ctor	Constructor
dtor	Destructor
ODR	One definition rule

Gotcha #10: Ignorance of Idiom

> It is an old observation that the best writers sometimes disregard the rules of rhetoric. When they do so, however, the reader will usually find in the sentence some compensating merit, attained at the cost of the violation. Unless he is certain of doing as well, he will probably do best to follow the rules. (Strunk and White, *The Elements of Style*)[1]

This often-quoted advice from the classic guide to clarity in English prose often finds its way into texts on programming style as well. I approve of the quote and the chastening sentiment behind it. However, I find it unsatisfying because, taken out of context, it doesn't indicate why it's generally profitable to follow the rules of rhetoric and how those rules come about. I've always preferred White's cow-path simile to Strunk's Olympian dictum:

> The living language is like a cowpath: it is the creation of the cows themselves, who, having created it, follow it or depart from it according to their whims or their needs. From daily use, the path undergoes change. A cow is under no obligation to stay in the narrow path she helped make, following the contour of the land, but she often profits by staying with it and she would be handicapped if she didn't know where it was and where it led to. (E. B. White, *Writings from The New Yorker*)

Programming languages are not as complex as natural languages, and our goal of writing clear code is not as difficult to achieve as that of writing clear sentences. A programming language like C++, however, is sufficiently complex that effective programming in the language depends upon a body of standard usage

---

1. The author of this quote is actually William Strunk, since it appeared in the original volume before the book's resurrection by White in 1959.

and idiom. The design of the C++ language is not proscriptive, in that it allows much flexibility in how it may be used, but idiomatic usage of language features allows efficient and clear communication of a design. Ignorance or willful disregard of idiom is an invitation to misunderstanding and misuse.

Much of the advice found in this book involves being aware of and employing idioms in C++ coding and design. Many of the gotchas listed here could be described simply as departing from a particular C++ idiom. The accompanying solution to the problem could often be described simply as following the appropriate idiom. There's a reason for this: the body of idiom in C++ coding and design has been built up and continuously refined by the community of C++ programmers as a whole. Approaches that don't work or that are out of date fall out of favor and are discarded. Idioms that survive are those that evolve to suit the environment of their use. Being aware of—and employing—C++ coding and design idioms is one of the surest ways of producing clear, effective, and maintainable C++ code and designs.

As competent professional programmers, we should be aware, always, that our code and designs exist within a context of idiom. If we are aware of coding and design idioms, we can choose to stay within their narrow path or make an educated decision to depart from them according to our needs. However, we can most often profit by staying within them, and we would be handicapped indeed if we were ignorant of them.

I don't mean to inadvertently give the impression that our C++ programming idioms are in some way a straitjacket that controls every aspect of the design process. Far from it. Properly used, idiom can simplify the process of design and communication of a design, leaving the designer free to expend creativity where it's needed. Sometimes even the most sensible and common programming idiom is inappropriate to the context of a design, and the designer is forced to depart from the standard approach.

One of the most common and useful C++ idioms is the copy operation idiom. Every abstract data type in C++ should make a decision about its copy assignment operator and copy constructor. Either the compiler should be allowed to write them, the programmer should write them, or they should be disallowed (see Gotcha #49).

If the programmer writes these operations, we know exactly how they should be written. However, the "standard" way of writing these operations has evolved over the years. This is one of the advantages of idiom over dictate; idiom evolves to suit the current context of use.

```
class X {
 public:
   X( const X & );
   X &operator =( const X & );
   // . . .
};
```

While the C++ language permits a lot of leeway in the definitions of copy operations, it's almost invariably a good idea to declare these operations as they are
above: both operations take a reference to a constant, and the copy assignment is
nonvirtual and returns a reference to a non-const. Clearly, neither of these operations will change its operand. It wouldn't make sense.

```
X a;
X b( a ); // a won't change
a = b; // b won't change
```

Except sometimes. The standard C++ auto_ptr template has some unusual
requirements. It's a resource handle charged with cleaning up heap-allocated
storage when the storage is no longer needed:

```
void f() {
   auto_ptr<Blob> blob( new Blob );
   // . . .
   // automatic deletion of allocated Blob
}
```

Fine, but what happens when the student interns are set loose on this code?

```
void g( auto_ptr<Blob> arg ) {
   // . . .
   // automatic deletion of allocated Blob
}
void f() {
   auto_ptr<Blob> blob( new Blob );
   g( blob );
   // another deletion of allocated Blob!!!
}
```

One approach might be to disallow copy operations for auto_ptr, but that would
severely limit their use and would make impossible a number of useful auto_ptr

idioms. Another approach might be to add a reference count to the `auto_ptr`, but that would increase the expense of employing a resource handle. The approach taken by the standard `auto_ptr` is to depart from the copy operation idiom intentionally:

```
template <class T>
class auto_ptr {
   public:
   auto_ptr( auto_ptr & );
   auto_ptr &operator =( auto_ptr & );
   // . . .
   private:
   T *object_;
};
```

(The standard `auto_ptr` also implements template member functions corresponding to these nontemplate copy operations, but the observations for those are similar. See also Gotcha #88.) Here the right side of each operation is nonconst! When one `auto_ptr` is initialized by or assigned to by another, the source of the initialization or assignment gives up ownership of the heap-allocated object to which it refers by setting its internal object pointer to null.

As is often the case when departing from idiom, some confusion initially arose about how to use `auto_ptr` properly. However, this departure from an existing idiom has allowed the development of a number of productive new idioms centered on object ownership issues, and the use of `auto_ptrs` as "sources" and "sinks" of data looks to be a profitable new design area. In effect, an educated departure from an existing, successful idiom has resulted in a family of new idioms.

Gotcha #11: Unnecessary Cleverness

C++ and C seem to attract a disproportionate number of showoffs. (Have you ever heard of an "Obfuscated Eiffel" contest?) These programmers seem to think the shortest distance between two points is the great circle route on a spherical distortion of Euclidean space.

Case in point: it's well-known in C++ circles (Euclidean or otherwise) that the formatting of code is entirely for the benefit of its human readers; it has no effect on the meaning of the code as long as the same sequence of tokens occurs. That last proviso is important, since (for example) the following two lines mean very different things (but see Gotcha #87):

```
a+++++b; // error!
a+++ ++b; // OK.
```

as do the following two lines (see Gotcha #17):

```
ptr->*m; // OK.
ptr-> *m; // error!
```

That said, most C++ programmers would concur that, apart from issues of tokenization of the input stream of characters, formatting is irrelevant to a program's meaning. So, for example, we can declare a variable on one line or several, with the same result. (Some programming environment debuggers and other tools are implemented in terms of line numbers rather than a more exact notion of program location. This often forces programmers to employ unnatural or inconvenient multiline formatting to get accurate error messages, be able to set accurate breakpoints, and so on. This is not a C++ language issue; it's an issue for the designers of C++ programming environments.)

```
long curLine = __LINE__; // current line number
long        curLine
     =                   __LINE__
  ; // same declaration
```

Most C++ programmers are wrong. Let's look at a simple template metaprogramming device for selecting a type at compile time:

➤➤ gotcha11/select.h

```
template <bool cond, typename A, typename B>
struct Select {
    typedef A Result;
};
template <typename A, typename B>
struct Select<false, A, B> {
    typedef B Result;
};
```

An instantiation of the `Select` template evaluates a condition at compile time, then instantiates one of two versions of the template, depending on the Boolean result of the expression. It's a compile-time if-statement that says, "If the condition is true, the nested `Result` type is A; otherwise, it's B."

➤➤ gotcha11/lineno.cpp

```
Select< sizeof(int)==sizeof(long), int, long >::Result temp = 0;
```

This statement declares `temp` to be an `int` if `int`s and `long`s occupy the same number of bytes. Otherwise, `temp` is declared to be a `long`.

Let's look at our earlier declaration of `curLine`. Why should we waste all that space on a `long` if we don't have to? Let's get unnecessarily complex for no good reason:

➤➤ gotcha11/lineno.cpp

```
const char CM = CHAR_MAX;
const Select<__LINE__<=CM,char,long>::Result curLine = __LINE__;
```

That works (and is also correct), but the line is rather long, so the maintainer who comes after us reformats a bit:

➤➤ gotcha11/lineno.cpp

```
const Select<__LINE__<=CM,char,long>::Result
   curLine = __LINE__;
```

Now we've got a bug. See it?

What if the declaration occurs on line number `CHAR_MAX` (which may be as small as 127)? The type of `curLine` will then be `char` and will be initialized with the maximum value of a `char`. As soon as we put the initializer on the following line, we'll attempt to initialize a `char` with one more than the maximum value of a `char`. The result is probably that the line number is a negative number (like –128). Clever.

Unnecessary cleverness is a common problem with C++ programmers. Remember that it's nearly always preferable to be conventional, clear, and slightly less efficient than unnecessarily clever, unclear, and unmaintainable.

Gotcha #12: Adolescent Behavior

We programmers are good at dispensing advice but often have a hard time following it. We preach against global variables, poor variable names, magic numbers and the like, but often insert them into our own code. This phenomenon confounded me for many years, until I read a magazine article that described the same phenomenon in adolescents. It's apparently common for adolescents to criticize risky behavior in others but, through a "personal fantasy," come to believe that they themselves are immune from any negative effects of engaging in that same behavior. As a class, then, programmers seem to suffer from arrested emotional development.

I've worked on projects where some programmers not only refused to follow coding standards but threatened to quit if they were required to indent four spaces instead of two. I've been in situations where one clique refused to attend meetings if the other clique was attending. I've seen programmers deliberately write undocumented and impenetrable code so no one else could maintain it. I've seen otherwise capable programmers refuse to accept advice from an older/younger/too straight/excessively pierced coworker, and head for disaster as a result.

Emotionally adolescent or not, as professional programmers we all have a number of adult, or at least professional, responsibilities. (See also the Association for Computing Machinery's positions on these issues, in the *ACM Code of Ethics and Professional Conduct* and *Software Engineering Code of Ethics and Professional Practice*.)

First, we have a duty to our chosen profession to do quality work to the best standards of which we are capable.

Second, we have a duty to the society in which we live and the planet on which we live. Our chosen profession is equal parts science and practical service. If our work does not contribute to making the world a better place to live, it is a waste of our talent, time, and, ultimately, our lives.

Third, we have the duty to our community to share our expertise in ways that affect governmental policy. In our increasingly technological society, most important decisions are made by persons schooled in the law or in politics but who are technologically illiterate and innumerate. For example, for a time one of the states had a law decreeing that the value of π was 3. That's funny (though wheeled transport was bumpy until the law was repealed), but a lot of the uninformed policy decisions we see are not. We have a duty to inform political debate with rational technical and numerate interpretation of policy.

Fourth, we have a duty to our colleagues to be collegial. This involves following local coding and design standards (if they're no good, we should change them, not ignore them), writing code that can be maintained, and listening to others while sharing our own perspectives.

This is in no way an exhortation to pick up pom-poms and be a "team player" or to encourage the adoption of the prevailing corporate uniform or social outlook. Some of my most satisfying professional collaborations have been with oddly dressed loners with unusual political positions and unique personal habits. But each of these cherished colleagues respected both me and my ideas (to the extent of telling me off when I deserved it, and letting me know I was wrong when I was), and worked with me to accomplish what we had together agreed to accomplish.

Fifth, we have a duty to others in our profession to share our knowledge and experience.

Sixth, we have a duty to ourselves. Our work and our thoughts should satisfy us and speak to the reasons for which we entered this profession. If we're passionate about what we do, if what we do is an essential part of what we are, the duties above will not be a burden; they will be a joy.

2 Syntax

C++ has a complex syntactic and lexical structure. Some of this complexity was inherited from C, and some is essential in the support of certain language features.

In this chapter, we'll examine a variety of syntax-related headaches. Some of these are common typos that nevertheless compile and execute in surprising ways. Others illustrate problems that arise due to a loose connection between the syntactic structure of a piece of code and its behavior at runtime. Still others will consider the problems occasioned by syntactic flexibility, when two programmers can examine the same piece of code and draw different conclusions about its meaning.

Gotcha #13: Array/Initializer Confusion

Let's allocate an array of 12 integers off the heap, shall we? No problem:

```
int *ip = new int(12);
```

So far, so good. Now let's use the array. When we've finished, we'll clean up after ourselves:

```
for( int i = 0; i < 12; ++i )
    ip[i] = i;
delete [] ip;
```

Notice the use of the empty brackets to let the compiler know that ip points to an array of integers instead of a single integer. Or does it?

Actually, ip points to a single integer initialized with the value 12. We've made the common typo of using parentheses instead of square brackets. Both the access within the loop (after index 0) and the deletion are illegal. However, the compiler is unlikely to catch the error at compile time. Because a pointer can refer to either a single object or an array of objects, both the index within the loop and the array deletion are perfectly correct syntactically, and we won't learn of an error until runtime.

Maybe not even then. It's illegal to access past the end of an object (although the language guarantees that you can point *one* element past an object), and it's illegal to delete a scalar as an array. But just because you do something illegal doesn't mean you'll get caught (think Wall Street). This code could run perfectly well on some platforms and fail at runtime on others, or exhibit flaky behavior on a particular platform, depending on runtime heap usage of a particular thread or process. The correct allocation is, of course, the following:

```
int *ip = new int[12];
```

However, the proper allocation is most probably not to allocate at all. Just use the standard library:

```
std::vector<int> iv( 12 );
for( int i = 0; i < iv.size(); ++i )
    iv[i] = i;
// no explicit deletion . . .
```

The standard `vector` template is nearly as efficient as the hand-coded version but is safer, faster to program, and self-documenting. In general, prefer `vector` to low-level arrays. By the way, the same syntax problem can occur with a simple declaration as well but is usually easier to detect:

```
int a[12]; // array of 12 ints
int b(12); // an int initialized to 12
```

Gotcha #14: Evaluation Order Indecision

C++'s C roots are nowhere more evident than in the evaluation order traps it lays for the unwary. This item looks at several manifestations of the same problem: the C and C++ languages permit a lot of leeway in how expressions are evaluated. This flexibility can result in highly optimized code, but it also requires careful attention on the part of the programmer to avoid unfounded assumptions about evaluation order.

Function Argument Evaluation Order

```
int i = 12;
int &ri = i;
int f( int, int );
//  . . .
int result1 = f( i, i *= 2 ); // unportable
```

Function argument evaluation is not fixed to a particular order. Therefore, the values passed to f could be 12 and 24 or 24 and 24. A careful programmer might decide not to modify an argument if it appears more than once in the same argument list, but this isn't safe either:

```
int result2 = f( i, ri *= 2 ); // unportable
int result3 = f( p(), q() ); // dicey . . .
```

In the first case, ri is an alias for i, so the value of result2 is as ambiguous as that of result1. In the second case, we're assuming that the order in which the functions p and q are called doesn't matter. Even if that is currently the case, it may not be in the future, but that constraint on the implementations of p and q isn't documented anywhere.

It's best to minimize side effects in function arguments:

```
result1 = f( i, i*2 );
result2 = f( i, ri*2 );
int a = p();
result3 = f( a, q() );
```

Subexpression Evaluation Order

The evaluation order of subexpressions isn't fixed either:

```
a = p() + q();
```

The function p may be called before q, or vice versa. Precedence and associativity of operators doesn't affect evaluation order:

```
a = p() + q() * r();
```

The three functions p, q, and r may be evaluated in any of six different orders. The higher precedence of the multiplication operator ensures only that the results of the calls to q and r will be multiplied before being added to the result of the call to p. Likewise, the left associativity of the plus operator doesn't guarantee the order in which p, q, and r are called below; it ensures only that the results of the calls will be added from left to right:

```
a = p() + q() + r();
```

Parentheses don't help either:

```
a = (p() + q()) * r();
```

The results of p and q will be added first, but r may (or may not) be the first function called. The only reliable way to fix the order of subexpression evaluation is to use explicit, programmer-defined temporaries:

```
a = p();
int b = q();
a = (a + b) * r();
```

How often does this problem occur? Often enough to ruin a weekend or two every year. Consider Figure 2–1, a fragment of an abstract syntax tree hierarchy used to implement an arithmetic calculator.

The following implementation is not portable:

➤➤gotcha14/e.cpp

```
int Plus::eval() const
    { return l_->eval() + r_->eval(); }
int Assign::eval() const
    { return id->set( e_->eval() ); }
```

The problem lies in the implementation of Plus::eval, because the order of evaluation of the left and right subtrees isn't fixed. Does this really matter for addition? After all, addition is supposed to be commutative. Consider evaluation of the following expression:

```
(a = 12) + a
```

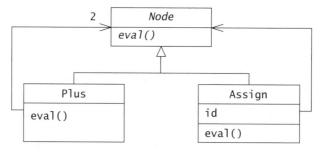

Figure 2–1 An abstract syntax tree node hierarchy for a simple calculator (abbreviated). A plus node has left and right subtrees; an assignment node has a single subtree representing the right side of the assignment.

Depending on the order of evaluation of the left and right subtrees within `Plus::eval`, the value of the expression will be either 24 or the previous value of a + 12. If our calculator requires that the assignment be performed before the addition, the implementation of `Plus::eval` must use an explicit temporary to fix the evaluation order:

➤➤gotcha14/e.cpp

```
int Plus::eval() const {
    int lft = l_->eval();
    return lft + r_->eval();
}
```

Placement new Evaluation Order

Admittedly, this one doesn't crop up a lot. The placement syntax for the new operator allows arguments to be passed not only to the initializer (generally a constructor) of the object being allocated but also to the `operator new` function that performs the allocation.

```
Thing *pThing =
    new (getHeap(), getConstraint()) Thing( initval() );
```

The first argument list is passed to an `operator new` that can accept the arguments, and the second to a constructor for `Thing`. Note that the general warning about function argument evaluation order applies to each of these argument lists: we don't know whether `getHeap` or `getConstraint` will be called first. Additionally, we don't know whether the arguments for the `operator new` or for the `Thing` constructor will be evaluated first, although we do know that `operator new` will be called before the constructor (since we need to get storage for an object before we can initialize it).

Operators That Fix Evaluation Order

Some operators have a more dependable nature than others, if they're left alone. The comma operator does fix the evaluation order of its subexpressions:

```
result = expr1, expr2;
```

This statement evaluates `expr1`, then evaluates `expr2`, the result of which is assigned to `result`. This can be used to write some unusual code:

```
return f(), g(), h();
```

This author of this code needs more socialization. Use a more conventional coding style unless you actually *want* to confuse maintainers of your code:

```
f();
g();
return h();
```

The only common use of the comma operator is in the increment part of a for-statement, when more than one iteration variable is in use:

```
for( int i = 0, j = MAX; i <= j; ++i, --j ) // . . .
```

Note that the first comma in the declaration of i and j is not a comma operator. It's part of the declaration of the two integers i and j.

The "short-circuiting" logical operators && and || are more useful, in that they allow us to write complex conditions in a compact and idiomatic way:

```
if( f() && g() ) // . . .
if( p() || q() || r() ) // . . .
```

The first expression says, "Call f. If the result is false, then the condition is false. If the result is true, then call g, and the value of the condition is the result of g." The second condition says, "Call p, q, and r in that order, but stop as soon as one of them succeeds. If all three calls fail, the condition is false; otherwise, it's true." Given their propensity for writing compact code, it's easy to see why C and C++ programmers use these operators so extensively.

The ternary conditional operator (pronounced "?:") also fixes the evaluation order of its arguments:

```
expr1 ? expr2 : expr3
```

The first expression, or condition, is evaluated first; then either the second or third expression is evaluated. The result of the conditional expression is the result of the expression that was evaluated.

```
a = f()+g() ? p() : q();
```

In this case, we have some assurance of evaluation order. We know that f and g will be called before p or q (although we don't know in what order they will be called) and that only one of p or q will be called. It might also be a good idea to add some strictly optional parentheses for readability:

```
a = (f()+g()) ? p() : q();
```

Otherwise, it's possible that a maintainer of the code, due to ignorance or haste, may make the erroneous assumption that the addition is performed after the conditional:

```
a = f()+(g() ? p() : q());
```

Improper Operator Overloading

However, as useful as the built-in versions of these operators are, it's not a good idea to overload them. In C++, operator overloading is "syntactic sugar"; we're just providing a more digestible syntax for a function call. For example, we could overload the && operator to accept two Thing arguments:

```
bool operator &&( const Thing &, const Thing & );
```

When we use the operator with infix notation, maintainers of our code will probably assume the short-circuiting behavior of the built-in operator, but they won't get it:

```
Thing &tf1();
Thing &tf2();
// . . .
if( tf1() && tf2() ) // . . .
```

This code is identical in meaning to a function call:

```
if( operator &&( tf1(), tf2() ) ) // . . .
```

As we've seen above, the functions tf1 and tf2 will both be called, and the order in which they're called is not fixed. This problem also occurs when overloading operator || and operator ,. Fortunately, operator ?: can't be overloaded.

Gotcha #15: Precedence Problems

This item doesn't speak to the issue of whether the Countess or the Baroness should sit next to the Ambassador at dinner (that problem has no solution). No, here we're going to discuss how the many levels of operator precedence in C++ expressions can give rise to some irksome problems.

Precedence and Associativity

It's usually beneficial for a programming language to have different levels of operator precedence, since this allows simplification of complex expressions without excessive and distracting use of parentheses. (Note, however, that it's usually a good idea to parenthesize complex or obscure expressions that may not be easily understood by all readers. Nevertheless, it's usually clearest to omit unnecessary parentheses in simple, universally understood cases.)

```
a = a + b * c;
```

In the expression above, we know that * has the highest precedence, or binding strength, so we'll execute that operation first. Assignment has the lowest precedence, so we'll perform that operation last.

```
b = a = a + b + c;
```

In this case, we know we'll perform the additions before the assignments, since + has higher precedence than =, but which addition and which assignment will be performed first? Here we have to examine the associativity of the operators. In C++, operators can be left-associative or right-associative. A left-associative operator like + will bind first with the argument to its left. Therefore, we'll first add a and b before adding the result of that subexpression to c.

Assignment is right-associative, so we'll first assign the result of a+b+c to a, then assign a to b. Some languages contain nonassociative operators; it would be illegal to have an expression like a@b@c if @ were a nonassociative operator. Congenial language that it is, C++ has no nonassociative operators.

Precedence Problems

The iostream library is designed to allow a minimum of parentheses:

```
cout << "a+b = " << a+b << endl;
```

The + operator has higher precedence than the left shift operator, so we get the desired parse; a+b is calculated first, then the result is sent to cout.

```
cout << a ? f() : g();
```

Here, the use of C++'s only ternary operator gets us into trouble, but it's not that ?: is ternary; it's that it has lower precedence than <<. Therefore, we're asking the compiler to generate code to shift a to cout, then use the result of that expression as the condition in the ?:. The tragic aspect of this situation is that the code is perfectly legal! (An output stream object like cout has a member operator void * that can be used implicitly to convert it to a void * value, which in turn can be converted to false or true, depending on whether the pointer value is null or not.) Here's a case where we reach for our parentheses:

```
cout << (a ? f() : g());
```

If you want to be considered completely normal, you can take things a step further:

```
if( a )
    cout << f();
else
    cout << g();
```

This approach doesn't have the same *je ne sais quoi* of the previous one, but it does have the advantage of being clear and maintainable.

Not many C++ programmers are fooled by precedence problems with pointers to classes, since it's well known that the -> and . operators have very high precedence. Therefore, an expression like a = ++ptr->mem means to increment the *member* mem of the object to which ptr refers. If we'd wanted to increment the *pointer* first, we'd have written a = (++ptr)->mem, or potentially ++ptr; a = ptr->mem;, or, on a really bad day, a = (++ptr, ptr->mem).

Pointers to class members are a different story. They must be dereferenced in the context of a class object (see Gotcha #46). For this purpose, two special-purpose dereference operators are defined: ->* to dereference a pointer to member with a pointer to a class object and .* to dereference a pointer to member with a class object.

Pointers to member functions are often a headache, but they don't cause any serious syntax problems:

```
class C {
    // . . .
```

```
    void f( int );
    int mem;
};
void (C::*pfmem)(int) = &C::f;
int C::*pdmem = &C::mem;
C *cp = new C;
// . . .
cp->*pfmem(12); // error!
```

We get a compile-time error because the function call operator has higher precedence than the ->* operator, but we can't call a pointer to member function without dereferencing it first. Parentheses are required here:

```
(cp->*pfmem)(12);
```

Pointers to data members are more problematic. Consider the following expression:

```
a = ++cp->*pdmem
```

The variable cp is the same pointer to class object above, and pdmem is not a member name but a pointer to member. In this case, because ->* has lower precedence
than ++, cp will be incremented before the pointer to member is dereferenced.
Unless cp is pointing into an array of class objects, this is likely to result in a bad
dereference.

Pointers to class members are not well understood by many C++ programmers.
For the future viability of the maintenance of your code, keep things as simple
and straightforward as possible when using them:

```
++cp;
a = cp->*pdmem;
```

Associativity Problems

Most C++ operators are left-associative, and C++ has no nonassociative operators. This doesn't stop some otherwise intelligent programmers from trying to
use operators that way:

```
int a = 3, b = 2, c = 1;
// . . .
if( a > b > c ) // legal, but probably wrong . . .
```

This code is perfectly legal but probably wrong. The value of the expression 3>2>1 is, of course, false. The greater-than operator, like most C++ operators, is left-associative, so we'll first evaluate the subexpression 3>2, which is true. That leaves us with the expression true>1. We convert true to an integer and evaluate the expression 1>1, which is false.

In this case, it's likely the programmer meant to write the condition as a>b && b>c. If, for some obscure reason, the programmer actually wanted the original result, a better way to write the condition would be a>b?1>c:0>c or perhaps (c-(a>b))<0, either of which is strange enough to cause a maintainer to take a second look. In this case, a comment would be permissible as well. (See Gotcha #1.)

Gotcha #16: for Statement Debacle

C++ has several places where it's legal to declare a variable in a restricted scope that's not simply a nested block. For example, it's possible to declare a variable in the condition of an if-statement. The variable will be available in the statements controlled by the condition, both the "true" and "false" branches:

```
if( char *theName = lookup( name ) ) {
    // do something with name . . .
}
// theName is out of scope here
```

Formerly, the variable would have been declared outside the if-statement, with the unfortunate consequence that it would still be hanging around, looking for trouble, after we'd finished with it:

```
char *theName = lookup( name );
if( theName ) {
    // do something with name . . .
}
// theName is still available here . . .
```

It's generally a good idea to restrict the scope of a variable to the region of the program in which it's used. Under maintenance, for reasons beyond my ability to understand, these variables tend to be reused for some wildly different purpose. The effect on documentation and maintenance is, shall we say, "negative." (See also Gotcha #48.)

```
theName = new char[ ISBN_LEN ]; // need buffer for ISBN
```

The same is true of the for-statement; an iteration variable can be declared as the first part of the statement:

```
for( int i = 0; i < bufSize; ++i ) {
    if( !buffer[i] )
        break;
}
if( i == bufSize ) // was legal, now illegal, i not in scope
    // . . .
```

This was legal C++ for many years, but the scope of the iteration variable has changed. Formerly, the scope of the variable extended from the point of its declaration (just before the initializer; see Gotcha #21) to the end of the block that contains the for-statement. Under the new semantics, the scope is restricted to the for-statement itself. Although most C++ programmers believe that the change makes good sense in most ways—it's more orthogonal to the rest of the language, makes it easier to optimize loops, and so on—it's something of a pain in the neck to go back and repair all the older uses of for.

Sometimes it's more than just a pain in the neck. Consider the possibility of a quiet change in meaning:

```
int i = 0;
void f() {
    for( int i = 0; i <bufSize; i++ ) {
        if( !buffer[i] )
        break;
    }
    if( i == bufSize ) // file scope i!
        // . . .
}
```

Fortunately, this kind of error is rare, and most quality compilers will warn about the condition. Take the warning seriously (and don't turn off warnings), and try to avoid hiding outer scope names in inner scopes. And lay off the global variables. (See Gotcha #3.)

Strangely, the most damaging effect of the scope change in the for-statement has been its effect on how some C++ programmers write their for-statements:

```
int i;
for( i = 0; i < bufSize; ++i ) {
```

```
    if( isprint( buffer[i] ) )
        massage( buffer[i] );
    // . . .
    if( some_condition )
        continue;
    // . . .
}
```

This is C code, not C++ code. It does have the advantage of having the same meaning under both the old and new for-statement semantics, but consider what's been lost. First, the iteration variable remains in force after the for-statement. Second, the variable i is not initialized. Neither of these is an issue when the code is first written, but under maintenance, less experienced programmers may attempt to use the uninitialized i before the for-statement as well as after, when the original designer had hoped i would quietly disappear.

Another problem is that the issue drives some programmers away from the for-statement entirely:

```
int i = 0;
while( i < bufSize ) {
    if( isprint( buffer[i] ) )
        massage( buffer[i] );
    // . . .
    if( some_condition )
        continue; // oops!
    // . . .
    ++i;
}
```

The problem here is that the while-statement is not equivalent to the for-statement. For example, if there's a continue within the body of the loop, the program will suffer a change in meaning that may not be easily detected. In this case the code will infinite loop, which is usually an indication of some sort of problem. We aren't always so lucky.

If you're fortunate enough to deal exclusively with platforms that support the new for-statement semantics, the best procedure for dealing with the change in meaning of the for-statement is to embrace the change as soon as your platforms allow.

Unfortunately, it's perhaps more often the case that code must be compiled on different platforms, with contradictory for-statement semantics. It may seem logical in this case to write for-statements that have the same meaning under either translation:

```
int i;
for( i = 0; i < bufSize; ++i ) {
    if( isprint( buffer[i] ) )
        massage( buffer[i] );
    // . . .
}
```

However, I recommend instead that all for-statements be written to the new semantics. To avoid problems with the scope of the iteration variable, the for-statement can be enclosed in a block:

```
{for( int i = 0; i < bufSize; ++i ) {
    if( isprint( buffer[i] ) )
        massage( buffer[i] );
    // . . .
}}
```

This is hideous enough that it will surely be noticed and removed when no longer needed. It also has the advantage of encouraging the original programmer to write the for-statement to the new semantics, avoiding the need to perform that bit of additional maintenance later.

Gotcha #17: Maximal Munch Problems

What do you do when faced with an expression like this?

```
++++p->*mp
```

Have you ever had occasion to deal with the "Sergeant operator"?

```
template <typename T>
class R {
    // . . .
    friend ostream &operator <<< // a sergeant operator?
        T >( ostream &, const R & );
};
```

Have you ever wondered whether the following expression is legal?

```
a+++++b
```

Welcome to the world of maximal munch. In one of the early stages of C++ translation, the portion of the compiler that performs "lexical analysis" has the task of breaking up the input stream into individual "words," or tokens. When faced with a sequence of characters like ->*, the lexical analyzer might reasonably identify three tokens (-, >, and *), two tokens (-> and *), or a single token (->*). To avoid this ambiguous state of affairs, the lexical analyzer always identifies the longest token possible, consuming as many characters as it legally can: maximal munch.

The expression a+++++b is illegal, because it's tokenized as a ++ ++ + b, and it's illegal to post-increment an rvalue like a++. If you had wanted to post-increment a and add the result to a pre-incremented b, you'd have to introduce at least one space: a+++ ++b. If you have any regard for the readers of your code, you'll spring for another space, even though it's not strictly necessary: a++ + ++b, and no one would criticize the addition of a few parentheses: (a++) + (++b).

Maximal munch solves many more problems than it causes, but in two common situations, it's an annoyance. The first is in the instantiation of templates with arguments that are themselves instantiated templates. For example, using the standard library, one might want to declare a list of vectors of strings:

```
list<vector<string>> lovos; // error!
```

Unfortunately, the two adjacent closing angle brackets in the instantiation are interpreted as a shift operator, and we'll get a syntax error. Whitespace is required:

```
list< vector<string> > lovos;
```

Another situation involves using default argument initializers for pointer formal arguments:

```
void process( const char *= 0 ); // error!
```

This declaration is attempting to use the *= assignment operator in a formal argument declaration. Syntax error. This problem comes under the "wages of sin" category, in that it wouldn't have happened if the author of the code had given the formal argument a name. Not only is such a name some of the best documentation one can provide, its presence would have made the maximal munch problem impossible:

```
void process( const char *processId = 0 );
```

Gotcha #18: Creative Declaration-Specifier Ordering

As far as the language is concerned, the ordering of declaration-specifiers is immaterial:

```
int const extern size = 1024; // legal, but weird
```

However, without a compelling reason to depart from convention, it's best to follow the de facto standard ordering of these specifiers: linkage-specifier, type-qualifier, type.

```
extern const int size = 1024; // normal
```

What's the type of ptr?

```
int const *ptr = &size;
```

Right. It's a pointer to a constant integer, but you wouldn't believe how many programmers read the declaration as constant pointer to integer:

```
int * const ptr2 = &size; // error!
```

These are two very different types, of course, since the first is allowed to refer to a constant integer, and the second isn't. Colloquially, many programmers refer to pointers to constant data as "const pointers." This is not a good idea, because it communicates the correct meaning (pointer to constant data) only to ignoramuses, and will mislead any competent C++ programmer who takes you at your word (a constant pointer to non-constant data).

Admittedly, the standard library contains the concept of a const_iterator that is, unforgivably, an iterator that refers to constant elements; the iterator itself is not constant. (Just because the standards committee has a bad day doesn't mean you should emulate them.) Distinguish carefully between "pointer to const" and "constant pointer." (See Gotcha #31.)

Because the order of declaration-specifiers is technically immaterial, a pointer to const can be declared in two different ways:

```
const int *pci1;
int const *pci2;
```

Some C++ experts recommend the second form of the declaration because, they claim, it's easier to read in more complex pointer declarations:

```
int const * const *pp1;
```

Placing the const qualifier last in the list of declaration-specifiers allows us to read the pointer modifiers in a declaration "backward"; that is, from right to left: pp1 is a pointer to a const pointer to a const int. The conventional arrangement doesn't allow such a simple rule:

```
const int * const *pp2; // same type as pp1
```

However, it's not inordinately more complex than the previous arrangement, and C++ programmers who read and maintain code containing such elaborate declarations are probably capable of figuring them out. More important, pointers to pointers and similarly complex declarations are rare, especially in interfaces where they're more likely to be encountered by less experienced programmers. Typically, one finds them deep in the implementation of a facility. Simple pointers to constant are much more common, and it therefore makes sense to follow convention in order to avoid misunderstanding:

```
const int *pci1; // correct: pointer to const
```

Gotcha #19: Function/Object Ambiguity

A default object initialization should not be specified with an empty initialization list, as this is interpreted as a function declaration.

```
String s( "Semantics, not Syntax!" ); // explicit initializer
String t;  // default initialization
String x(); // a function declaration
```

This is an inherent ambiguity in the C++ language. Effectively, the language standard has "tossed a coin" and decided that x is a function declaration. Note that this ambiguity does not apply to new-expressions:

```
String *sp1 = new String();  // no ambiguity here . . .
String *sp2 = new String;  // same as this
```

However, the second form is preferable, because it's more common and is orthogonal with the object declaration.

Gotcha #20: Migrating Type-Qualifiers

There are no constant or volatile arrays, so type-qualifiers (const or volatile) applied to an array will migrate to an appropriate position within the type:

```
typedef int A[12];
extern const A ca; // array of 12 const ints
typedef int *AP[12][12];
volatile AP vm; // 2-D array of volatile pointers to int
volatile int *vm2[12][12]; // 2-D array of pointers to volatile int
```

This makes sense, since an array is really just a kind of literal pointer to its elements. It has no associated storage that could be constant or volatile, so the qualifiers are applied to its elements. Be warned, however: compilers often implement this incorrectly in more complex cases. For example, the type of vm above is often (erroneously) determined to be the same as that of vm2.

Things are a bit loopier with respect to function declarators. In the past, the behavior of common C++ implementations was to allow the same migration for function declarations:

```
typedef int FUN( char * );
typedef const FUN PF; // earlier: function that returns const int
                      // now: illegal
```

The standard now says that a type-qualifier can be applied to a function declarator in a "top-level" typedef and that typedef may be used only to declare a nonstatic member function:

```
typedef int MF() const;
MF nonmemfunc; // error!
class C {
    MF memfunc; // OK.
};
```

It's probably best to avoid this usage. Current compilers don't always implement it correctly, and it's confusing to human readers as well.

Gotcha #21: Self-Initialization

What is the value of the inner var in the following code?

```
int var = 12;
{
    double var = var;
    // . . .
```

It's undefined. In C++, a name comes into scope before its initializer is parsed, so any reference to the name within the initializer refers to the name being declared! Not many programmers will compose as strange a declaration as the one above, but it's possible to cut and paste your way into trouble:

```
int copy = 12; // some deeply buried variable
// . . .
int y = (3*x+2*copy+5)/z; // cut this . . .
// . . .
void f() {
    // need a copy of y's initial value . . .
    int copy = (3*x+2*copy+5)/z; // and paste it here!
    // . . .
```

Use of the preprocessor can produce essentially the same error as indiscriminate cutting and pasting (see Gotcha #26):

```
int copy = 12;
#define Expr ((3*x+2*copy+5)/z)
// . . .
void g() {
    int copy = Expr; // déjà vu all over again . . .
    // . . .
```

Other manifestations of this problem occur when naming conventions fail to distinguish adequately between type names and non-type names:

```
struct buf {
    char a, b, c, d;
};
```

```
// . . .
void aFunc() {
    char *buf = new char[ sizeof( buf ) ];
    // . . .
```

The local buf will (probably) refer to a 4-byte buffer, big enough to hold a char *. This error could go undetected for a long time, especially if a struct buf happens to be the same size as a pointer. Following a naming convention that distinguishes type names from non-type names would have circumvented this problem (see Gotcha #12):

```
struct Buf {
    char a, b, c, d;
};
// . . .
void aFunc() {
    char *buf = new char[ sizeof( Buf ) ]; // OK
    // . . .
```

OK, so we now know to avoid the canonical manifestation of this gotcha:

```
int var = 12;
{
    double var = var;
    // . . .
```

How about a variation on this theme?

```
const int val = 12;
{
    enum { val = val };
    // . . .
```

What's the value of the enumerator val? Undefined? Guess again. The value is 12, and the reason is that the point of declaration for the enumerator val is, unlike that of a variable, after its initializer (or, more formally, after its enumerator-definition). The val after the = symbol in the enum refers to the outer-scope const. This could lead to discussion of an even more involved situation:

```
const int val = val;
{
    enum { val = val };
    // . . .
```

Thankfully, this enumerator-definition is illegal. The initializer is not an integer constant-expression, because the compiler can't determine the value of the outer-scope `val` at compile time.

Gotcha #22: **Static and Extern Types**

No such thing. However, experienced C++ programmers sometimes lead inexperienced ones astray with declarations that appear to apply a linkage-specifier to a type (see Gotcha #11):

```
static class Repository {
  // . . .
} repository; // static
Repository backUp;  // not static
```

Even though types may have linkage, linkage-specifiers always refer to an object or function, not a type. It's better to be clear:

```
class Repository {
  // . . .
};
static Repository repository;
static Repository backUp;
```

Note also that use of an anonymous namespace may be preferable to use of the `static` linkage-specifier:

```
namespace {
Repository repository;
Repository backUp;
}
```

The names `repository` and `backUp` now have external linkage and can therefore be used for a wider variety of purposes than a static name can (for instance, in a template instantiation). However, like statics, they're not accessible outside the current translation unit.

Gotcha #23: Operator Function Lookup Anomaly

Overloaded operators are really just standard member or non-member functions that may be invoked using infix syntax. They're syntactic sugar:

```
class String {
 public:
    String &operator =( const String & );
    friend String operator +( const String &, const String & );
    String operator -();
    operator const char *() const;
    // . . .
};
String a, b, c;
// . . .
a = b;
a.operator =( b ); // same
a + b;
operator +( a, b ); // same
a = -b;
a.operator =( b.operator -() ); // same
const char *cp = a;
cp = a.operator const char *(); // same
```

I think we can make a case for superior clarity in the case of the infix notation. Typically, we would employ infix notation when using an overloaded operator; after all, that's why we overloaded the operator in the first place.

Common exceptions to the use of infix notation would be when the function call syntax is clearer than the corresponding infix call. One standard example is the invocation of a base class's copy assignment operator from the implementation of the derived class copy assignment operator:

```
class A {
 protected:
    A &operator =( const A & );
    // . . .
};
```

```
class B : public A {
 public:
    B &operator =( const B & );
    // . . .
};

B &B::operator =( const B &b ) {
    if( &b != this ) {
        A::operator =( b ); // clearer than
                            // (*static_cast<A*const>(this))=b
        // assign local members . . .
    }
    return *this;
}
```

The function call form is also used in preference to infix when the infix usage—though perfectly correct—is so weird that it would cost a reader a couple of minutes to figure it out:

```
value_type *Iter::operator ->() const
    { return &operator *(); } // rather than &*(*this)
```

There are also ambiguous cases, in which neither the infix nor non-infix syntax offers a clear advantage :

```
bool operator !=( const Iter &that ) const
    { return !(*this == that); } // or !operator ==(that)
```

However, note that the lookup sequence for the infix syntax differs from that of the function call syntax. This can produce unexpected results:

```
class X {
 public:
    X &operator %( const X & ) const;
    void f();
    // . . .
};
X &operator %( const X &, int );
```

```
void X::f() {
    X &anX = *this;
    anX % 12; // OK, non-member
    operator %( anX, 12 ); // error!
}
```

The use of the function call syntax follows the standard lookup sequence in searching for the function name. In the case of the member function X::f, the compiler will first look in the class X for a function named operator %. Once it finds the name, it won't continue looking in outer scopes for additional functions named operator %.

Unfortunately, we're attempting to pass three arguments to a binary operator. Because the member function operator % has an implicit this argument, the two explicit arguments imply to the compiler that we're attempting to make binary % a ternary operator. A correct call would either identify the nonmember function explicitly (::operator %(anX, 12)) or pass the correct number of arguments to the member function (operator %(anX)).

Using the infix notation causes the compiler to search in the scope indicated by the left operand (that is, in class X, since anX is of type X) for a member operator % and to search for a non-member operator %. In the case of the expression anX % 12, the compiler will identify two candidate functions and correctly match on the non-member function.

Gotcha #24: Operator -> Subtleties

The predefined -> operator is binary: the left operand is a pointer, and the right operand is the name of a class member. Overloaded operator -> is a unary member function!

➤➤gotcha24/ptr.h

```
class Ptr {
  public:
    Ptr( T *init );
    T *operator ->();
    // . . .
  private:
    T *tp_;
};
```

An invocation of overloaded -> must return something that may then be used with an -> operator to access a member:

➤➤gotcha24/ptr.cpp

```
Ptr p( new T );
p->f(); // p.operator ->()->f()!
```

One way to look at it is that the -> token is not "consumed" by an overloaded operator -> but is instead retained for eventual use as the predefined -> operator. Typically, some additional semantics are attached to the overloaded -> to create a "smart pointer" type:

➤➤gotcha24/ptr.cpp

```
T *Ptr::operator ->() {
    if( today() == TUESDAY )
        abort();
    else
        return tp_;
}
```

We mentioned that an overloaded operator -> must return "something" that may be then used to access a member. That something doesn't have to be a predefined pointer. It could be a class object that itself overloads operator ->:

➤➤gotcha24/ptr.h

```
class AugPtr {
 public:
    AugPtr( T *init ) : p_( init ) {}
    Ptr &operator ->();
    // . . .
 private:
    Ptr p_;
};
```

➤➤gotcha24/ptr.cpp

```
Ptr &AugPtr::operator ->() {
    if( today() == FRIDAY )
      cout << '\a' << flush;
    return p_;
}
```

This allows the cascading of smart pointer responsibilities:

➤➤gotcha24/ptr.cpp

```
AugPtr ap( new T );
ap->f(); // ap.operator ->().operator ->()->f()!
```

Note that the sequence of `operator ->` activations is always determined statically by the type of the object that contains the `operator ->` definition, and the sequence of `operator ->` member function calls always terminates in a call that returns a predefined pointer to class. For example, applying the `->` operator to an `AugPtr` will always result in the sequence of calls `AugPtr::operator ->` followed by `Ptr::operator ->`, followed by a predefined `->` operator applied to a `T *` pointer. (See Gotcha #83 for a more realistic example of the use of `operator ->`.)

3 | The Preprocessor

Preprocessing is probably the most dangerous phase of C++ translation. The preprocessor is concerned with tokens (the "words" of which the C++ source is composed) and is ignorant of the subtleties of the rest of the C++ language, both syntactic and semantic. In effect, the preprocessor doesn't know its own strength and, like many powerful ignoramuses, is capable of much damage.

The advice of this chapter is to allow the preprocessor to perform only tasks that require much power but little knowledge of C++ and to avoid its use for anything that requires finesse.

Gotcha #25: #define Literals

C++ programmers don't use #define to define literals, because in C++ such usage causes bugs and portability problems. Consider a standard C-like use of a #define:

```
#define MAX 1<<16
```

The basic problem with preprocessor symbols is that the preprocessor expands them before the C++ compiler proper has the opportunity to examine them. The preprocessor knows nothing about the scoping or type rules of C++.

```
void f( int );
void f( long );
// . . .
f( MAX ); // which f?
```

The preprocessor symbol MAX is just the integral value 1<<16 by the time the compiler performs overload resolution. The value 1<<16 could be an int or a long, depending on the target platform of the compilation. Compiling this code on a different platform could result in invocation of a different function.

The #define directive does not respect scope. Most C++ facilities are now encapsulated in namespaces. This has a number of benefits, not the least of which is that different facilities are less likely to interfere with each other. Unfortunately, a #define is not scoped inside a namespace:

```
namespace Influential {
#       define MAX 1<<16
// . . .
}
namespace Facility {
const int max = 512;
// . . .
}
// . . .
int a[MAX]; // oops!
```

The programmer forgot to import the name max and also misspelled it as MAX. However, the preprocessor replaced MAX with 1<<16, so the code compiled anyway. "I wonder why I'm using so much memory…"

The solution to all these problems is, of course, to use an initialized constant:

```
const int max = 1<<9;
```

Now the type of max is the same on all platforms, and the name max follows the usual scoping rules. Note that use of max will probably be just as efficient as use of the #define, since the compiler is free to optimize away storage for the variable and simply substitute its initial value wherever it's used as an rvalue. However, because max is an lvalue (it just happens to be a nonmodifiable lvalue; see Gotcha #6), it has an address, and we can point to it. This isn't possible with a literal:

```
const int *pmax = &Facility::max;
const int *pMAX = &MAX; // error!
```

Another problem with #define literals concerns the lexical, rather than syntactic, nature of their substitution by the preprocessor. Our #define of MAX didn't cause any problems in how we used it above, but it wouldn't be hard to make it do so:

```
int b[MAX*2];
```

That's right. Because we didn't parenthesize the expression in the #define, we've actually attempted to declare a truly large array of integers:

```
int b[ 1<<16*2 ];
```

Admittedly, this error is the result of an improperly constructed #define, but it's an error that can't occur with the corresponding use of an initialized constant.

We have the same problem in class scope. Here, we'd like to make a value available throughout the scope of the class and nowhere else. The traditional C++ solution to this problem is to employ an enumerator:

```
class Name {
    // . . .
    void capitalize();
    enum { nameLen = 32 };
    char name_[nameLen];
};
```

The enumerator nameLen occupies no storage, has a well-defined type, and is available only within the scope of the class—including, of course, the class's member functions:

```
void Name::capitalize() {
    for( int i = 0; i < nameLen; ++i )
        if( name_[i] )
            name_[i] = toupper( name_[i] );
        else
            break;
}
```

It's also legal, but not yet universally supported, to declare and initialize a constant static integral data member with an integral constant expression within the body of a class (see Gotcha #59):

```
class Name {
    // . . .
    static const int nameLen_ = 32;
};
// . . .
const int Name::nameLen_; // no initializer here!
```

However, it's possible that the space for this static data member will not be optimized away, and the traditional use of an enumerator is preferred for simple integral constants.

Gotcha #26: #define Pseudofunctions

In C, #define is often used to define pseudofunctions, where the efficiency of avoiding the cost of a function call is considered more important than safety:

```
#define repeated(b, m) (b & m & (b & m)-1)
```

Of course, all the usual caveats apply with respect to any use of the preprocessor. In particular, the above definition is flawed.

```
typedef unsigned short Bits;
enum { bit01 = 1<<0, bit02 = 1<<1, bit03 = 1<<2, // . . .
Bits a = 0;
const Bits mask = bit02 | bit03 | bit06;
// . . .
if( repeated( a+bit02, mask ) ) // oops!
    // . . .
```

Here, we've committed the common error of insufficient parenthesization of the pseudofunction. The correct definition doesn't leave anything to chance:

```
#define repeated(b, m) ((b) & (m) & ((b) & (m))-1)
```

Except side effects. A moderately different use of the pseudofunction will yield a result that's both incorrect and ambiguous:

```
if( repeated( a+=bit02, mask ) ) // double oops!
    // . . .
```

The first argument to the pseudofunction has a side effect. If repeated were a real function, the side effect would take place exactly once, before the function was called. In the case of this particular definition of repeated, the side effect will occur twice, and in an unspecified order (see Gotcha #14). Pseudofunctions are particularly dangerous because their use resembles that of real functions, but they have very different semantics. Because of this resemblance to real functions, even experienced C++ programmers tend to misuse pseudofunctions, because they assume they're calling a function.

In C++, an inline function is almost always preferable to a pseudofunction, because it will display proper function call semantics; it has the same meaning as a non-inline function:

```
inline Bits repeated( Bits b, Bits m )
    { return b & m & (b & m)-1; }
```

Macros used as pseudofunctions also suffer from the same scoping problems that affect macros used as manifest constants (see Gotcha #25):

➤➤ gotcha26/execbump.cpp

```
int kount = 0;
#define execBump( func ) (func(), ++kount)
// . . .
void aFunc() {
    extern void g();
    int kount;
    while( kount++ < 10 )
        execBump( g ); // increment local kount!
}
```

The user of the execBump pseudofunction is (one hopes) unaware that it references a variable spelled kount and has inadvertently modified the value of the local kount variable rather than the global one. A better solution would employ a function:

➤➤ gotcha26/execbump.cpp

```
int kount = 0;
inline void execBump( void (*func)() )
    { func(); ++kount; }
```

The use of an inline function binds the identifier kount to the global variable when the function body is compiled. The name will not be re-bound to a different kount variable when the function is called. (But we're still using a global variable; see Gotcha #3.)

An even better solution might employ a function object to better encapsulate the count:

➤➤ gotcha26/execbump.cpp

```
class ExecBump { // Monostate. See Gotcha #69.
  public:
    void operator ()( void (*func)() )
        { func(); ++count_; }
    int get_count() const
                { return count_; }
  private:
    static int count_;
};
// . . .
```

```
int ExecBump::count_ = 0;
// . . .
void aFunc() {
    extern void g();
    ExecBump exec;
    int count = 0;
    while( count++ < 10 )
        exec( g );
}
```

The proper uses of pseudofunctions are relatively rare and usually involve the use of the __LINE__, __FILE__, __DATE__, or __TIME__ preprocessor symbols:

➤➤ gotcha28/myassert.h

```
#define myAssert( e ) ((!(e))?void(std::cerr << "Failed: " \
    << #e << " line " << __LINE__ << std::endl): void())
```

See also Gotcha #28.

Gotcha #27: Overuse of `#if`

`#if` for Debugging

How do we insert debugging code into our programs? Everyone knows we use the preprocessor:

```
void buggy() {
#ifndef NDEBUG
    // some debugging code . . .
#endif
    // some actual code . . .
#ifndef NDEBUG
    // more debug code . . .
#endif
}
```

Everyone's wrong. Most veteran programmers have long and tedious stories about how the debug version of a program worked perfectly, but "simply" defining NDEBUG caused the production version to fail mysteriously.

Well, there's nothing mysterious about it. We're actually discussing two unrelated programs that happen to be generated from the same source files. You'd have to compile the same source code twice to see if it's even syntactically correct. The correct way to write the code is to dispense with the idea of a debugging version and write just a single program:

```
void buggy() {
    if( debug ) {
        // some debugging code . . .
    }
    // some actual code . . .
    if( debug ) {
        // more debugging code . . .
    }
}
```

What about the problem of all the debug code remaining in the executable of the production version? Isn't that going to waste space? Aren't the unnecessary conditional branches going to cost time? Not if the debug code isn't present in the executable. Compilers are very, very good at identifying and removing unusable code. They're a whole lot better at this than we are with our pathetic #ifndefs. All we have to do is make things unambiguous:

```
const bool debug = false;
```

The expression debug is what the standard calls an integer constant-expression. Every C++ compiler must be able to evaluate constant-expressions like this at compile time to translate array bound expressions, case labels, and bitfield lengths. Every minimally competent compiler can perform elimination of unreachable code of the form

```
if( false ) {
    // unreachable code . . .
}
```

Yes, even the compiler you've been complaining about to your management for the last five years can handle this. Even though the compiler removes the unreachable code, it must still perform a full parse and static semantic check.

Given the definition of constant-expression in the standard, your compiler can even eliminate unreachable code guarded by more complex expressions:

```
if( debug && debuglvl > 5 && debugopts&debugmask ) {
    // potentially unreachable code . . .
}
```

Your compiler may even perform the code elimination in more complex cases. For example, we might attempt to involve my favorite inline function in the conditional expression:

```
typedef unsigned short Bits;
inline Bits repeated( Bits b, Bits m )
    { return b & m & (b & m)-1; }
// . . .
if( debug && repeated( debugopts, debugmask ) ) {
    // potentially unreachable code . . .
    error( "One option only" );
}
```

However, with the use of a function call (whether inline or not), the expression is no longer a constant-expression, we have no guarantee that the compiler will be able to evaluate it at compile time, and therefore the code elimination may not take place. If you require the code elimination, this approach is not portable. Some programmers who have been coding in C for too long may suggest the following fix:

```
#define repeated(b, m) ((b) & (m) & ((b) & (m))-1)
```

Don't do it. (See Gotcha #26.)

Note that it may be advisable to have some conditionally compiled code in an application, to be able to set the values of constants from the compile line:

```
const bool debug =
#ifndef NDEBUG
    false
#else
    true
#endif
    ;
```

Even the presence of this minimal conditionally compiled code is not necessary, however. A generally better approach would be to select between debug and production versions in a makefile or similar facility.

Using `#if` for Portability

"However," you state with a knowing look, "my code is platform independent. I have to use `#if` to handle the different platform requirements." To prove your point, such as it is, you display the following code:

```
void operation() {
    // some portable code . . .
#ifdef PLATFORM_A
    // do something . . .
    a(); b(); c();
#endif
#ifdef PLATFORM_B
    // do same thing . . .
    d(); e();
#endif
}
```

This code is not platform-independent. It's multiplatform dependent. Any change to any of the platforms requires not only a recompilation of the source but change to the source for all platforms. You've achieved maximal coupling among platforms: a remarkable achievement, if somewhat impractical.

But that's a minor annoyance compared to the real problem that lurks inside this implementation of `operation`. Functions are abstractions. The `operation` function is an abstraction of an operation that has different implementations on different platforms. When we use high-level languages, we can often use the same source code to implement the same abstraction for different platforms. For example, the expression a = b + c, where a, b, and c are ints, has to be rendered in different ways for different processors, but the meaning of the expression is sufficiently close across processors that we can (generally) use the same source code for all platforms. This isn't always the case, particularly when our operation must be defined in terms of operating-system or library-specific operations.

The implementation of `operation` indicates that the "same" thing is supposed to happen under both supported platforms, and this may even be the case initially.

Under maintenance, however, bug reports tend to be reported and repaired on a platform-specific basis. Over a breathtakingly short period of time, the meaning of operation on different platforms will diverge, and you really will be maintaining totally different applications for each platform. Note that these different behaviors are different required behaviors, because users will come to depend on the platform-specific meanings of operation. A correct initial implementation of operation would have accessed platform dependent code through a platform-independent interface:

```
void operation() {
    // some portable code . . .
    doSomething(); // portable interface . . .
}
```

In making the abstraction explicit, it's far more likely that, under maintenance, different platforms will remain in conformance with the meaning of the operation. The declaration of doSomething belongs in the platform-independent portion of the source. The various implementations of doSomething are defined in the various platform-dependent portions of the source (if doSomething is inline, then it will be defined in a platform-specific header file). Selection of platform is handled in the makefile. No #ifs. Note also that adding or removing a particular platform requires no source code changes.

What About Classes?

Like a function, a class is an abstraction. An abstraction has an implementation that can vary at either compile time or runtime, depending on its implementation. As with a function, use of #if for varying a class's implementation is fraught with peril:

```
class Doer {
#       if ONSERVER
    ServerData x;
#       else
    ClientData x;
#       endif
    void doit();
    // . . .
};
```

```
void Doer::doit() {
#       if ONSERVER
    // do server things . . .
#       else
    // do client things . . .
#       endif
}
```

Strictly speaking, this code is not illegal unless the Doer class is defined with the ONSERVER symbol both defined and undefined in different translation units. But sometimes it would be nice if it were illegal. It's common for different versions of Doer to be defined in different translation units and then linked together without error. The runtime errors that appear are unusually arcane and difficult to track down.

Fortunately, this technique for introducing bugs is not now as common as it once was. The most obvious way to express variation of this kind is to use polymorphism:

```
class Doer { // platform-independent
 public:
    virtual ~Doer();
    virtual void doit() = 0;
};
class ServerDoer : public Doer { // platform-specific
    void doit();
    ServerData x;
};
class ClientDoer : public Doer { // platform-specific
    void doit();
    ClientData x;
};
```

Reality Check

We've looked at some fairly simple manifestations of attempts to make a single source represent different programs. From these simple examples, it looks like a straightforward task to reengineer the source code to be more maintainable through application of the idioms and patterns illustrated above.

Unfortunately, the reality is often far worse and far more complex. Typically, the source is not parameterized by a single symbol (like NDEBUG) but is subject to several symbols, each of which may take on a number of values; these symbols may also be used in combination. As we illustrated above, each combination of symbols and symbol values gives rise to an essentially different application with different required, abstract behaviors. From a practical standpoint, even if it's possible to tease apart the separate applications defined by these symbols, reengineering will unavoidably result in a change in behavior of the application on at least one platform.

However, such reengineering eventually becomes necessary when the abstract meaning of the program can no longer easily be determined and when many hundreds of compilations with different symbol settings are required simply to determine whether the source code is syntactically correct. It's far better to avoid the use of #if for versioning of source.

Gotcha #28: Side Effects in Assertions

I don't like many of the ways in which #define is used, but I do put up with the standard assert defined in <cassert>. In fact, I encourage its use, provided it's used properly. Proper use is often the problem.

There are many variations, but the assert macro is usually defined something like this:

➤➤ gotcha28/myassert.h

```
#ifndef NDEBUG
#define assert(e) ((e) \
    ? ((void)0) \
    :__assert_failed(#e,__FILE__,__LINE__) )
#else
#define assert(e) ((void)0)
#endif
```

If the NDEBUG symbol is defined, then we're not debugging, and assert is a no-op. Otherwise, we're debugging, and assert expands (in this implementation) to a conditional expression that tests a condition. If the condition is false, we produce a diagnostic message and abort.

Use of `assert` is generally superior to that of comments for documenting pre-
conditions, postconditions, and invariants. An `assert`, if enabled, performs a
runtime check on these conditions and so cannot be as easily ignored as a comment (see Gotcha #1). Unlike comments, `assert`s that become invalid are usually
corrected, since the invocation of `abort` is a potent reminder of the need for
maintenance:

➤➤ gotcha28/myassert.cpp

```cpp
template <class Cont>
void doit( Cont &c, int index ) {
    assert( index >= 0 && index < c.size() ); // #1
    assert( process( c[index] ) ); // #2
    // . . .
}
```

In the code above, however, we're misusing the `assert` facility. The line marked #2
is an obvious misuse, since we're calling a function that may have a side effect from
within an `assert`. The behavior of the code will be substantially different, depending on whether the NDEBUG symbol is set or not. This use of `assert` could result in
correct behavior while debugging and a bug when debugging is turned off. So
you'll turn on debugging and the bug will disappear. Then you'll turn off debugging, and . . .

The line marked #1 is more nuanced. The `size` member function of the `Cont`
class is probably a const member function, so it should have no side effect, right?
Wrong. Nothing except the conventional meaning of `size` promises const semantics. Even if the `size` function is const, there's no guarantee that calling it will not
have a side effect. Even if the logical state of c is unchanged by the call, its physical
state may be (see Gotcha #82). Finally, keep in mind that assertions are for catching bugs. Even if calling `size` isn't intended to have a discernible effect on the
code's subsequent behavior, its implementation may contain a bug. We'd prefer
that our uses of `assert` uncover bugs rather than hide them. Proper use of
`assert` avoids even a potential side effect in its condition:

```cpp
template <class Cont>
void doit( Cont &c, int index ) {
    const int size = c.size();
    assert( index >= 0 && index < size ); // correct
    // . . .
```

Assertions are not a cure-all, obviously, but they do occupy a useful niche situated somewhere between comments and exceptions for documenting and detecting illegal behavior. The major drawback to assertions is that `assert` is a pseudofunction and is therefore subject to all our earlier provisos about pseudofunctions (see Gotcha #26). However, it does have the advantage of being a standard pseudofunction, with the implication that its failings are well known. When used with caution, assertions can be of value.

4 | Conversions

C++'s type system is appropriately complex for a language of its expressive power. This base complexity is complicated further by the presence of user-defined conversions that may be applied implicitly during translation. In effect, the ability to extend the C++ language through the addition of abstract data types gives the designer the responsibility of designing an effective, safe, and coherent type system. Because C++ is largely statically typed, it should be possible to tame this complexity with effective design.

Unfortunately, poor coding practices can compromise even the most coherent designs. In this chapter, we'll look at some common practices that defeat static type safety. We'll also look at some frequently misunderstood areas of the C++ language that can result in compromised static type safety.

Gotcha #29: Converting through void *

Even C programmers know that a void * is second cousin to a cast and should be avoided to the extent possible. As with a cast, converting a typed pointer to void * removes all useful type information. Typically, the original type of the pointer must be "remembered" and restored when the void * is used. If the type is resupplied correctly, everything will work fine (except, of course, that having to remember types for later casting implies that the design needs work).

```
void *vp = new int(12);
// . . .
int *ip = static_cast<int *>(vp); // will work
```

Unfortunately, even this simple use of void * can open the door to portability problems. Remember that static_cast is the cast operator we use (when we must cast) for relatively safe and portable conversions. For example, one might use a static_cast to cast from a base class pointer to a publicly derived class pointer. For unsafe, platform-dependent conversions, we're forced to use rein-terpret_cast. For example, one might use a reinterpret_cast to cast from an integer to a pointer or between pointers to unrelated types:

```
char *cp = static_cast<char *>(ip); // error!
char *cp = reinterpret_cast<char *>(ip); // works.
```

The use of reinterpret_cast is a clear indication to you and to the readers and maintainers of your code that you're not only casting but that you're casting in a potentially nonportable way. Use of a void * intermediary allows that important warning to be circumvented:

```
char *cp = static_cast<char *>(vp); // put int addr into a char *!
```

It gets worse. Consider a user interface that allows the address of a "Widget" to be stored and later retrieved:

```
typedef void *Widget;
void setWidget( Widget );
Widget getWidget();
```

Users of this interface recognize that they have to remember the type of Widget they set, so they can restore its type information when it's retrieved:

```
// In some header file . . .
class Button {
    // . . .
};
class MyButton : public Button {
    // . . .
};
// elsewhere . . .
MyButton *mb = new MyButton;
setWidget( mb );

// somewhere else entirely . . .
Button *b = static_cast<Button *>(getWidget()); // might work!
```

This code will usually work, even though we lose some type information when we extract the Widget. The stored Widget refers to a MyButton but is extracted as a Button. The reason this code will often work has to do with the likely way that the storage for a class object is laid out in memory.

Typically, a derived class object contains the storage for its base class subobject starting at offset 0, as if its base class part were the first data member of the derived class, and simply appends any additional derived class data below that, as in Figure 4–1. Therefore, the address of a derived class object is generally the same as that of its base class. (Note, however, that the standard guarantees correct results only if the address in the void ∗ is converted to exactly the same type used to set the void ∗. See Gotcha #70 for one way this code could fail even under single inheritance.)

However, this code is fragile, in that a remote change during maintenance may introduce a bug. In particular, a straightforward and proper use of multiple inheritance may break the code:

```
// in some header file . . .
class Subject {
    // . . .
};
class ObservedButton : public Subject, public Button {
    // . . .
};
// elsewhere . . .
ObservedButton *ob = new ObservedButton;
setWidget( ob );
// . . .
Button *badButton = static_cast<Button *>(getWidget()); // disaster!
```

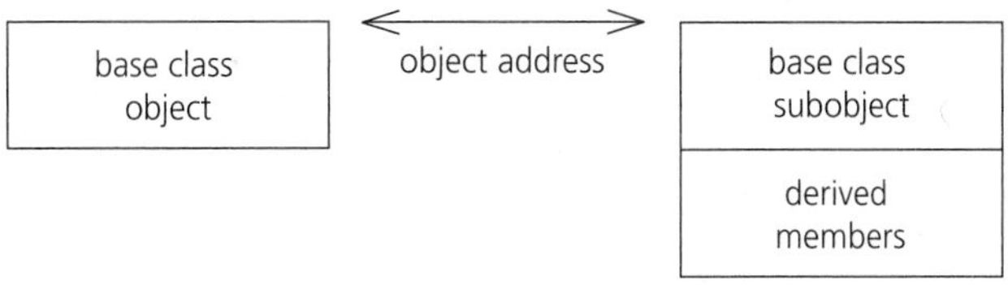

base class object	object address	base class subobject
		derived members

Figure 4–1 | Likely layout of a derived class under single inheritance

The problem is with the layout of the derived class object under multiple inheritance. An ObservedButton has two base class parts, and only one of them can have the same address as the complete object. Typically, storage for the first base class (in this case, Subject) is placed at offset 0 in the derived class, followed by the storage for subsequent base classes (in this case, Button), followed by any additional derived class data members, as in Figure 4–2. Under multiple inheritance, a single object commonly has multiple valid addresses.

Ordinarily this is not a problem, since the compiler is aware of the various offsets and can perform the correct adjustments at compile time:

```
Button *bp = new ObservedButton;
ObservedButton *obp = static_cast<ObservedButton *>(bp);
```

In the code above, bp correctly points to the Button part of the ObservedButton object, not to the start of the object. When we cast from a Button pointer to an ObservedButton pointer, the compiler is able to adjust the address so that it points to the start of the ObservedButton object. It's not hard, since the compiler knows the offset of each base class part within a derived class, as long as it knows the type of the base and derived classes.

And that's our problem. When we use setWidget, we throw away all useful type information. When we cast the result of getWidget to Button, the compiler can't perform the adjustment to the address. As a result, the Button pointer is actually referring to a Subject!

Void pointers do have their uses, as do casts, but they should be used sparingly. It's never a good idea to use a void * as part of an interface that requires one use of the interface to resupply type information lost through another use.

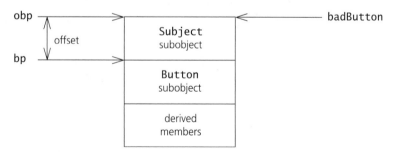

Figure 4–2 | Likely layout of an object under multiple inheritance. An Observed-Button object contains subobjects for both its Subject and Button base classes. Loss of type information caused **badButton** to refer to a non-**Button** address.

Gotcha #30: Slicing

Slicing occurs when a derived class object is copied onto a base class object. As a result, the derived class-specific data and behavior will be "sliced off," usually resulting in an error or unpredictable behavior:

```
class Employee {
 public:
   virtual ~Employee();
   virtual void pay() const;
   // . . .
 protected:
   void setType( int type )
       { myType_ = type; }
 private:
   int myType_; // bad idea, see Gotcha #69
};
class Salaried : public Employee {
   // . . .
};
Employee employee;
Salaried salaried;
employee = salaried; // slice!
```

The assignment of `salaried` to `employee` is perfectly legal, since a `Salaried` is-a `Employee`, but the result is probably not what we wanted. After the assignment, the behavior of `employee`, both of its virtual and nonvirtual functions, will be `Employee` behavior. Additionally, any `Salaried`-specific data members will not be copied.

Most damaging, however, is that the state of `employee` will be a copy of the `Employee` part of `salaried`. What's wrong with that? Well, a derived `Salaried` object may use its `Employee` base class part to store `Salaried`-appropriate values that may not make sense in the context of an `Employee` object (see Gotcha #91).

As an illustration, suppose classes derived from `Employee` were to store some sort of type identification code in their `Employee` subobject. (Please note that this is not actually good design practice; it's just an illustration. See Gotcha #69.) After the slice, `employee` will behave like an `Employee` but will claim to be a `Salaried`.

In actual practice, the disconnect between the state of the sliced object and its behavior tends to be much more subtle and therefore much more damaging.

The most common source of slicing occurs when a derived class object is passed by value to initialize a base class formal parameter:

```
void fire( Employee victim );
// . . .
fire( salaried ); // slice!
```

This problem can be avoided through passing by reference (or pointer) instead of by value. In that case, no slicing will occur, since the derived class object is not actually copied and the formal argument is simply an alias for the actual argument (see Gotcha #5):

```
void rightSize( Employee &asset );
// . . .
rightSize( salaried ); // no slice
```

Other slicing problems are also possible, though less common. For example, it's possible to copy a base class subobject from one derived class object to another derived class object of a different type:

```
Employee *getNextEmployee(); // get an object derived from Employee
// . . .
Employee *ep = getNextEmployee();
*ep = salaried; // slice!
```

Problems with slicing generally indicate deeper design flaws in a hierarchy. The best and simplest way to avoid slicing problems is to avoid concrete base classes (see Gotcha #93):

```
class Employee {
 public:
   virtual ~Employee();
   virtual void pay() const = 0;
   // . . .
};
```

```
void fire( Employee ); // error, fortunately
void rightSize( Employee & ); // OK
Employee *getNextEmployee(); // OK
Employee *ep = getNextEmployee(); // OK
*ep = salaried; // error, fortunately
Employee e2( salaried ); // error, fortunately
```

An abstract base class can't be instantiated, so most situations that could lead to slicing will be caught at compile time.

Note that in rare situations, slicing is used intentionally in an implementation to modify the behavior or type of a derived class object. Typically, no data are sliced off, and slicing is used to "reinterpret" the base class data with different derived class behaviors. These techniques are useful but rare and should never be exposed as part of a general-purpose interface.

Gotcha #31: Misunderstanding Pointer-to-Const Conversion

First, let's get some terminology straight. A "const pointer" is a pointer that is constant. It doesn't imply that what the pointer refers to is constant. True, the C++ standard library has a concept of `const_iterator`, which is a non-constant iterator into a sequence of constant elements, but that is a symptom of design-by-committee or some similar disease.

```
const char *pci; // pointer to const
char * const cpi = 0; // const pointer
char const *pci2; // pointer to const, see Gotcha #18
const char * const cpci = 0; // const pointer to const
char *ip; // pointer
```

The standard permits conversions that "increase constness." For example, we can copy a pointer to non-const to a pointer to const. This allows us to, among other things, pass a pointer to non-constant character to the standard `strcmp` or `strlen` functions, even though they're declared to accept pointers to constant character. Intuitively, we understand that in allowing a pointer to const to refer to non-constant data, we're not violating any constraint implied by the data's declaration. We also understand the reverse conversion is invalid, because it would grant greater permission than the declaration of the data specifies:

```
size_t strlen( const char * );
// . . .
int i = strlen( cpi ); // OK . . .
pci = ip; // OK . . .
ip = pci; // error!
```

Note that the language rules take the conservative point of view: it may actually be "OK," in the sense of not dumping core immediately, to modify the data referred to by a pointer to const if those data actually aren't const, or if they are const but the platform doesn't allocate const data in a read-only area of memory. However, the use of const is typically a statement of design intent as well as a physical property. The language can be seen to enforce the intent of the designer.

Gotcha #32: Misunderstanding Pointer-to-Pointer-to-Const Conversion

The happily simple state of conversions that holds for pointer to const does not hold in the case of pointer to pointer to const. Consider an attempt to convert a pointer to a pointer to a char to a pointer to a pointer to a const char (that is, to convert char ** to const char **):

```
char **ppc;
const char **ppcc = ppc; // error!
```

It looks harmless, but, like many harmless-looking conversions, it opens the door to a subversion of the type system:

```
const T t = init;
T *pt;
const T **ppt = &pt; // error, fortunately
*ppt = &t;   // put a const T * into a T *!
*pt = value; // trash t!
```

This compelling subject is treated in section 4.4 of the standard, under "Qualification Conversions." (Technically, const and volatile are known in C as "type-qualifiers," but the C++ standard tends to refer to them as "cv-qualifiers." I tend to refer to them as type-qualifiers.) There we find the following simple rules for determining convertibility:

A conversion can add cv-qualifiers at levels other than the first in multi-level pointers, subject to the following rules:

Two pointer types T1 and T2 are similar if there exists a type T and integer n > 0 such that:

T1 is $cv_{1,0}$ pointer to $cv_{1,1}$ pointer to ... $cv_{1,n-1}$ pointer to $cv_{1,n}$ T

and

T2 is $cv_{2,0}$ pointer to $cv_{2,1}$ pointer to ... $cv_{2,n-1}$ pointer to $cv_{2,n}$ T

where each $cv_{i,j}$ is const, volatile, const volatile, or nothing.

In other words, two pointers are similar if they have the same base type and have the same number of `*`'s. So, for example, the types char `*` const `**` and const char `***`const are similar, but int `*` const `*` and int `***` are not.

The n-tuple of cv-qualifiers after the first in a pointer type, e.g., $cv_{1,1}$, $cv_{1,2}$, ..., $cv_{1,n}$ in the pointer type T1, is called the *cv-qualification* signature of the pointer type. An expression of type T1 can be converted to type T2 if and only if the following conditions are satisfied:

- The pointer types are similar.

- For every $j > 0$, if const is in $cv_{1,j}$ then const is in $cv_{2,j}$, and similarly for volatile.

- If the $cv_{1,j}$ and $cv_{2,j}$ are different, then const is in every $cv_{2,k}$ for $0 < k < j$.

Armed with these rules—and a little patience—we can determine the legality of pointer conversions such as the following:

```
int * * * const cnnn = 0;
    // n==3, signature == none, none, none
int * * const * ncnn = 0;
    // n==3, signature == const, none, none
int * const * * nncn = 0;
    // signature == none, const, none
int * const * const * nccn = 0;
    // signature == const, const, none
const int * * * nnnc = 0;
    // signature == none, none, const


// examples of application of rules
ncnn = cnnn; // OK
```

```
nncn = cnnn; // error!
nccn = cnnn; // OK
ncnn = cnnn; // OK
nnnc = cnnn; // error!
```

These rules may seem esoteric, but their use arises fairly often. Consider the following common situation:

```
extern char *namesOfPeople[];
for( const char **currentName = namesOfPeople; // error!
        *currentName; currentName++ ) // . . .
```

In my experience, the typical response to this error is to file a bug report with the compiler vendor, cast away the error, and dump core later on. As usual, the compiler is right and the developer is not.

Let's reconsider a more specific version of our earlier example:

```
typedef int T;
const T t = 12345;
T *pt;
const T **ppt = (const T **)&pt; // an evil cast!
*ppt = &t;  // put a const T * into a T *!
*pt = 54321; // trash t!
```

The truly tragic aspect of this code is that the bug may remain undetected for years before manifesting itself under simple maintenance. For example, we can use the value of t:

```
cout << t; // output 12345, probably
```

Because the compiler may freely substitute the initializer of a constant for the constant itself, this statement is likely to output the value 12345 even after the value of the constant has been changed to 54321. Later, a slightly different use of t will unveil the bug:

```
const T *pct = &t;
// . . .
cout << t; // output 12345
cout << *pct; // output 54321!
```

It's often better design to avoid the complexities of pointers to pointers through use of references or the standard library. For example, it's common in C to pass the address of a pointer (that is, a pointer to a pointer) to modify the value of the pointer:

➤➤ gotcha32/gettoken.cpp

```cpp
// get_token returns a pointer to the next sequence of
// characters bounded by characters in ws.
// The argument pointer is updated to point past the
// returned token.
char *get_token( char **s, const char *ws = " \t\n" ) {
    char *p;
    do
        for( p = ws; *p && **s != *p; p++ );
    while( *p ? *(*s)++ : 0 );
    char *ret = *s;
    do
        for( p = ws; *p && **s != *p; p++ );
    while( *p ? 0 : **s ? (*s)++ : 0 );
    if( **s ) {
        **s = '\0';
        ++*s;
    }
    return ret;
}

extern char *getInputBuffer();
char *tokens = getInputBuffer();
// . . .
while( *tokens )
    cout << get_token( &tokens ) << endl;
```

In C++, we prefer to pass the pointer argument as a reference to non-constant. This cleans up the implementation of the function somewhat and, more important, makes its use less clumsy:

➤➤ gotcha32/gettoken.cpp

```cpp
char *get_token( char *&s, const char *ws = " \t\n" ) {
    char *p;
    do
        for( p = ws; *p && *s != *p; p++ );
```

```
    while( *p ? *s++ : 0 );
    char *ret = s;
    do
        for( p = ws; *p && *s != *p; p++ );
    while( *p ? 0 : *s ? s++ : 0 );
    if( *s ) *s++ = '\0';
    return ret;
}
// . . .
while( *tokens )
    cout << get_token( tokens ) << endl;
```

Our original example can be more safely rendered with standard library components:

```
extern vector<string> namesOfPeople;
```

Gotcha #33: Misunderstanding Pointer-to-Pointer-to-Base Conversion

We face a similar situation with pointers to pointers to derived classes:

```
D1 d1;
D1 *d1p = &d1; // OK
B **ppb1 = &d1p; // error, fortunately
D2 *d2p;
B **ppb2 = &d2p; // error, fortunately
*ppb2 = *ppb1; // now d2p points to a D1!
```

Look familiar? Just as the const-conversion property doesn't hold if one introduces another level of indirection, the same is the case with the is-a property. While a pointer to a derived class is-a pointer to a public base, a pointer to a pointer to a derived class is not a pointer to a pointer to a public base. As with the analogous const example, the situation that results in an error initially looks contrived. However, it's easy to construct a situation that produces an error as a cooperative effort between a bad interface design and an incorrect use of the interface:

```
void doBs( B *bs[], B *pb ) {
    for( int i = 0; bs[i]; ++i )
        if( somecondition( bs[i], pb ) )
            bs[i] = pb; // oops!
}
```

```
// . . .
extern D1 *array[];
D2 *aD2 = getMeAD2();
doBs( (B **)array, aD2 ); // another casted death wish . . .
```

Once again, the developer assumes the compiler is in error and circumvents the type system with a cast. In this case, though, the designer of the function interface has a lot to answer for as well. A safer design would have employed a container that didn't permit spoofing by cast, as an array does.

Gotcha #34: Pointer-to-Multidimensional-Array Problems

C and C++ arrays are pretty minimal. In fact, an array name is really not much more than a pointer literal that refers to the first element of the array:

```
int a[5];
int * const pa = a;
int * const *ppa = &pa;
const int alen = sizeof(a)/sizeof(a[0]); // alen == 5
```

The only practical differences between an array name and a constant pointer are that the array name gives the array size in a `sizeof` expression rather than giving the size of a pointer, and an array name occupies no storage and therefore has no address. To be clear: an array has an address, and that address is indicated by the array name; the array name itself has no address:

```
int *ip = a; // a is a ptr to first element of array
int (*ap)[5] = &a; // &a is the address of the array, not a
int (*ap2)[sizeof(a)/sizeof(a[0])] = &a; // same thing
int **pip = &ip; // &ip is the address of a pointer, not an array
```

This is also the case for multidimensional arrays or, more properly, arrays of arrays. But remember that the type of the first element of a multidimensional array is an array, not the base type:

```
int aa[2][3];
const int aalen = sizeof(aa)/sizeof(aa[0]); // aalen = 2
```

Therefore, aa is essentially a pointer literal to the first element of an array of three integers. It's not a pointer to an integer. This can lead to some surprising, if technically correct, results:

```
void processElems( int *, size_t );
void processElems( void *, size_t );
// . . .
processElems( a, alen );
processElems( aa, aalen ); // oops!
```

The first call to the overloaded processElems function matches the version that takes an int * argument; the array name a is just an int * in disguise. The second call matches the version of processElem that takes a void *, which is probably not what the programmer intended. The type of the multidimensional array name is a pointer to its first element, which is an array of a particular size, not a pointer to the base type of the array. There is no implicit conversion of an int(*)[3] (that is, a pointer to an array of three integers) to an int *, but there is such a conversion to a void *.

```
int (* const paa)[3] = aa;
int (* const *ppaa)[3] = &paa;
void processElems( int (*)[3], size_t );
// . . .
processElems( aa, aalen ); // OK.
```

Multidimensional arrays are problematic. A better alternative is generally to use the standard library containers or special-purpose containers that implement abstract multidimensional arrays. If a situation does require the use of raw multidimensional arrays, encapsulating them is usually best. It's just not responsible to expose a naive user of your interface to

```
int *(*(*aryCallback)(int *(*)[n]))[n];
```

This is (of course) a pointer to a function that takes a pointer to an array of n pointers to int and returns a pointer of the same type. All right, that's just showing off. (See Gotcha #11.) A typedef would have simplified things considerably:

```
typedef int *(*PA)[n];
PA (*aryCallback)(PA); // more humane
```

Gotcha #35: Unchecked Downcasting

Casting a base class pointer to a derived class pointer ("downcasting") may result in a bad address, as illustrated in the example below and in Figure 4–3. The delta arithmetic performed by the compiler on the casted pointer assumes that the base class address belongs to a base class part of the derived class:

```
class A { public: virtual ~A(); };
class B { public: virtual ~B(); };
class D : public A, public B {};
class E : public B {};
B *bp = getMeAB(); // get an object derived from B
D *dp = static_cast<D*>(bp); // safe???
```

The best approach is to design so that downcasting is unnecessary; systematic use of downcasts is often an indication of bad design. If a downcast really is required, it's often a good idea to use a dynamic_cast, which will perform a runtime check to ensure that the cast is correct:

```
if( D *dp = dynamic_cast<D *>(bp) ) {
    // cast succeeded
}
else {
    // cast failed
}
```

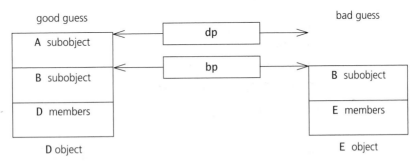

Figure 4–3 Effect of a bad static cast: casting a pointer to the B subobject of an E object to a D pointer

Gotcha #36: Misusing Conversion Operators

Overuse of conversion operators increases code complexity. Because the compiler applies them implicitly, the presence of too many conversion operators in a class can result in ambiguity:

```
class Cell {
 public:
   // . . .
   operator int() const;
   operator double() const;
   operator const char *() const;
   typedef char **PPC;
   operator PPC() const;
   // etc . . .
};
```

A Cell can answer so many different requirements that its users may frequently find it answers more than one simultaneously, with the result of compile-time ambiguity. Worse, in cases with no ambiguity and no compile-time error, it's still often difficult to determine precisely what implicit conversion the compiler has employed. It's generally better to dispense with conversion operators where many conversions are required and employ the more straightforward alternative of explicit conversion functions:

```
class Cell {
 public:
   // . . .
   int toInt() const;
   double toDouble() const;
   const char *toPtrConstChar() const;
   char **toPtrPtrChar() const;
   // etc . . .
};
```

Ordinarily, one would expect to have no more than a single conversion operator in a class, if that. The presence of two is worth a second look. The presence of three or more is an indication that it's time to get a second opinion.

Even a single conversion operator may provoke ambiguity in combination with a constructor:

```
class B;

class A {
  public:
    A( const B & );
    // . . .
};

class B {
  public:
    operator A() const;
    // . . .
};
```

There are two ways to convert a B to an A implicitly: A's constructor or B's conversion operator. The result is an ambiguity:

```
extern A a;
extern B b;
a = b; // error! ambiguous
a = b.operator A(); // OK, but odd
a = A(b); // error! ambiguous
```

Note the lack of a direct way to invoke a constructor or take its address. The expression A(b) is, therefore, not a constructor call, even though such expressions often result in the invocation of a constructor. It's a request to convert b to type A by any means whatsoever, and it's still ambiguous. (Unfortunately, most compilers will nevertheless not flag the error and will use class A's constructor to perform the conversion.)

It's typically better to dispense with conversion operators, declare single-argument constructors explicit, and avoid implicit conversions, except in cases where their presence is really appropriate. Where nonexplicit constructors and conversion operators are indicated, a rule of thumb is to prefer the use of constructors to convert from user-defined types and conversion operators to convert only to predefined types.

The purpose of conversion operators is to further integrate an abstract data type into an existing type system, by providing implicit conversions that mirror the implicit conversions supported by the predefined types. It's a mistake to use a conversion operator to implement a "value-added" conversion:

```
class Complex {
    //  . . .
    operator double() const;
};
Complex velocity = x + y;
double speed = velocity;


class Container {
    //  . . .
    virtual operator Iterator *() const = 0;
};
Container &c = getNewContainer();
Iterator *i = c;
```

Here, the designer of the `Complex` class wants to be able to determine the length of the vector defined by the complex number. However, a user of this interface may assume that the conversion to `double` returns the real part of the complex, the imaginary part, the angle of the vector, or any other reasonable interpretation. The intent of the conversion is unclear.

The designer of the abstract `Container` interface would like to implement a Factory Method that returns a pointer to an appropriate iterator into the concrete container derived from `Container`. However, we're not converting a `Container` into an `Iterator`, and implementation of the Factory Method as a conversion is confusing and inappropriate. It could also cause maintenance problems if the Factory Method should require an argument in the future. Because the conversion operator cannot take an argument, it would have to be replaced by a nonoperator function. This, in turn, would force all users of the `Container` class to locate and rewrite all the implicit uses of the conversion operator.

It's much better to reserve conversion operators for their intended use as conversions. Better interfaces for all these design goals are better achieved with nonoperator functions:

```
class Complex {
    // . . .
    double magnitude() const;
};
Complex velocity = x + y;
double speed = velocity.magnitude();

class Container {
    // . . .
    virtual Iterator *genIterator() const = 0;
};
Container &c = getNewContainer();
Iterator *i = c.genIterator();
```

This advice holds, I claim, even in the case of a simple conversion to bool (or, sometimes, void *) to indicate that an object is in a valid or usable state:

```
class X {
 public:
    virtual operator bool() const = 0;
    // . . .
};
// . . .
extern X &a;
if( a ) {
    // a is usable . . .
```

Once again, this "value-added" use of the conversion operator results in imprecision. In the future, we may wish to distinguish among X objects that are invalid, unusable, or corrupted. It's better to be precise:

```
class X {
 public:
    virtual bool isValid() const = 0;
    virtual bool isUsable() const = 0;
    // . . .
};
```

```
// . . .
if( a.isValid() ) {
    // . . .
```

The standard iostream library employs conversion operators to allow an easy check on the state of an iostream:

```
if( cout ) // is cout in a good state?
    // . . .
```

An `operator void *` provides this capability, and the statement above would be translated in a way similar to this:

```
if( static_cast<bool>(cout.operator void *()) ) // . . .
```

If the iostream is in a bad state, the conversion operator returns a null pointer; otherwise, it returns a non-null pointer. Since the conversion from a pointer to a `bool` is predefined, it may be used to test the state of the iostream. Unfortunately, it may also be used to set the value of a `void` pointer:

```
void *coutp = cout; // odd and almost useless
cout << cout << cin << cerr; // print some void *'s
```

However, the existence of a conversion from an iostream to a `void *`, while odd, is not as problematic as the existence of a conversion to `bool` would be:

```
cout >> 12; // won't compile, fortunately
```

Here, we've made the common mistake of using the right-shift operator rather than the left-shift operator with an output stream. If it were possible to convert an output stream directly to a `bool`, this statement would compile. `cout` would be converted to a `bool` value, which, in turn, would be converted to `int`, and the result would be shifted 12 bit positions to the right. Clearly, the conversion of `cout` to `void *` is preferable to a conversion to `bool`, but it would have been an even better design to dispense with conversion operators entirely, in preference to a clear and unambiguous member function:

```
if( !cout.fail() )
    // . . .
```

Gotcha #37: Unintended Constructor Conversion

A single-argument constructor specifies both an initialization and a conversion. As with a conversion operator, a constructor conversion may be applied implicitly by the compiler. This is sometimes convenient:

```
class String {
 public:
    String( const char * );
    operator const char *() const;
    // . . .
};
String name1( "Fred" ); // direct init
name1 = "Joe"; // implicit conversion
const char *cname = name1; // implicit conversion
String name2 = cname; // implicit conversion, copy init
String name3 = String( cname ); // explicit conversion, copy init
```

(See Gotcha #56.) However, implicit constructor conversions can often render code hard to understand and can introduce obscure bugs. Consider a container template for a stack of fixed, maximum size:

```
template <class T>
class BoundedStack {
 public:
    BoundedStack( int maxSize );
    ~BoundedStack();
    bool operator ==( const BoundedStack & ) const;
    void push( const T & );
    void pop();
    const T &top() const;
    // . . .
};
```

Our BoundedStack types have the usual stack operations of push, pop, and so on, as well as the ability to compare two stacks for equality. When we create a BoundedStack<T>, we must provide its maximum size.

```
BoundedStack<double> s( 128 );
s.push( 37.0 );
s.push( 232.78 );
// . . .
```

Unfortunately, the single-argument constructor may be applied as a conversion in cases where we would probably have preferred a compile-time error:

```
if( s == 37 ) { // oops!
   // . . .
```

In this case, chances are that we intended to have a condition like s.top() == 37. Unfortunately, the condition will compile without error, because the compiler is able to convert the integer value 37 into a BoundedStack<double> and pass it as an argument to BoundedStack<double>::operator ==. Effectively, the compiler generates the following code:

```
BoundedStack<double> stackTemp( 37 );
bool resultTemp( s.operator ==( stackTemp ) );
stackTemp.~BoundedStack<double>();
if( resultTemp ) {
   // . . .
```

The resulting code is legal, incorrect, and expensive. A safer alternative would be to declare the BoundedStack constructor to be explicit. The explicit keyword tells the compiler that it may not use the constructor as an implicit conversion, although it may still be used as an explicit conversion:

```
template <class T>
class BoundedStack {
 public:
    explicit BoundedStack( int maxSize );
    // . . .
};
// . . .
if( s == 37 ) { // error, fortunately
    // . . .
if( s.top() == 37 ) { // correct, no conversion
    // . . .
```

```
if( s == static_cast< BoundedStack<double> >(37) ) { // correct . . .
  // . . .
```

Insidious implicit conversions are much more to be feared than the occasional necessity of performing an explicit conversion, so it's common and recommended to declare most single-argument constructors `explicit`.

Note that declaring a constructor `explicit` also affects the set of legal initialization syntaxes one may employ when declaring an object of a class. Let's make a change to our `String` class above and see how it affects the set of legal initializations:

```
class String {
 public:
   explicit String( const char * );
   operator const char *() const;
   // . . .
};
String name1( "Fred" ); // OK.
name1 = "Joe"; // error!
const char *cname = name1; // implicit conversion, OK
String name2 = cname; // error!
String name3 = String( cname ); // explicit conversion, OK
```

The implicit temporary generation that is part of the copy initializations of `name2` and the argument of `String::operator` = are now illegal. The initialization of `name3` is still legal, because the conversion is explicit (although it would have been better form to perform the initialization with a `static_cast`; see Gotcha #40). As usual, it's best to use direct initialization in preference to copy initialization. (See Gotcha #56.)

Before we leave the subject of `explicit` behind, let's have a look at an instructive, but now outmoded, technique for implementing the semantics of `explicit` without use of the keyword:

```
class StackInit {
 public:
   StackInit( size_t s ) : size_( s ) {}
   int getSize() const { return size_; }
 private:
   int size_;
};
```

```
template <class T>
class BoundedStack {
 public:
    BoundedStack( const StackInit &init );
    // . . .
};
```

Because the BoundedStack constructor isn't declared to be explicit, the compiler will attempt to convert implicitly any StackInit objects to BoundedStack. However, the compiler won't make the attempt to convert an integer to a Stack-Init and follow that implicit conversion with a second implicit conversion of StackInit to BoundedStack. The standard specifies that the compiler will attempt only a single implicit user-defined conversion at a time:

```
BoundedStack<double> s( 128 ); // OK.
BoundedStack<double> t = 128; // OK.
if( s == 37 ) { // error!
    // . . .
```

This technique gives us behavior almost identical to that of explicit. The declaration of s and t is legal, because only a single user-defined conversion is necessary to convert 128 into a StackInit to pass to the constructor. However, the compiler will not attempt to convert 37 to a BoundedStack<double>, because that would require a sequence of two user-defined conversions: int to StackInit and StackInit to BoundedStack<double>.

Gotcha #38: Casting under Multiple Inheritance

Under multiple inheritance, an object may have many valid addresses. Each base class subobject of a complete object may have a unique address, and each of these addresses is a valid address for the complete object. (In a poorly designed single-inheritance hierarchy, an object might have two valid addresses. See Gotcha #70.)

```
class A { /* . . .*/ };
class B { /* . . .*/ };
class C : public A, public B { /* . . .*/ };
// . . .
```

```
C *cp = new C;
A *ap = cp; // OK
B *bp = cp; // OK
```

In the example above, the B subobject of the C complete object is likely to be allocated at a fixed offset, or "delta," from the start of the C object. Conversion of the derived class pointer cp to B * will therefore result in adjustment of cp by the delta to produce a valid B address. The conversion is type safe, efficient, and automatically implemented by the compiler.

Similarly, the existence of multiple valid addresses for an object forces C++ to be precise about the meaning of pointer comparison:

```
if( bp == cp ) // . . .
```

The question we are asking is not "Do these two pointers contain the same bit pattern?" but rather "Do these two pointers refer to the same object?" The implementation of the condition may be more complex, but it's still efficient, safe, and automatic. The compiler probably implements the pointer comparison in a way similar to the following:

```
if( bp ? (char *)bp-delta==(char *)cp : cp==0 )
```

Both old- and new-style casts may be used to perform conversions that respect delta arithmetic on class object addresses. However, unlike the conversions above, there is no guarantee that the result of the cast will be a valid address. (A dynamic_cast will give such a guarantee but may introduce other problems. See Gotchas #97, #98, and #99.)

```
B *gimmeAB();
bp = gimmeAB();
cp = static_cast<C *>(bp); cp = (C *) bp;
typedef C *CP;
cp = CP( bp );
```

All three casts will perform delta arithmetic on bp, but the result will be valid only if the B object to which bp refers is part of a containing C object. If this assumption is incorrect, the result will be a bad address, equivalent to some creative C-style code:

```
cp = (C *)((char *)bp-delta)
```

A `reinterpret_cast` will do just what it says. It will simply reinterpret the bit pattern of its argument to mean something else, probably without modifying the bits. Effectively, it "turns off" the delta arithmetic. (To be perfectly precise, the standard says the behavior of this cast is implementation-defined, but it's universally understood to "turn off hierarchy traversal." However, this behavior is not guaranteed by the standard, and `reinterpret_cast` may actually change the bit representation of the pointer.)

```
cp = reinterpret_cast<C *>(bp);   // yes, I do want to dump core . . .
```

All these uses of casts are asking the object referred to by the B pointer to take on more responsibility than its interface can guarantee. We have a bad design, because we know too little about an object's capabilities and are using a static cast to force the object into a role it may not be able to fulfill. It's best to avoid static casts on class objects. Later, I'll argue that it's best to avoid dynamic casts as well. You get the picture.

Gotcha #39: Casting Incomplete Types

Incomplete class types have no definition, but it's still possible to declare pointers and references to them and to declare functions that take arguments and return results of the incomplete types. This is a common and useful practice:

```
class Y;
class Z;
Y *convert( Z * );
```

The problem arises when a programmer tries to force the issue; ignorance is bliss only to a certain extent:

```
Y *convert( Z *zp )
    { return reinterpret_cast<Y *>(zp); }
```

The `reinterpret_cast` is necessary here, because the compiler doesn't have any information available about the relationship between the types Y and Z. Therefore, the best it can offer us is to "reinterpret" the bit pattern in the Z pointer as a Y pointer. This may even work for a while:

```
class Y { /* . . .*/ };
class Z : public Y { /* . . .*/ };
```

It's likely that the Y base class subobject in a Z object has the same address as the complete object. However, this may not continue to be the case, and a remote change could affect the legality of the cast. (See Gotchas #38 and #70.)

```
class X { /* . . .*/ };
class Z : public X, public Y { /* . . .*/ };
```

The use of a `reinterpret_cast` will probably cause the delta arithmetic to be "turned off," and we'll get a bad Y address.

Actually, the `reinterpret_cast` is not the only available choice, since we could have used an old-style cast as well. This may initially seem the better choice, because an old-style cast will perform the delta arithmetic if it has enough information at its disposal. However, this flexibility actually compounds the problem, because we may get different behavior from the ostensibly same conversion, depending on what information is available when the conversion is defined:

```
Y *convert( Z *zp )
   { return (Y *)zp; }
// . . .
class Z : public X, public Y { // . . .
// . . .
Z *zp = new Z;
Y *yp1 = convert( zp );
Y *yp2 = (Y *)zp;
cout << zp << ' ' << yp1 << ' ' << yp2 << endl;
```

The value of yp1 will match that of either zp or yp2, depending on whether the definition of `convert` occurs before or after the definition of class Z.

The situation can become immeasurably more complex if `convert` is a template function with many instantiations in many different object files. In this case, the ultimate meaning of the cast may depend on the idiosyncrasies of your linker. (See Gotcha #11.)

The use of `reinterpret_cast` is preferable to that of an old-style cast, in this case, because it will be more consistently incorrect. My preference would be to avoid either.

Gotcha #40: Old-Style Casts

Don't use old-style casts. They simply do too much for and to you and are entirely too easy to use. Consider a header file:

```
// emp.h
// . . .
const Person *getNextEmployee();
// . . .
```

This header is used throughout the application, including the following section of code:

```
#include "emp.h"
// . . .
Person *victim = (Person *)getNextEmployee();
dealWith( victim );
// . . .
```

Now, any casting away of constness is potentially dangerous and unportable. Suppose, however, the author of this code is more clairvoyant than the rest of us and has determined that this particular use of the cast is correct and portable. The code is still wrong for two reasons. First, the conversion requested is much stronger than is necessary. Second, the author has fallen into the beginner's fallacy of depending on "secondary semantics": this code assumes that the observed, but unadvertised, behavior of the abstraction expressed by the getNextEmployee function will continue to be supported in the future.

Essentially, this use of getNextEmployee assumes that the function will never change after its initial implementation. Of course, this is not the case. Soon the implementer of the emp.h header file will recognize that employees are not people and will correct the design accordingly:

```
// emp.h
// . . .
const Employee *getNextEmployee();
// . . .
```

Unfortunately, the cast is still legal, although it has changed its meaning from modifying the constness of its object to changing the set of operations available on the object. In using the cast, we're telling the compiler that we know more about the type system than the compiler does. Originally, this may have been the case, but when the header file is maintained, it's unlikely that all uses of the header will be revisited, and our imperious command to the compiler will stand uncorrected. The use of the appropriate new-style cast would have allowed the compiler to detect the change in usage and flag the error:

```
#include "emp.h"
// . . .
Person *victim = const_cast<Person *>(getNextEmployee());
dealWith( victim );
```

Note that the use of a `const_cast`, while an improvement over an old-style cast, is still dangerous. We're still relying on the assumption that, under maintenance, the unadvertised—and perhaps accidental—collaboration between the functions `getNextEmployee` and `dealWith` that permit the `const_cast` will continue to hold.

Gotcha #41: Static Casts

By "static casts" we mean—unsurprisingly—non-dynamic casts. Under this definition, we include not only the `static_cast` operator but also `reinterpret_cast`, `const_cast`, and old-style casts.

The basic problem with static casts is that they're static. In employing such a construct, we're asking the compiler to accept our version of an object's capabilities rather than the object's version. While many uses of static casts may result in code that is initially correct, that code is not able to adjust itself automatically to future changes in an object's type structure. Because these changes are generally remote from the point of the cast, maintainers often do not modify the code containing the cast. At the same time, the cast has the additional effect of turning off any diagnostics the compiler would otherwise have provided.

Casts are not essentially evil, but they must be used in moderation and in such a way that maintenance of code remote from the cast will not invalidate the cast. From a practical perspective, these requirements imply that one should, in general, avoid casting abstract data types and, most particularly, abstract data types in a hierarchy.

Consider a simple hierarchy:

```
class B {
 public:
    virtual ~B();
    virtual void op1() = 0;
};
```

```
class D1 : public B {
 public:
   void op1();
   void op2();
   virtual int thisop();
};
```

Associated with the hierarchy is a function that serves as a factory to create some sort of B object. Initially, we may have only a single derived class, so its implementation is trivial:

```
B *getAB() { return new D1; }
```

Unfortunately, the original developer or a maintainer may require access to the D1-specific functionality of the object returned from getAB. The proper procedure in this case is to redesign so that the type of the object is known statically. If that isn't possible or practical, a dynamic_cast may be used (after appropriate soul-searching). It's almost never a good idea to use a static cast, as we have here:

```
B *bp = getAB();
D1 *d1p = static_cast<D1 *>(bp);
d1p->op1();
d1p->op2();
int a = d1p->thisop();
```

This code works only because the returned object is actually a D1. This simple situation is not likely to last, and a new derived class will be added to the hierarchy along with an updated factory:

```
class D2 : public B {
 public:
   void op1();
   void op2();
   virtual char thatop();
};
// . . .
B *getAB() {
   if( rand() & 1 )
       return new D1;
```

```
    else
        return new D2;
}
```

Note that these changes probably take place in a remote part of the code not frequented by the maintainer of code containing the static cast. One would hope that the modification of the getAB function would at least provoke a recompilation of this code, but even that is not guaranteed. Even if the code is recompiled, the use of a static cast ensures that the compiler will issue no diagnostic. Few guarantees can be made about the behavior of this code when getAB returns an object of type D2, but it's quite possible it could actually run, after a fashion. The comments below indicate commonly observed behavior:

```
B *bp = getAB(); // gets a D2
D1 *d1p = static_cast<D1 *>(bp); // pretend D2 is a D1
d1p->op1(); // #1: call D2::op1!
d1p->op2(); // #2: call D1::op2!!
int a = d1p->thisop(); // #3: call D2::thatop!!!
```

In spite of the lack of a guarantee of this behavior, the line marked #1 is probably going to do "the right thing." Of course, it would have been preferable if the function op1 were invoked through the base class interface, because this would guarantee correct behavior.

The line marked #2 is more problematic. It's a nonvirtual member function call to a member of D1. Unfortunately it's being passed a D2 object, which will result in undefined runtime behavior. It may even work.

The line marked #3 is perhaps the most problematic. Statically, we invoke a virtual function of D1 named thisop that returns an int. Dynamically, we invoke a virtual function of D2 named thatop that returns a char. If this code manages to run without aborting, we'll attempt to copy a char result into an int.

Use of a static cast is often, as Scott Meyers has observed, "a sign that negotiations between you and your compiler have broken down." In effect, a static cast not only tells your compiler "Because I say so" (and, as with a similar discussion with a human interlocutor, guarantees the end of any useful communication); it shows a lack of respect to the public interface offered by the abstract data type being cast. Thoughtful, negotiated solutions that respect the advertised capabilities of objects often require more finesse than a heavy-handed cast, but they generally result in more robust, portable, and usable code and interfaces.

Gotcha #42: Temporary Initialization of Formal Arguments

Consider a `String` class with equality operators:

```
class String {
 public:
    String( const char * = "" );
    ~String();
    friend bool operator ==( const String &, const String & );
    friend bool operator !=( const String &, const String & );
    // . . .
 private:
    char *s_;
};
inline bool
operator ==( const String &a, const String &b )
    { return strcmp( a.s_, b.s_ ) == 0; }


inline bool
operator !=(const String &a, const String &b )
    { return !(a == b); }
```

Notice that this particular design employs a nonexplicit single-argument constructor and non-member equality operators. We are, therefore, inviting our users to take advantage of implicit conversions to simplify their code:

```
String s( "Hello, World!" );
String t( "Yo!" );
if( s == t ) {
  //  . . .
}
else if( s == "Howdy!" ) { // implicit conversion
  //  . . .
}
```

The first condition, s == t, is efficient. The two reference formal arguments of `operator ==` are initialized with s and t, and `strcmp` is used to perform the comparison. If the compiler chooses to inline the call to operator == (it probably will, unless a heavy-duty debugging flag is turned on), the runtime effect will be a simple call to strcmp.

The second condition, s == "Howdy!", is less efficient, though correct. To initialize the second argument of the call to operator ==, the compiler must create a temporary String object and initialize it with the character string literal "Howdy!". This temporary is then used to initialize the argument. After the function returns, the temporary must be destroyed. The effect of the call is something like this:

```
String temp( "Howdy!" );
bool result = operator ==( s, temp );
temp.~String();
if( result ) {
   // . . .
}
```

In this case, the convenience of the implicit conversion may well be worth the extra expense, since its presence renders both the code that implements the String class and the user code short and clear.

However, the implicit conversion is not acceptable on at least two occasions. The first is, of course, the case where the conversions are heavily used and are causing significant size or speed problems. The second is when the availability of an implicit conversion from a const char * to a String is causing ambiguity and complexity elsewhere in the use of Strings, and the designer of the String class wishes to address these problems by making the String constructor explicit.

Overloading the String equality operators easily solves this problem:

```
class String {
 public:
   explicit String( const char * = "" );
   ~String();
   friend bool operator ==( const String &, const String & );
   friend bool operator !=( const String &, const String & );
   friend bool operator ==( const String &, const char * );
   friend bool operator !=( const String &, const char * );
   friend bool operator ==( const char *, const String & );
   friend bool operator !=( const char *, const String & );
   // . . .
};
```

Now any legal combination of arguments for the operation will result in an exact match, and the compiler will generate no temporary String objects. Unfortunately, the String class is now larger and harder to understand, so this approach to optimization is usually appropriate only after profiling reveals the need.

A common error committed by C++ novices is to pass class objects by value when passing by reference would be preferable. Consider a function that takes a String argument:

```
String munge( String s ) {
    // munge s . . .
    return s;
}
// . . .
String t( "Munge Me" );
t = munge( t );
```

It's hard to find anything nice to say about this code, yet such code is common in many novice attempts to use C++. The call to munge requires a copy construction of the s formal argument as well as a copy construction of the return value and a destruction of the local s. Since we're assigning the munged t back to itself, we might expect that the assignment operator will recognize that and perform a no-op. No such luck. The compiler is required to dump the return value of munge into a temporary (which must be destroyed later), so the assignment will not be optimized. So we're looking at a total of six function calls.

A better approach is to rewrite the munge function to use an alias for the String it will munge:

```
void munge( String &s ) {
    // munge s . . .
}
// . . .
munge( t );
```

One function call. The two functions have slightly different meanings, in that any munging performed on s is reflected immediately in the actual argument t rather than on return. (This difference might be noticeable if an exception or interrupt were to occur within munge or if munge should call another function that referenced t.) However, the overall complexity is reduced, and the code is smaller and faster.

Passing by reference is particularly important when implementing templates, since it's not possible to predict in advance the expense of argument passing for a particular instantiation:

```
template <typename T>
bool operator >( const T &a, const T &b )
   { return b < a; }
```

Passing an argument by reference has a low, fixed cost that doesn't vary from argument to argument. It may be that some arguments, such as predefined types and small, simple class types, are more efficiently passed by value. If these cases are important, the template can be overloaded (if it's a function template) or specialized (if it's a class template).

Additionally, convention sometimes encourages passing by value. For example, in the C++ standard template library, it's conventional to pass "function objects" by value. (A function object is an object of a class that overloads the function call operator. It's just a class object like any other class object, but it allows one to use it with function call syntax.)

For example, we can declare a function object to serve as a "predicate": a function that answers a yes-or-no question about its argument:

```
struct IsEven : public std::unary_function<int,bool> {
   bool operator ()( int a ) const
      { return !(a & 1); }
};
```

An `IsEven` object has no data members, no virtual functions, and no constructor or destructor. Passing such an object by value is inexpensive (and often free). In fact, it's considered good form when using the STL to pass function objects as anonymous temporaries:

```
extern int a[n];
int *thatsOdd = partition( a, a+n, IsEven() );
```

The expression `IsEven()` creates an anonymous temporary object of type `IsEven`, which is then passed by value to the `partition` algorithm (see Gotcha #43). Of course, this convention presumes the additional convention that function objects used with the STL will be small and efficiently passed by value.

Gotcha #43: Temporary Lifetime

In certain circumstances, the compiler is forced to create temporary objects. The standard states that the lifetime of such a temporary is from its point of creation to the end of the largest enclosing expression (what the standard calls the "full-expression"). A common problem is unintended dependence on the continued existence of these temporaries after they've been destroyed:

```
class String {
public:
  // . . .
  ~String()
       { delete [] s_; }
  friend String operator +( const String &, const String & );
  operator const char *() const
       { return s_; }
private:
  char *s_;
};
// . . .
String s1, s2;
printf( "%s", (const char *)(s1+s2) ); // #1
const char* p = s1+s2; // #2
printf( "%s", p ); // #3
```

The implementation of String's binary + operator often requires that the return value be stored in a temporary. This is the case for both its uses above. In the instance marked #1 above, the result of s1+s2 is dumped into a temporary, which is then converted to a const char * prior to being passed to printf. After the call to printf returns, the temporary String object is destroyed. This works because the temporary has lived as long as any of its uses.

In the instance marked #2, the result of s1+s2 is dumped into a temporary, which is then converted to a const char * as before. The difference in this case is that the String temporary is destroyed at the end of the initialization of the pointer p. When p is used in the call to printf, it's referring to a buffer held by a destroyed String object. Undefined behavior.

The truly unfortunate aspect of this particular bug is that the code may well continue to work (as least during testing). For example, when the String temporary deletes its character array buffer, the array delete operator may simply mark the storage as unused, without changing its content. If the storage is not reused between lines #2 and #3, the code will appear to work. If this piece of code is later embedded in a multithreaded application, it will fail sporadically.

It's better to either employ a complex expression or declare an explicit temporary with an extended lifetime:

```
String temp = s1+s2;
const char *p = temp;
printf( "%s", p );
```

Note, however, that the limited lifetime of temporaries can often be used to advantage. One common practice when programming with the standard library is to customize components with function objects:

```
class StrLenLess
    : public binary_function<const char *, const char *, bool> {
 public:
    bool operator() ( const char *a, const char *b ) const
        { return strlen(a) < strlen(b); }
};
// . . .
sort( start, end, StrLenLess() );
```

The expression StrLenLess() causes the compiler to generate an anonymous temporary object that exists until the return from the sort algorithm. The alternative of using an explicitly named variable is longer and pollutes the current scope with a useless name (see Gotcha #48):

```
StrLenLess comp;
sort( start, end, comp );
// comp is still in scope . . .
```

Another complication with temporary lifetimes can occur with legacy code written to a pre-standard C++ compiler. Prior to publication of the standard, there was no universal rule for temporary lifetime. As a result, some compilers would destroy temporaries at the end of the block in which they came into existence, some would destroy them at the end of the statement in which they came into existence, and so on. When refactoring legacy code, be alert for any silent changes of meaning due to changes in temporary lifetime.

Gotcha #44: References and Temporaries

A reference is an alias for its initializer (see Gotcha #5). After initialization, a reference may be freely substituted for its initializer with no change in meaning. Well…mostly.

```
int a = 12;
int &r = a;
++a; // same as ++r
int *ip = &r; // same as &a
int &r2 = 12; // error! 12 is a literal
```

A reference has to be initialized with an lvalue; basically, this means that its initializer must have an address as well as a value (see Gotcha #6). Things are a little more complex with a reference to const. The initializer for a reference to const must still be an lvalue, but the compiler is willing, in this case, to create an lvalue from a non-lvalue initializer:

```
const int &r3 = 12; // OK.
```

The reference r3 is an alias for an anonymous temporary int allocated and initialized implicitly by the compiler. Ordinarily, the lifetime of a compiler-generated temporary is limited to the largest expression that contains it. However, in this case, the standard guarantees that the temporary will exist as long as the reference it initializes. Note that the temporary has no connection to its initializer, so the rather unsightly and dangerous code below will, fortunately, not affect the value of the literal 12:

```
const_cast<int &>(r3) = 11; // assign to temporary, or abort . . .
```

The compiler will also manufacture a temporary for an lvalue initializer that is a different type from the reference it initializes:

```
const string &name = "Fred"; // OK.
short s = 123;
const int &r4 = s; // OK.
```

Here we can run into some semantic difficulties, since the notion of reference as an alias for its initializer is becoming tenuous. It's easy to forget that the reference's initializer is actually an anonymous temporary and not the initializer that appears in the source text. For example, any change to the short s won't be reflected in the reference r4:

```
s = 321; // r4 still == 123
const int *ip = &r4; // not &s
```

Is this really a problem? It can be, if you help it along. Consider an attempt at portability through the use of typedefs. Perhaps a project-wide header file attempts to fix platform-independent standard names for different-sized integers:

```
// Header big/sizes.h
typedef short Int16;
typedef int Int32;
// . . .
```

```
// Header file small/sizes.h
typedef int Int16;
typedef long Int32;
// . . .
```

(Please note that we didn't use #if to jam the typedefs for all platforms into a single file. That's evil and will end up ruining your weekends, reputation, and life. See Gotcha #27.) There's nothing wrong with this, as long as all developers use the names consistently. Unfortunately, they don't always do that:

```
#include <sizes.h>
// . . .
Int32 val = 123;
const int &theVal = val;
val = 321;
cout << theVal;
```

If we develop on the "large" platform, theVal is an alias for val, and we'll shift 321 to cout. If we later take advantage of our supposed platform independence and recompile for the "small" platform, theVal will refer to a temporary, and we'll shift 123. This change in meaning will occur silently, of course, and will typically not be as obvious as a changed line of output.

Another potential problem is that the initialization of a reference to constant can open up a temporary-lifetime problem. We've seen that the compiler will make sure that such a temporary lives as long as the reference it initializes, which seems like a safe procedure. Let's look at a simple function:

```
const string &
select( bool cond, const string &a, const string &b ) {
    if( cond )
        return a;
    else
        return b;
}
// . . .
string first, second;
bool useFirst = false;
// . . .
const string &name = select( useFirst, first, second ); // OK
```

At first glance, this function seems innocuous. After all, it simply returns one of its arguments. The problem is in that `return`. Let's have a look at another function that's more obviously problematic:

```
const string &crashAndBurn() {
    string temp( "Fred" );
    return temp;
}
// . . .
const string &fred = crashAndBurn();
cout << fred; // oops!
```

Here, we're explicitly returning a reference to a local variable. On return, the local variable will be destroyed, and a user of the function will be left with a handle to the destroyed object. Luckily, most compilers will warn about this situation. But they won't warn about the following one, because, in general, they can't:

```
const string &name = select( useFirst, "Joe", "Besser" );
cout << name; // oops!
```

The problem is that the second and third arguments to the `select` function are references to constant, so they'll be initialized with temporary string objects. While these temporaries aren't local to the select function, they'll live only until the end of the largest enclosing expression, which is after the return from `select` but before the return value is used. A working alternative would be to embed the function call in a larger expression:

```
cout << select( useFirst, "Joe", "Besser" ); // works, fragile
```

This is the kind of code that works when written by an expert and breaks when maintained by a novice.

A safer procedure is to avoid returning a formal argument that's a reference to constant. In the case of our `select` function, we have at least two reasonable choices. The standard `string` is not a polymorphic type (that is, it has no virtual functions), and therefore we're allowed to assume that the reference arguments are bound to `strings` and not to objects of a type derived from `string`. We can therefore return by value without fear of slicing, but we'll incur some cost in invoking `string`'s copy constructor to initialize the return value:

```
string
select( bool cond, const string &a, const string &b ) {
    if( cond )
        return a;
    else
        return b;
}
```

Another alternative would be to declare the formal arguments to be reference to non-const, which would cause a compile-time error if temporaries were required for their initialization. This would simply render our example above illegal:

```
string &
select( bool cond, string &a, string &b ) {
    if( cond )
        return a;
    else
        return b;
}
```

Neither of these options is attractive, but either is better than the alternative of leaving your code open to an insidious bug.

Gotcha #45: Ambiguity Failure of `dynamic_cast`

Sure, you feel guilty about it. You probably won't discuss it with your colleagues. It may even start to affect your personal relationships. But when your back is to the wall, you're dealing with a poorly designed module and impossible demands from your management, and you need to be finished yesterday, it may be time to employ a `dynamic_cast`.

Let's say the problem has to do with the need to determine whether a particular screen object is an entry screen rather than some other type of screen. The problem is that you're in the middle of some otherwise generic code that should apply to screens in general. Your first impulse might be to augment the interface of all screen types to provide the required information:

```cpp
class Screen {
 public:
    //...
    virtual bool isEntryScreen() const
        { return false; }
};
class EntryScreen : public Screen {
 public:
    bool isEntryScreen() const
        { return true; }
};
//  . . .
Screen *getCurrent();
//  . . .
if( getCurrent()->isEntryScreen() )
    //  . . .
```

The problem with this approach is that it legitimizes asking a prying question of a `Screen` object. The base `Screen` class is explicitly inviting maintainers to ask the personal question "Are you an `EntryScreen`?" With that, the floodgates are open, and future maintainers will add more prying questions (see Gotcha #98):

```cpp
class Screen {
 public:
    //...
    virtual bool isEntryScreen() const
        { return false; }
```

```
    virtual bool isPricingScreen() const
        { return false; }
    virtual bool isSwapScreen() const
        { return false; }
    // ad infinitum . . .
};
```

Of course, the presence of such an interface pretty much guarantees it will be used:

```
// . . .
if( getCurrent()->isEntryScreen() )
    // . . .
else if( getCurrent()->isPricingScreen() )
    // . . .
else if( getCurrent()->isSwapScreen() )
    // . . .
```

It's kind of like a `switch`, except slower and less maintainable. A lesser evil is just to bite the bullet and perform a single `dynamic_cast`. The use of the cast will, one hopes, be sufficiently hidden not to inspire imitation and will be removed at some future date when the code is refactored:

```
if( EntryScreen *es = dynamic_cast<EntryScreen *>(sp) ) {
    // do stuff with the entry screen...
}
```

If the cast succeeds, `es` will refer to an `EntryScreen`, which may be the actual type of the screen object or simply an `EntryScreen` subobject of a more specialized screen object. But what does failure mean?

A `dynamic_cast` can produce a null result for any of four reasons. First, the cast can be incorrect. If `sp` doesn't refer to an `EntryScreen` or something derived from an `EntryScreen`, the cast will fail. Second, if `sp` is null, the result of the cast will also be null. Third, the cast will fail if we attempt to cast to or from an inaccessible base class. Finally, the cast can fail due to an ambiguity.

Type conversion ambiguities are uncommon in well-designed hierarchies, but it's possible to get into trouble with hierarchies that are poorly constructed or improperly accessed.

Figure 4–4 shows a simple multiple-inheritance hierarchy. We'll assume A is polymorphic (it has a virtual function) and that only public inheritance is used. In this case, a D object has two A subobjects; that is, at least one A is a nonvirtual base class:

```
D *dp = new D;
A *ap = dp; // error! ambiguous
ap = dynamic_cast<A *>(dp); // error! ambiguous
```

The initialization of ap is ambiguous, because it can refer to two reasonable A addresses. However, once we have the address of one of the two A subobjects, reference to any of the other subtypes in the hierarchy is unambiguous:

```
B *bp = dynamic_cast<B *>(ap); // works
C *cp = dynamic_cast<C *>(ap); // works
```

No matter which A subobject ap refers to, converting it to refer to the B or C subobjects or to the D complete object is unambiguous, because the complete object contains a single instance of each of those subobjects.

It's interesting to note that if both As were virtual base classes, there would be no ambiguity, since a D object would then contain a single A subobject:

```
D *dp = new D;
A *ap = dp; // OK, not ambiguous
ap = dynamic_cast<A *>(dp); // OK, not ambiguous
```

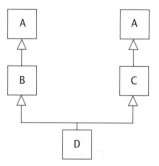

Figure 4–4 | A multiple-inheritance hierarchy without virtual base classes. A D complete object contains two A subobjects.

We can reintroduce ambiguity by making the hierarchy a little more complex, as in Figure 4–5. For this modified hierarchy, the earlier ambiguity is not present, because a D object still contains a single A subobject:

```
A *ap = new D; // no ambiguity
```

However, we now have an ambiguity going the other way:

```
E *ep = dynamic_cast<E *>(ap); // fails!
```

The pointer ap could be converted to either of two E subobjects. We can circumvent this ambiguity by being more specific:

```
E *ep = dynamic_cast<B *>(ap); // works
```

A D contains a single B subobject, so converting an A * into a B * is unambiguous, and the subsequent conversion from B * to its public base doesn't require a cast. However, note that this solution embeds detailed knowledge of the structure of the hierarchy below classes A and E into the code. It's better to simplify the structure of the hierarchy to avoid the possibility of dynamic ambiguity.

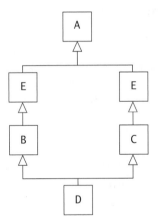

Figure 4–5 | A multiple-inheritance hierarchy with virtual and nonvirtual inheritance of multiple subobjects of the same type. A D complete object contains a single A subobject but two E subobjects.

Since we're on the subject of dynamic_cast, we should point out a couple of subtleties of its semantics. First, a dynamic_cast is not necessarily dynamic, in that it may not perform a runtime check. When performing a dynamic_cast from a derived class pointer (or reference) to one of its public base classes, no runtime check is needed, because the compiler can determine statically that the cast will succeed. Of course, no cast of any kind is needed in this case, since conversion from a derived class to its public base classes is predefined. (While language rules of this type may initially seem extraneous, they often facilitate template programming, where the types to be manipulated are generally not known in advance.)

It's also legal to cast a pointer or reference to a polymorphic type to void *. In this case, the result will refer to the start of the "most derived," or complete, object to which the pointer refers. Of course, we still won't know what we're pointing to, but at least we'll know where it is . . .

Gotcha #46: Misunderstanding Contravariance

The rules for conversion of pointers to member are logical but often counterintuitive. An examination of an implementation of pointers to member often helps clear things up.

A pointer refers to a region of memory; it contains an address that can be dereferenced to access the memory. (The code that follows makes use of two reprehensible practices: public data and hiding of a base class nonvirtual function. This is done for illustration only and is not intended as an implicit recommendation of these practices. See Gotchas #8 and #71.)

```
class Employee {
 public:
    double level_;
    virtual void fire() = 0;
    bool validate() const;
};
class Hourly : public Employee {
 public:
    double rate_;
    void fire();
    bool validate() const;
};
```

```
// . . .
Hourly *hp = new Hourly, h;
// . . .
*hp = h;
```

Note that the address of a data member of a particular object is not a pointer to member. It's a simple pointer that refers to a specific member of a specific object:

```
double *ratep = &hp->rate_;
```

A pointer to member is not a pointer. A pointer to member is not an address of anything, and it doesn't refer to any particular object or location. A pointer to member refers to a specific member of an unspecified object. Therefore, an object must be supplied to dereference the pointer to member:

```
double Hourly::*hvalue = &Hourly::rate_;
hp->*hvalue = 1.85;
h.*hvalue = hp->*hvalue;
```

The .* and ->* operators are binary dereference operators that dereference a pointer to member with a class object or class pointer, respectively (but see Gotchas #15 and #17). The pointer to member hvalue was initialized to refer to the rate_ member of the Hourly class, then dereferenced to access the rate_ members of the Hourly object h and the Hourly object referred to by hp.

A pointer to data member is generally implemented as an offset. That is, taking the address of a data member, as we did above with &Hourly::rate_, gives the number of bytes from the start of the class object at which the data member occurs. Typically, this offset value is incremented by 1, so that the value 0 can represent a null pointer to data member. Dereferencing a pointer to data member typically involves manufacturing an address by adding the offset (decremented by 1) stored in the pointer to data member to the address of a class object. The resultant pointer is then dereferenced to access the corresponding data member of the class object. For example, the expression

```
h.*hvalue = 1.85
```

could be translated like this:

```
*(double *)((char *)&h+(hvalue-1)) = 1.85
```

Let's look at another pointer to data member:

```
double Employee::*evalue = &Employee::level_;
Employee *ep = hp;
```

Because an `Hourly` is-a `Employee`, we can dereference the `evalue` pointer to member with either type of pointer. This is the well-known implicit conversion from a derived class to its public base class:

```
ep->*evalue = hp->*evalue;
```

An `Hourly` is substitutable for an `Employee`. However, an attempt to perform a similar conversion with pointers to member fails:

```
evalue = hvalue; // error!
```

There is no conversion from a pointer to member of a derived class to a pointer to member of a public base class. However, the opposite conversion is legal:

```
hvalue = evalue; // OK
```

This phenomenon is known as "contravariance"; the implicit conversions for pointers to member are precisely the inverse of those for pointers to classes. (Don't confuse contravariance with covariant return types; see Gotcha #77.) After a little reflection, the logic behind this somewhat counterintuitive rule is obvious. Since an `Hourly` is-a `Employee`, it contains an `Employee` subobject. Therefore, any offset within `Employee` is also a valid offset within `Hourly`. However, some offsets within `Hourly` are not valid for `Employee`. This implies that a pointer to member of a public base class may be safely converted to a pointer to member of a derived class, but not the reverse:

```
T SomeClass::*mptr;
 . . . ptr->*mptr  . . .
```

In the code snippet above, the pointer `ptr` can legally be a pointer to an object of type `SomeClass` or of any publicly derived class of `SomeClass`. The pointer to member `mptr` can contain the address of a member of `SomeClass` or the address of a member of any accessible base class of `SomeClass`.

Contravariance also applies to pointers to function member. It's just as counterintuitive and makes just as much sense, on reflection:

```
void (Employee::*action1)() = &Employee::fire;
(hp->*action1)(); // Hourly::fire
bool (Employee::*action2)() const = &Employee::validate;
(hp->*action2)(); // Employee::validate
```

Implementations of pointers to function member vary widely but are typically small structures. The structure contains information necessary to distinguish virtual from nonvirtual members as well as other platform-specific information necessary for dealing with implementation-specific details of the structure of objects under inheritance. In the first call, through `action1` above, we'll make an indirect virtual call and invoke `Hourly::fire`, because `&Employee::fire` is a pointer to a virtual member function. In the second call, through `action2`, we'll invoke `Employee::validate`, because `&Employee::validate` is a pointer to a nonvirtual function:

```
action2 = &Hourly::validate; // error!
bool (Hourly::*action3)() = &Employee::validate; // OK
```

Contravariance again. It's illegal to assign the address of the derived class's `validate` function to a pointer to member of the base class, but it's fine to initialize a pointer to member of a derived class with the address of a base class member function. As with pointers to data member, the reason concerns safety of member access. The implementation of `Hourly::validate` may attempt to access data (and function) members not present in `Employee`. On the other hand, any members accessed by `Employee::validate` will also be present in `Hourly`.

5 | Initialization

The semantics of initialization in C++ are subtle, complex, and important.

The reasons behind this complexity are not frivolous. Much of programming in C++ consists of using classes to design abstract data types. Essentially, we extend the base C++ language with new data types integrated into the rest of the type system. On one hand, we're engaged in programming-language design to produce usable, integrated types. On the other hand, we're engaged in translator design, in that we must convince the compiler to translate our implementations of these abstract data types efficiently. The details of initialization and copying of class objects are essential to efficient, production-quality use of data abstraction.

Equally important to efficiency, of course, is correctness. Unfamiliarity with the necessarily complex semantics of initialization in C++ can lead to misuse.

In this chapter, we'll examine issues of implementing initialization as well as how to convince the compiler to optimize user-defined initialization and copy operations. We'll also examine several common problems associated with misunderstanding the semantics of initialization.

Gotcha #47: Assignment/Initialization Confusion

Technically, assignment has little to do with initialization. They're separate operations, used in different circumstances. Initialization is the process of turning raw storage into an object. For a class object, this could entail setting up internal mechanisms for virtual functions and virtual base classes, runtime type information, and other type-dependent information (see Gotchas #53 and #78). Assignment is the process of replacing the existing state of a well-defined object with a new state. Assignment doesn't affect internal mechanisms that implement type-dependent behavior of an object. Assignment is never performed on raw storage.

Idiomatically, however, if copy construction semantics are important in one set of circumstances, chances are that copy assignment semantics are important in the others, and vice versa. Forgetting to consider both assignment and initialization will result in bugs:

```
class SloppyCopy {
 public:
   SloppyCopy &operator =( const SloppyCopy & );
   // Note: compiler default SloppyCopy(const SloppyCopy &) . . .
 private:
   T *ptr;
};


void f( SloppyCopy ); // pass by value


SloppyCopy sc;
f( sc );        // alias what ptr points to, probable error
```

Argument passing is accomplished with initialization, not assignment; the formal argument to f is initialized by the sc actual argument. The initialization will be accomplished with SloppyCopy's copy constructor. In the absence of an explicitly declared copy constructor, the compiler will write one. In this case, the compiler's version will be incorrect. (See Gotchas #49 and #53.)

The idiomatic assumption is that, even though copy construction and copy assignment are different operations, they should have similar, or conformant, meaning:

```
extern T a, b;
b = a;
T c( a );
```

In the code above, users of the type T would expect the values of b and c to be conformant. In other words, it should be immaterial to subsequent execution whether an object of type T received its current value as the result of an assignment or an initialization. This assumption of conformance is so ingrained in the C++ programming community that the standard library depends on it:

➤➤gotcha47/rawstorage.h

```
template <class Out, class T>
class raw_storage_iterator
   : public iterator<output_iterator_tag,void,void,void,void> {
```

```cpp
public:
    raw_storage_iterator& operator =( const T& element );
    // . . .
protected:
    Out cur_;
};
template <class Out, class T>
raw_storage_iterator<Out, T> &
raw_storage_iterator<Out,T>::operator =( const T &val ) {
    T *elem = &*cur_; // get a ptr to element
    new ( elem ) T(val); // placement and copy constructor
    return *this;
}
```

A raw_storage_iterator is used to assign to uninitialized storage. Ordinarily, an assignment operator requires that both its arguments be properly initialized objects; otherwise, a problem is likely when the assignment attempts to "clean up" the left argument before setting its new value. For example, if the objects being assigned contain a pointer to a heap-allocated buffer, the assignment will typically delete the buffer before setting the new value of the object. If the object is uninitialized, the deletion of the uninitialized pointer member will result in undefined behavior:

➤➤gotcha47/rawstorage.cpp

```cpp
struct X {
    T *t_;
    X &operator =( const X &rhs ) {
        if( this != &rhs )
            { delete t_; t_ = new T(*rhs.t_); }
        return *this;
    }
    // . . .
};
// . . .
X x;
X *buf = (X *)malloc( sizeof(X) ); // raw storage . . .
X &rx = *buf; // foul trickery . . .
rx = x; // probable error!
```

The copy algorithm from the standard library copies an input sequence to an output sequence, using assignment to perform the copy of each element:

```
template <class In, class Out>
Out std::copy( In b, In e, Out r ) {
    while( b != e )
        *r++ = *b++; // assign src element to dest element
    return r;
}
```

Use of copy on an uninitialized array of X will most probably fail:

➤➤gotcha47/rawstorage.cpp

```
X a[N];
X *ary = (X *)malloc( N*sizeof(X) );
copy( a, a+N, ary ); // assign to raw storage!
```

Assignment is a bit like (but not exactly like!) a destruction followed by a copy construction. The raw_storage_iterator allows assignment to uninitialized storage by reinterpreting the assignment as a copy construction, skipping the problematic "destruction" step. This will work only under the assumption that copy assignment and copy construction produce acceptably similar results.

➤➤gotcha47/rawstorage.cpp

```
raw_storage_iterator<X *, X> ri( ary );
copy( a, a+N, ri ); // works!
```

This is not to imply that the designer of class X must be intimately aware of all the (admittedly difficult and obscure) details of the standard library to produce a correct implementation. However, the designer does have to be aware of the general, idiomatic assumption that copy initialization and copy assignment are conformant. An abstract data type that doesn't support this conformance can't be leveraged effectively with the standard library and will be less useful than a type that does conform.

Another common misapprehension is that assignment is somehow involved in the following initialization:

```
T d = a; // not an assignment
```

That = symbol is not an assignment operator, and d is initialized by a. This is fortunate, since otherwise we'd have an assignment to uninitialized storage. (But see Gotcha #56.)

Gotcha #48: Improperly Scoped Variables

One of the most common sources of bugs in C and C++ programs is uninitialized variables, and it's a problem that simply does not have to exist. Separating the declaration of a variable from its initializer rarely offers any advantage:

```
int a;
a = 12;
string s;
s = "Joe";
```

That's just silly. The integer will have an indeterminate value until its assignment in the following statement. The string will be properly initialized by its default constructor but will be immediately overwritten by the following assignment (see also Gotcha #51). Both these declarations should have employed explicit initialization in the declaration-statement:

```
int a = 12;
string s( "Joe" );
```

The real danger is that, under maintenance, code may be inserted between the uninitialized declaration and its first assignment. The typical scenario is a bit subtler than the code above:

```
bool f( const char *s ) {
    size_t length;
    if( !s ) return false;
    length = strlen( s );
    char *buffer = (char *)malloc( length+1 );
    // . . .
}
```

Not only is `length` uninitialized, but it should be a constant. The author of this code has forgotten that in C++, as opposed to C, a declaration is a statement; to be precise, it's a declaration-statement, and a declaration can occur anywhere a statement can:

```cpp
bool f( const char *s ) {
    if( !s ) return false;
    const size_t length = strlen( s );
    char *buffer = (char *)malloc( length+1 );
    // . . .
}
```

Let's look at another common problem that generally occurs under maintenance. The following code is fairly unexceptional:

```cpp
void process( const char *id ) {
    Name *function = lookupFunction( id );
    if( function ) {
        // . . .
    }
}
```

The declaration of `function` is not too bad right now, but under maintenance, it can become a problem. As we mentioned earlier, maintainers will often reuse a local variable for a wildly different purpose. Why? Because it's there, I suppose:

```cpp
void process( const char *id ) {
    Name *function = lookupFunction( id );
    if( function ) {
        // process function . . .
    }
    else if( function = lookupArgument( id ) ) {
        // process argument . . .
    }
}
```

No bug yet, though I imagine the code for processing an argument is going to be pretty heavy going for the uninitiated reader ("In this section of the code, wherever I say 'function,' I mean 'argument.' ") But what happens when the original author comes back to do a little maintenance on function processing?

```
void process( const char *id ) {
   Name *function = lookupFunction( id );
   if( function ) {
      // process function . . .
   }
   else if( function = lookupArgument( id ) ) {
      // process argument . . .
   }
   // . . .
   if( function ) {
      // postprocess function . . .
   }
}
```

Now we may attempt to postprocess an argument as a function.

It's usually best to restrict a name's scope to coincide precisely with where the original author intends that the name be used. Names still in scope but no longer used are a bit like unoccupied teenagers; they're just hanging out, waiting to get into trouble. The original function should have restricted the scope of the variable function to the scope of its intended use:

```
void process( const char *id ) {
   if( Name *function = lookupFunction( id ) ) {
      // . . .
   }
}
```

Scoping the variable name removes the temptation to reuse it, and the eventual implementation of the function after maintenance will be more rational:

```
void process( const char *id ) {
   if( Name *function = lookupFunction( id ) ) {
      // . . .
      postprocess( function );
   }
   else if( Name *argument = lookupArgument( id ) ) {
      // . . .
   }
}
```

C++ recognizes the importance of initialization and scoping of names. It provides a variety of language features to assist the programmer to ensure that every name is initialized and has scope corresponding precisely to its intended area of use.

Gotcha #49: Failure to Appreciate C++'s Fixation on Copy Operations

C++ takes its copy operations seriously. Copy operations are extremely important in C++ programming, particularly copy operations of class objects. These operations are so important that if you don't provide them for a class, the compiler will. Sometimes, even if you try to provide these operations yourself, the compiler will push you aside and provide them anyway. Sometimes the compiler implements the operations correctly; sometimes it doesn't. That's why it's a good idea to know precisely what the compiler expects with respect to copy operations.

Note that copy assignment and copy construction (along with other constructors and the destructor) are not inherited from base classes. Therefore, every class defines its own copy operations.

The default implementation of copy construction is to perform a member-by-member initialization. Member-by-member initialization has nothing to do with C-style bitwise copying of structures. Consider a simple class implementation:

```
template <int maxlen>
class NBString {
 public:
    explicit NBString( const char *name );
    // . . .
 private:
    std::string name_;
    size_t len_;
    char s_[maxlen];
};
```

Assuming no copy operations are defined, the compiler will write some for us implicitly. These will be defined as public, inline members.

```
NBString<32> a( "String 1" );
// . . .
NBString<32> b( a );
```

The implicit copy constructor will perform a member-by-member initialization, invoking string's copy constructor to initialize b.name_ with a.name_, b.len_ with a.len_, and the elements of b.s_ with those of a.s_. (Actually, in an inspired burst of weirdness, the standard specifies that "scalar" types such as predefined types, enums, and pointers will be assigned within the implicit copy constructor rather than initialized. The group mental processes of the standards committee that led to this definition are beyond my ken, but the result will be the same—for these scalar types, anyway—whether assignment or initialization is used.)

```
b = a;
```

Similarly, the implicit copy assignment operator will perform a member-by-member assignment, invoking string's assignment operator to assign a.name_ to b.name_, a.len_ to b.len_, and the elements of a.s_ to the corresponding elements of b.s_.

These implicit definitions of the copy operations will provide correct, conventional copy semantics. (See also Gotcha #81.) However, consider a slightly different implementation of the named, bounded string class:

```
class NBString {
 public:
   explicit NBString( const char *name, int maxlen = 32 )
        : name_(name), len_(0), maxlen_(maxlen),
          s_(new char[maxlen] )
        { s_[0] = '\0'; }
   ~NBString()
        { delete [] s_; }
   // . . .
 private:
   std::string name_;
   size_t len_;
   size_t maxlen_;
   char *s_;
};
```

The constructor now sets the maximum size of the string, and storage for the character string is no longer physically within the NBString object. Now the implicit, compiler-provided copy operations are incorrect:

```
NBString c( "String 2" );
NBString d( c );
NBString e( "String 3" );
e = c;
```

The implicit copy constructor sets the s_ members of both c and d to the same heap-allocated buffer. The buffer will suffer a double deletion when the destructors for d and then c attempt to delete the same memory. Similarly, when c is assigned to e, the memory to which e.s_ refers is left dangling when e.s_ is set to the same buffer as c.s_, with results similar to those above. (See also Gotcha #53 for a short discussion of the implications of compiler-generated copy assignment in the presence of virtual base classes.)

A correct implementation must take over from the compiler the task of writing the copy operations in their entirety:

```
class NBString {
 public:
   // . . .
   NBString( const NBString & );
   NBString &operator =( const NBString & );
 private:
   std::string name_;
   size_t len_;
   size_t maxlen_;
   char *s_;
};
// . . .
NBString::NBString( const NBString &that )
   : name_(that.name_), len_(that.len_), maxlen_(that.maxlen_),
     s_(strcpy(new char[that.maxlen_], that.s_))
   {}
NBString &NBString::operator =( const NBString &rhs ) {
   if( this != &rhs ) {
      name_ = rhs.name_;
```

```
        char *temp = new char[rhs.maxlen_];
        len_ = rhs.len_;
        maxlen_ = rhs.maxlen_;
        delete [] s_;
        s_ = strcpy( temp, rhs.s_ );
    }
    return *this;
}
```

Every class designer must take careful consideration of copy operations. They must either be supplied explicitly (and maintained with every change to the class's implementation), be generated implicitly by the compiler (with this decision revisited with every change to the class's implementation), or be denied using the coding idiom below:

```
class NBString {
 public:
   // . . .
 private:
   NBString( const NBString &);
   NBString &operator =( const NBString & );
   // . . .
};
```

Declaring—but not defining—private copy operations has the effect of "turning off" copying for the class. The compiler will not attempt to provide implicit versions of the operations, and most code will not have access to the private members. Any accidental copying performed by members or friends of the class will be caught as an undefined function at link time.

It's pretty much impossible to talk your way past the compiler on the subject of implementing copy operations. The code below shows three creative but futile attempts to defeat the compiler:

```
class Derived;
class Base {
 public:
   Derived &operator =( const Derived & );
   virtual Base &operator =( const Base & );
};
```

```
class Derived : public Base {
 public:
    using Base::operator =; // hidden
    template <class T>
    Derived &operator =( const T & ); // not a copy assign
    Derived &operator =( const Base & ); // not a copy assign
};
```

We already know that copy operations aren't inherited, but the using-declaration that imports the rather accommodating nonvirtual base class assignment operator doesn't prevent the compiler from writing one either, and the compiler's implicit version hides the one imported explicitly. (Note also that the base class mentions the derived class explicitly, which is poor design. See Gotcha #69.)

The use of a template assignment member function doesn't help; template members are never used to implement copy operations (see Gotcha #88). The virtual copy assignment from the base class is overridden in the derived class, but the overriding derived class assignment operator is not a copy assignment (see Gotcha #76). The C++ language is insistent: either you write the copy operations or the compiler will, and no fooling around.

Gotcha #50: Bitwise Copy of Class Objects

Nothing is essentially wrong with allowing the compiler to write copy operations implicitly, though it's generally best to allow these implicit definitions only for simple classes or, to be more precise, only for classes that have simple structure. In fact, for simple classes, it's often a good idea to cede this job to the compiler for reasons of efficiency. Consider a class that's really just a simple collection of data:

```
struct Record {
    char name[maxname];
    long id;
    size_t seq;
};
```

It makes a lot of sense to allow the compiler to implement copy operations for this simple class. A class of this kind is known as a POD (for Plain Old Data; see Gotcha #9), which is basically a C-like struct. The implicit copy operations in such cases are carefully defined by the standard to match the copy semantics of C structs, which are implemented as bitwise copy.

In particular, if a given platform has a "copy *n* bytes real fast" instruction, the compiler is free to use it in the implementation of the bitwise copy. This kind of optimization can be appropriate even for non-POD classes. The copy operations for the original, templated implementation of `NBString` of Gotcha #49 could reasonably be implemented by invoking the appropriate copy operation for the `string` member `name_` followed by a fast bitwise copy of the remainder of the object.

Occasionally, an implementer of a class decides to take control of the bitwise copy decision. This is usually a mistake, because the compiler is much more cognizant of both the class implementation details and the platform specifics than the programmer. A handcrafted bitwise copy is usually both slower and buggier than the compiler's version:

```cpp
class Record {
  public:
    Record( const Record &that )
        { *this = that; }
    Record &operator =( const Record &that )
        { memcpy( this, &that, sizeof(Record) ); return *this; }
    // . . .
  private:
    char name[maxname];
    long id;
    size_t seq;
};
```

Our Record POD is growing into a real class, so we've provided some explicit copy operations for it. This was unnecessary, since the compiler would have provided perfectly efficient and correct versions. The real problem comes when the Record class continues its development:

```cpp
class Record {
  public:
    virtual ~Record();
    Record( const Record &that )
        { *this = that; }
    Record &operator =( const Record &that )
        { memcpy( this, &that, sizeof(Record) ); return *this; }
    // . . .
```

```
    private:
      char name[maxname];
      long id;
      size_t seq;
  };
```

Now things don't look so good. A bitwise copy no longer serves the structure of the class. The addition of a virtual function causes the compiler to add mechanism to the class implementation, typically a pointer to a virtual function table (see Gotcha #78).

Implicit copy operations generated by the compiler take care to handle the implicit class mechanism appropriately: the copy constructor sets the pointer appropriately, and the copy assignment operator takes care not to modify it. Our memcpy implementation, however, will overwrite the virtual function table pointer immediately after it's set in the copy constructor, and the copy assignment will overwrite it as well. Many other changes to the class could provoke similar bugs: derivation from a virtual base class, adding a data member that defines nontrivial copy operations, use of a pointer to unencapsulated storage, and so on.

In general, it's unwise to employ a hand-coded bitwise copy of any class object without hard data that show both a need and a sizable improvement in performance. If you are employing such an approach, carefully revisit the decision with every change to the implementation of the class.

Of course, using bitwise class copy outside a class's implementation is even less recommended. Implementing a copy operation with memcpy is daring. Bit-blasting on the sly is suicidal:

```
extern Record *exemplaryRecord;
char buffer[sizeof(Record)];
memcpy( buffer, exemplaryRecord, sizeof(buffer) );
```

Whoever wrote this code is probably embarrassed about it (or should be) and has hidden it away in an implementation file remote from the code that implements Record. Any changes to Record that are incompatible with a bitwise copy won't be detected until they manifest as a runtime error. If it's essential to write code like this, it must be done in such a way that the class's own copy operations are invoked (see Gotcha #62):

```
(void) new (buffer) Record( *exemplaryRecord );
```

Gotcha #51: Confusing Initialization and Assignment in Constructors

In a constructor, all class members that legally require initialization will be initialized. Not assigned, initialized. Members that require initialization are constants, references, class objects that have constructors, and base class subobjects. (But see Gotcha #81 regarding const and reference data members.)

```
class Thing {
 public:
    Thing( int );
};
class Melange : public Thing {
 public:
    Melange( int );
 private:
    const int aConst;
    const int &aRef;
    Thing aClassObj;
};
// . . .
Melange::Melange( int )
    {} // errors!
```

The compiler will flag four separate errors in the `Melange` constructor for failure to initialize its base class and its three data members. Any error flagged at compile time isn't too serious, since we can fix it before it negatively affects anyone's life:

```
Melange::Melange( int arg )
    : Thing( arg ), aConst( arg ), aRef( aConst ), aClassObj( arg )
    {}
```

A more insidious problem occurs when the programmer neglects to perform an initialization, but the resulting code is nevertheless legal:

```
class Person {
 public:
    Person( const string &name );
    // . . .
```

```
  private:
    string name_;
};
// . . .
```
```
Person::Person( const string &name )
    { name_ = name; }
```

This perfectly legal code increases the code size and nearly doubles the runtime of the Person constructor. The string type has a constructor, so it must be initialized. It also has a default constructor that will be called if no explicit initializer is present. The Person constructor therefore invokes string's default constructor, only to immediately overwrite the result with an assignment. A better implementation would just initialize the string member and be done with it:

```
Person::Person( const string &name )
    : name_( name )
    {}
```

Generally, prefer initialization in the member initialization list to assignment in the body of the constructor.

Of course, we wouldn't want to push this advice beyond its logical limit. Moderation in all things. Consider a constructor for a nonstandard String class:

```
class String {
  public:
    String( const char *init = "" );
    // . . .
  private:
    char *s_;
};
// . . .
String::String( const char *init )
    : s_(strcpy(new char[strlen(init?init:"")+1],init?init:"") )
    {}
```

This is carrying things a bit far, and a more appropriate constructor would simply assign within its body:

```
String::String( const char *init ) {
   if( !init ) init = "";
   s_ = strcpy( new char[strlen(init)+1], init );
}
```

Two kinds of data members cannot be initialized in the member initialization list: static data members and arrays. Static data members are dealt with in Gotcha #59. The individual elements of array members must be assigned within the body of the constructor. Alternatively, and often preferably, a standard container, such as a vector, may be used in preference to the array member.

Gotcha #52: Inconsistent Ordering of the Member Initialization List

The order in which a class object's components are initialized is fixed to a precise order by the C++ language definition (see also Gotcha #49).

- Virtual base class subobjects, no matter where they occur in the hierarchy

- Nonvirtual immediate base classes, in the order they appear on the base class list

- The data members of the class, in the order they are declared

This implies that any constructor for a class must perform its initializations in this order. Specifically, this implies that the order in which items are specified on a constructor's member initialization list is immaterial, as far as the compiler is concerned:

```
class C {
public:
   C( const char *name );
private:
   const int len_;
   string n_;
};
// . . .
C::C( const char *name )
   : n_( name ), len_( n_.length() ) // error!!!
   {}
```

The len_ member is declared first, so it will be initialized before n_, even though its initialization appears after that of n_ on the member initialization list. In this case, we'll attempt to call a member function of an object that hasn't been initialized, with an undefined result.

It's considered good form to put the elements of the member initialization list in the same order as the base class and data members of the class; that is, in the order the initializations will actually be performed. To the extent possible, it's also good practice to avoid order dependencies within the member initialization list:

```
C::C( const char *name )
    : len_( strlen(name) ), n_( name )
    {}
```

See Gotcha #67 for the reasons why the initialization ordering is divorced from the ordering of the member initialization list.

Gotcha #53: Virtual Base Default Initialization

A virtual base subobject is laid out differently from a nonvirtual base subobject. A nonvirtual base class is typically laid out as if it were a simple data member of a derived class object, as in Figure 5–1. It may therefore occur more than once within an object:

```
class A { members };
class B : public A { members };
class C : public A { members };
class D : public B, public C { members };
```

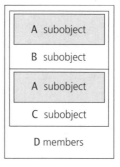

Figure 5–1 | Likely object layout under multiple inheritance without virtual inheritance. A D object has two A subobjects.

A virtual base class occurs only once within an object, even if it occurs many times in the class lattice (hierarchy structure) of the complete object (as in Figure 5–2):

```
class A { members };
class B : public virtual A { members };
class C : public virtual A { members };
class D : public B, public C { members };
```

For ease of illustration, we've shown a rather outmoded pointer implementation of virtual base classes. In the location where a nonvirtual base class A would appear in the complete object, we have instead a pointer to the shared storage for a single A subobject. More typically, the link to the shared virtual base subobject would be accomplished with an offset or with information stored in the virtual function table. However, the discussion that follows applies to any implementation.

Typically, the storage for the shared virtual base subobject is appended to the complete object. In the example above, the complete object is of type D, and the storage for A is appended after any D data members. An object whose "most derived class" is B would have a different storage layout.

A moment's reflection will convince you that only the most derived class knows precisely where the storage for a virtual base subobject is located. An object of type B may be a complete object, or it may be embedded as a subobject in another object. For this reason, it's the task of the most derived class to initialize all the virtual base subobjects in the class lattice as well as the mechanism used to access those subobjects.

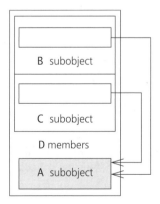

Figure 5–2 | Likely object layout under multiple inheritance with virtual inheritance. A D object has a single A subobject.

In the case of an object whose most derived type is B, as in Figure 5–3, the B constructors will initialize the A subobject and set the pointer to it:

```
B::B( int arg )
    : A( arg ) {}
```

In the case of an object whose most derived type is D, as in Figure 5–2, the D constructors will initialize the A subobject and the pointers to it in B and C as well as D's immediate base classes:

```
D::D( int arg )
    : A( arg ), B( arg ), C( arg+1 ) {}
```

Once the A subobject is initialized by D's constructor, it will not be reinitialized by B's or C's constructor. (One way the compiler might accomplish this is to have the D constructor pass a flag or A pointer to the B and C constructors that says "Oh, by the way, don't initialize A." Nothing mystical here.) Let's look at another constructor for D:

```
D::D()
    : B( 11 ), C( 12 ) {}
```

This is a common source of misunderstanding and bugs in the use of virtual base classes. The D constructor still initializes the virtual A subobject, but it does so implicitly, by calling A's default constructor. When D's constructor invokes the constructor for the B subobject, it doesn't reinitialize A, and therefore the explicit call to A's nondefault constructor doesn't take place.

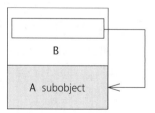

Figure 5–3 Likely layout of an object under single inheritance with a virtual base class. A B object has a single A subobject, but it must still be referenced indirectly.

For simplicity, it's best to use virtual base classes only when a design clearly indicates their use. (By the same token, virtual bases should not be avoided when a design clearly indicates their use.) In addition, it's usually simplest to design classes used as virtual bases as "interface classes." Interface classes have no data, generally all their member functions (except perhaps the destructor) are pure virtual, and they typically have no declared constructor or a simple default constructor:

```
class A {
 public:
    virtual ~A();
    virtual void op1() = 0;
    virtual int op2( int src, int dest ) = 0;
    // . . .
};
inline A::~A()
    {}
```

Following this advice will help avoid bugs in the implementation not only of constructors but also of assignment. In particular, the standard specifies that a compiler-provided version of copy assignment may, or may not, assign multiple times to a virtual base subobject. If all virtual base classes are interface classes, then assignment is a no-op (remember that class mechanism, like virtual function table pointers, is not affected by assignment, only by initialization), and multiple assignment does not pose a problem.

General solutions to implementing assignment in a hierarchy containing virtual base classes usually involve imitating, in some sense, the semantics of construction of objects that contain virtual base class subobjects.

Consider the first implementation of class D above, shown in Figure 5–1, which contains two (nonvirtual) A subobjects. In this case, as with D's constructor, a programmer-supplied copy assignment operator can be implemented entirely in terms of its immediate base classes:

➤➤gotcha53/virtassign.cpp

```
D &D::operator =( const D &rhs ) {
    if( this != &rhs ) {
        B::operator =( rhs ); // assign B subobject
        C::operator =( rhs ); // assign C subobject
        // assign any D-specific members . . .
    }
    return *this;
}
```

This assignment makes the reasonable assumption that the B and C base classes will perform an appropriate assignment of their (nonvirtual) A subobjects. As with construction, this simple, layered approach to assignment does not hold up under virtual inheritance. As with construction, the most derived class should assign the virtual base subobjects and somehow prevent intermediary base class subobjects from reassigning:

➤➤gotcha53/virtassign.cpp

```
D &D::operator =( const D &rhs ) {
    if( this != &rhs ) {
        A::operator =( rhs ); // assign virtual A
        B::nonvirtAssign( rhs ); // assign B, except A part
        C::nonvirtAssign( rhs ); // assign C, except A part
        // assign any D-specific members . . .
    }
    return *this;
}
```

Here, we've introduced special assignment-like member functions in B and C. They perform identically to their copy assignment operators but don't perform assignment on any virtual base subobjects. This is effective but clearly complex and requires that D be intimately aware of the structure of the hierarchy beyond its immediate base classes. Any change to that structure will require reimplementation of D. As mentioned above, it's generally best that classes used as virtual bases be interface classes.

One implication of the layout of virtual base class subobjects is that it's illegal to perform a static downcast from a virtual base class to one of its derived classes:

```
A *ap = gimmeanA();
D *dp = static_cast<D *>(ap); // error!
dp = (D *)ap; // error!
```

It is possible to perform a reinterpret_cast from a virtual base to one of its derived classes. As shown in Figure 5–4, this will probably result in a bad address and so is not of much use. The only reliable way to perform a downcast from a virtual base pointer or reference is to use a dynamic_cast (but see Gotcha #45):

```
if( D *dp = dynamic_cast<D *>(ap) ) {
  // do something with dp . . .
}
```

However, systematic use of dynamic_cast may indicate a poor design. (See Gotchas #98 and #99.)

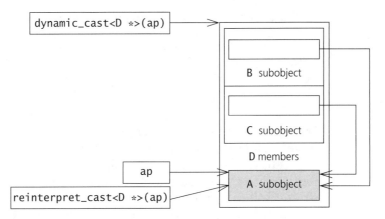

Figure 5–4 Likely effect of static and dynamic casting under multiple inheritance with virtual base classes. Under this implementation, a **D** object has three valid addresses, and a correct cast depends on knowledge of the offsets of the various subobjects within the complete object.

Gotcha #54: Copy Constructor Base Initialization

Here are a couple of simple components:

```
class M {
 public:
   M();
   M( const M & );
   ~M();
   M &operator =( const M & );
   // . . .
};
class B {
 public:
   virtual ~B();
 protected:
   B();
   B( const B & );
   B &operator =( const B & );
   // . . .
};
```

Let's leverage these components to produce a new class—and try to get the compiler to do as much work for us as is reasonable:

```
class D : public B {
    M m_;
};
```

While class D doesn't inherit constructors, destructor, or the copy assignment operator from its base class, the compiler will write these operations for us implicitly, leveraging the corresponding implementations of the components. (See Gotcha #49.) For example, the compiler's implementation of D's default constructor will be as a public inline member function. The constructor will first invoke the base class B's default constructor, then the default constructor for the M member. The destructor will, as always, do the inverse: it will first destroy the member, then call the base class destructor.

The copy operations are more interesting. The compiler-generated copy constructor will perform a member-by-member initialization, as if we had written it like this:

```
D::D( const D &init )
    : B( init ), m_( init.m_ )
    {}
```

The compiler-generated assignment operator performs a member-by-member assignment, as if we had written it like this:

```
D &D::operator =( const D &that ) {
    B::operator =( that );
    m_ = that.m_;
    return *this;
}
```

Suppose we add a data member to our class that doesn't define these operations? For example, we could add a data member that points to a heap-allocated X:

```
class D : public B {
 public:
    D();
    ~D();
    D( const D & );
    D &operator =( const D & );
```

```
private:
  M m_;
  X *xp_; // new data member
};
```

Now we should write all these operations explicitly. The default constructor and the destructor are straightforward, and we can let the compiler do most of the work for us:

```
D::D()
    : xp_( new X )
    {}
D::~D()
    { delete xp_; }
```

The compiler invokes the default constructors and destructors for the base class and member m_ implicitly. It's tempting to think we can get away with the same approach when implementing copy construction and copy assignment, but we can't:

```
D::D( const D &init )
    : xp_( new X(*init.xp_) )
    {}
D &D::operator =( const D &rhs ) {
    delete xp_;
    xp_ = new X(*rhs.xp_);
    return *this;
}
```

Both these implementations will compile without error and do the wrong thing at runtime. Our copy constructor implementation correctly initializes the member xp_ with a copy of what its initializer's xp_ refers to, but the base class and m_ member are initialized using B's and M's default constructors respectively, rather than their copy constructors. In the case of the assignment, the values of the base class part and m_ are unchanged.

Once you take over the job of writing any of these member functions from the compiler, you're responsible for the entire implementation:

```
D::D( const D &init )
    : B( init ), m_( init.m_ ), xp_( new X(*init.xp_) )
    {}
```

```
D &D::operator =( const D &rhs ) {
   if( this != &rhs ) {
      B::operator =( rhs );
      X *tmp = new X(*rhs.xp_);
      m_ = rhs.m_;
      delete xp_;
      xp_ = tmp;
   }
   return *this;
}
```

This is the case for the default constructor and destructor as well, but the implicit invocation of the default constructors for the base class and m_ member resulted in correct code in that case. I prefer the approach that minimizes typing, but if you prefer, you can be explicit:

```
D::D()
   : B(), m_(), xp_( new X )
   {}
```

Gotcha #55: Runtime Static Initialization Order

All static data in a C++ program are initialized before access. Most of these static initializations are accomplished when the program image is loaded, before execution begins. If no explicit initializer is provided, the data are initialized to "all zeros":

```
static int question; // 0
extern int answer = 42;
const char *terminalType; // null
bool isVT100; // false
const char **ptt = &terminalType;
```

These initializations all take place "simultaneously," with no issue of initializer ordering.

We can also employ runtime static initialization. In this case, there is no guarantee of initialization order between translation units. (A translation unit is basi-

```
// in file term.cpp
const char *terminalType = getenv( "TERM" );


// in file vt100.cpp
extern const char *terminalType;
bool isVT100 = strcmp( terminalType, "vt100" )==0; // error?
```

There is an implicit ordering dependency between the initializations of terminal-Type and isVT100, but the C++ language does not, and cannot, guarantee a particular initialization order. This gotcha typically occurs when an existing, working program is ported to a different platform that happens to implement a different translation unit ordering for runtime static initializations. It may also pop up without source changes due to changes in a build procedure or if a facility that was formerly statically linked is changed to use dynamic linking.

Keep in mind that default initialization of static class objects also constitutes a runtime static initialization:

```
class TermInfo {
  public:
    TermInfo()
        : type_( ::terminalType )
        {}
  private:
    std::string type_;
};
// . . .
TermInfo myTerm; // runtime static init!
```

The best way to avoid runtime static initialization difficulties is to minimize the use of external variables, including static class data members (see Gotcha #3).

Failing that, another possibility is to depend only on the initialization order within a given translation unit. This ordering is well defined, and the static variables within a translation unit are initialized in the order in which they are defined. For example, if the definitions for terminalType and isVT100 occurred in that order within the same file, there would be no portability issue. Even with this procedure, however, an initialization order problem may occur if an external function, including member functions, uses a static variable, since that function may be called, directly or indirectly, from runtime static initializations of other translation units:

```
extern const char *termType()
    { return terminalType; }
```

Failing that, another approach might be to substitute lazy evaluation for initialization. Typically, this is accomplished with some variation of the Singleton pattern (see Gotcha #3).

As a last resort, we can code the initialization order explicitly, using standard techniques. One such standard technique is a Schwarz counter, so called because it was devised by Jerry Schwarz and is employed in his implementation of the iostream library:

➤➤gotcha55/term.h

```
extern const char *terminalType;
//other things to initialize . . .
class InitMgr { // Schwarz counter
 public:
   InitMgr()
       { if( !count_++ ) init(); }
   ~InitMgr()
       { if( !--count_ ) cleanup(); }
   void init();
   void cleanup();
 private:
   static long count_; // one per process
};
namespace { InitMgr initMgr; } // one per file inclusion
```

➤➤gotcha55/term.cpp

```
extern const char *terminalType = 0;
long InitMgr::count_ = 0;
void InitMgr::init() {
   if( !(terminalType = getenv( "TERM" )) )
       terminalType = "VT100";
   // other initializations . . .
}
void InitMgr::cleanup() {
   // any required cleanup . . .
}
```

A Schwarz counter counts how many times the header file in which it resides is #included. There is a single instance, per process, of the static member count_ of InitMgr. However, every time the header file term.h is included, a new object of type InitMgr is allocated, and each of these requires a runtime static initialization. The InitMgr constructor checks the count_ member to see if this is the "first" initialization of an InitMgr object of the process. If it is, the initializations are performed.

Conversely, when the process terminates normally, static objects that have destructors will be destroyed. With each InitMgr object destruction, the InitMgr destructor decrements the count_. When count_ reaches zero, any required cleanup is performed.

Although they are robust, particularly boneheaded coding can defeat even Schwarz counters. In general, it's best to minimize use of static variables and avoid runtime static initializations.

Gotcha #56: Direct versus Copy Initialization

I've seen some pretty sloppy initializations in my day. Consider a simple class Y:

```
class Y {
 public:
    Y( int );
    ~Y();
};
```

It's not uncommon to see a simple initialization of a Y object written any of three different ways, as if they were equivalent. As if it didn't matter. As if.

```
Y a( 1066 );
Y b = Y(1066);
Y c = 1066;
```

In point of fact, all three of these initializations will probably result in the same object code being generated, but they're not equivalent. The initialization of a is known as a direct initialization, and it does precisely what one might expect. The initialization is accomplished through a direct invocation of Y::Y(int).

The initializations of b and c are more complex. In fact, they're too complex. These are both copy initializations. In the case of the initialization of b, we're requesting the creation of an anonymous temporary of type Y, initialized with the value 1066. We then use this anonymous temporary as a parameter to the copy constructor for class Y to initialize b. Finally, we call the destructor for the anonymous temporary. Essentially, we've requested that the compiler generate something like the following code:

```
Y temp( 1066 ); // initialize temporary
Y b( temp ); // copy construction
temp.~Y(); // destructor activation
```

The semantics of the initialization of c are the same, but the creation of the anonymous temporary is implicit.

Let's change the implementation of Y somewhat by adding our own copy constructor and see what happens:

```
class Y {
  public:
    Y( int );
    Y( const Y & )
        { abort(); }
    ~Y();
};
```

Clearly, Y objects have no intention of putting up with any copy construction. However, when we recompile and run our little program, all three initializations may well go off without terminating the process. What gives?

What gives is that the standard explicitly allows the compiler to perform a program transformation to remove the temporary generation and copy constructor call and to generate the same code as in the case of a direct initialization. Note that this is not a simple "optimization," since the actual behavior of the program is altered (in this case, we didn't terminate the process). Most C++ compilers will perform the transformation, but they're not required to do so by the standard. Given this uncertainty, it's always a good idea to say precisely what you mean and to use direct initialization in declaration of class objects:

```
Y a(1066), b(1066), c(1066);
```

Perversely, you may want to ensure that the compiler does not perform the transformation, because you want some side effect that temporary generation and copy construction provide, or you may just want to produce a large, slow application.

Unfortunately, it's not easy to ensure these semantics, since any standard compiler is free to perform the transformation. Avoiding the transformation in a portable way (without benefit of a platform-specific compile switch or #pragma) is too horrible to contemplate, so let's just have a quick look at it:

```
struct {
    char b_[sizeof(Y)];
} aY; // aligned buffer as big as a Y
new (&aY) Y(1066); // create temp
Y d( reinterpret_cast<Y &>(aY) ); // copy ctor
reinterpret_cast<Y &>(aY).~Y(); // destroy temp
```

This will almost duplicate the meaning of the untransformed initialization. (The storage for aY will probably not be reused later in the stack frame, the way the storage for a compiler-generated temporary might. See Gotcha #66.) But there are easier ways to write big and slow programs.

An important point to understand about this program transformation is that the compiler applies it after the original semantics have been checked. If the untransformed initialization is incorrect, the compiler will issue an error, even if the transformation would have produced correct code. Consider a class X:

```
class X {
  public:
    X( int );
    ~X();
    // . . .
  private:
    X( const X & );
};
```

```
X a( 1066 ); // OK
X b = 1066; // error!
X c = X(1066); // error!
```

The untransformed initializations of b and c require access to X's copy constructor, but the designer of X has decided to disallow copy construction of X objects by making the copy constructor private. Even though the transformation would have eliminated the copy constructor calls, the code is still incorrect.

Direct and copy initialization apply to non-class types as well, but the results are predictable and portable:

```
int i(12); // direct
int j = 12; // copy, same result
```

For the initialization of these types, feel free to use whichever form is clearest. However, note that it's usually best to use direct initialization within a template, where the type of variable is not known until template instantiation. Consider a simplified sequence-length generic algorithm parameterized on not only the iterator type of the sequence (In) but also the type of its numeric counter (N):

➤➤gotcha56/seqlength.cpp

```
template <typename N, typename In>
void seqLength( N &len, In b, In e ) {
   N n( 0 ); // this way, NOT "N n = 0;"
   while( b != e ) {
       ++n;
       ++b;
   }
   len = n;
}
```

With this implementation, the use of direct initialization allows us to employ an (admittedly unusual) user-defined numeric type that doesn't permit copy construction. An implementation of seqLength that employs copy initialization of an N object will not allow us to do so.

For simplicity and portability, it's a good idea to use direct initialization in declarations of class objects or of objects that might be of class type.

Gotcha #57: Direct Argument Initialization

We all know that formal arguments are initialized by actual arguments, but by what kind of initialization—direct or copy? That should be easy to test experimentally:

```
class Y {
public:
   Y( int );
   ~Y();
```

```
  private:
    Y( const Y & );
    // . . .
};
void f( Y yFormalArg ) {
    // . . .
}
// . . .
f( 1337 );
```

If argument passing is implemented as a direct initialization, the call to f should be correct. If the argument is initialized with copy initialization, the compiler should issue an error about the implicit attempt to access the private copy constructor for Y. Most compilers will permit the call, so we might conclude that argument passing is implemented with direct initialization. But most compilers are wrong, or at least out of date. The standard says that argument passing is accomplished with copy initialization, so the call to f above is incorrect. The initialization of yFormalArg is entirely analogous to the declaration below:

```
Y yFormalArg = 1337; // error!
```

If we want to write code that's standard, portable, and that will remain correct as compilers move to implement the details of the standard, we should avoid writing code like the call to f.

There may also be performance issues. If the function that calls f had access to Y's private copy constructor, the call would be correct but would mean something like the following:

```
Y temp( 1337 );
yFormalArg( temp );
// body of f . . .
yFormalArg.~Y();
temp.~Y();
```

In other words, the initialization of the formal argument would consist of a temporary creation, copy construction of the formal argument, destruction of the formal argument on function return, and destruction of the temporary. Four function calls, not counting the call to f. Fortunately, most compilers will perform the program transformation to get rid of the temporary generation and copy constructor and will generate the same object code that would have been generated for a direct initialization:

```
yFormalArg( 1337 );
//body of f . . .
yFormalArg.~Y();
```

However, even this solution is not optimal in all cases. What if we initialize yFormalArg with a Y object?

```
Y aY( 1453 );
f( aY );
```

Here we will have a copy construction of yFormalArg with aY and destruction of yFormalArg on return from f. A much better solution is to avoid, if possible, passing class objects by value in favor of passing by reference to constant:

```
void fprime( const Y &yFormalArg );
// . . .
fprime( 1337 ); // works! no copy ctor
fprime( aY ); // works, efficient.
```

In the first case, the compiler will create a temporary Y initialized with the value 1337 and will use this temporary to initialize the reference formal argument. The temporary will be destroyed immediately after fprime returns. (See Gotcha #44, where I discuss the extreme danger of returning such an argument.) This is equivalent in efficiency to the transformed solution above and has the additional benefit of being legal C++. The second call to fprime incurs no temporary generation overhead at all and, in addition, avoids the necessity of a destructor call on return.

Gotcha #58: Ignorance of the Return Value Optimizations

It is often necessary for a function to return a result by value. For instance, the String class below implements a binary concatenation operator that must return the newly created concatenation of two existing Strings by value:

```
class String {
public:
    String( const char * );
    String( const String & );
```

```
    String &operator =( const String &rhs );
    String &operator +=( const String &rhs );
    friend String
        operator +( const String &lhs, const String &rhs );
    // . . .
  private:
    char *s_;
};
```

As with formal argument initialization, initialization of the function return value by the return expression is accomplished with copy initialization:

```
String operator +( const String &lhs, const String &rhs ) {
    String temp( lhs );
    temp += rhs;
    return temp;
}
```

Logically, a copy constructor is used to initialize a return area in the caller with `temp`, and then `temp` is destroyed. Generally, the compiler chooses to implement the return by including the destination of the return value as an implicit argument to the function, as if the function were written something like this:

```
void
operator +( String &dest, const String &lhs, const String &rhs ) {
    String temp( lhs );
    temp += rhs;
    dest.String::String( temp ); // copy ctor
    temp.~String();
}
```

Note that the compiler is generating the call to the copy constructor above, but we're not allowed to do that. Mere programmers have to resort to subterfuge:

```
new (&dest) String( temp ); // placement new trick, see Gotcha #62
```

One implication of this transformation is that it's generally more efficient to initialize a class variable with the return value of a function than to assign to it:

```
String ab( a+b ); // efficient
ab = a + b; // probably not efficient
```

In the declaration of ab, the compiler is free to copy the result of a+b directly into ab. However, this is not possible in the case of the assignment. The assignment operator for `String` is a member function that performs operations similar to a destruction of ab followed by a reinitialization of it; therefore, we should never attempt to assign to uninitialized storage (see Gotcha #47):

```
String &String::operator =( const String &rhs );
```

To initialize the `rhs` argument of `String`'s member `operator =`, the compiler will be obliged to copy the value of a+b into a temporary, initialize `rhs` with the temporary, and destroy the temporary after `operator =` returns. For efficiency, prefer initialization to assignment.

Consider the meaning of copy initialization when returning the result of an expression that is not the same as the return type:

```
String promote( const char *str )
  { return str; }
```

Here, the copy initialization semantics demand that `str` be used to initialize a local temporary `String`, which will then be used to copy-construct the return value. Finally, the local temporary will be destroyed. However, the compiler is permitted to apply the same program transformation on the return initialization that it applies to declarations and formal argument initializations. It's likely that `str` will be used to initialize the return value directly with a call of the non–copy constructor of `String` and avoid the creation of a local temporary. When the program transformation of the copy initialization to the direct initialization is performed in the context of function return, it's often called the "return value optimization," or RVO.

Programmers commonly attempt to achieve greater efficiency by using a lower-level approach:

```
String operator +( const String &lhs, const String &rhs ) {
    char *buf = new char[ strlen(lhs.s_)+strlen(rhs.s_)+1];
    String temp( strcat( strcpy( buf, lhs.s_ ), rhs.s_ ) );
    delete [] buf;
    return temp;
}
```

Unfortunately, this code may well be slower than our previous implementation of operator +. We're allocating a local character buffer in which to concatenate the representation of the two argument Strings, only to use the buffer to initialize a temporary String return value. The buffer is then tossed away.

In cases like this, it's sometimes useful to employ a "computational constructor" in the implementation of a class. A computational constructor is a constructor that is really part of the implementation of a class and is typically private. It's basically a "helper" function implemented as a constructor, to access the special properties constructors possess that regular member functions do not. Generally, the property of interest is the guarantee that the constructor is working with uninitialized storage, not an object. This guarantee means that there is nothing to "clean up":

```
class String {
    // . . .
  private:
    String( const char *a, const char *b ) { // computational
        s_ = new char[ strlen(a)+strlen(b)+1];
        strcat( strcpy( s_, a ), b );
    }
    char *s_;
};
```

This computational constructor can then be used to facilitate efficient return by value for other functions in the implementation of the class:

```
inline String operator +( const String &a, const String &b )
    { return String( a.s_, b.s_ ); }
```

Recall that the copy initialization of the return value is analogous to that of a declaration:

```
String retval = String( a.s_, b.s_ );
```

If the compiler applies the transformation to the initialization, we have the functional equivalent of direct initialization:

```
String retval( a.s_, b.s_ );
```

Often, computational constructors are simple and can be inlined. The invoking `operator +` is now also a suitable candidate for inlining, resulting in a highly efficient implementation, equivalent to a hand-coded solution. However, note that computational constructors typically do nothing to enhance the public interface of a type. They should therefore generally be considered part of a class's implementation and be declared in the private section. Any single-argument computational constructors should without exception be declared to be `explicit`, so as not to affect the set of implicit conversions applied to a class (see Gotcha #37).

C++ compilers also implement one other common transformation in the context of function return, known as the "named return value optimization," or NRV. This transformation is similar to the RVO but allows the use of a named local variable to hold the return value. Consider our initial implementation of `operator +`:

```
String operator +( const String &lhs, const String &rhs ) {
    String temp( lhs );
    temp += rhs;
    return temp;
}
```

If a compiler applies the NRV to this code, the local variable `temp` will be replaced by a reference to the eventual destination of the return value in the caller. It's as if the function were written as follows:

```
void
operator +( String &dest, const String &lhs, const String &rhs ) {
    dest.String::String( lhs ); // copy ctor
    dest += rhs;
}
```

The NRV is typically applied only if the compiler can determine that all return expressions from a function are identical and refer to the same local variable. To increase the likelihood that the NRV will be applied, it is best to have a single return of a local variable or, failing that, have all returns return the same local variable. The simpler the better. Note that the NRV is a program transformation and not an optimization, because any side effects of the temporary initialization and destruction will be removed.

The performance gain from the application of these transformations can be significant, and it's often a good idea to facilitate their application through the use of computational constructors or the use of simple local variables to hold return values.

Gotcha #59: Initializing a Static Member in a Constructor

Static data members exist independently of any object of their class and generally come into existence before any objects of the class. (Beware of constraints that are generally true.) Like member functions (both static and non-static), static data members have external linkage and occur in the scope of their class:

```
class Account {
    // . . .
  private:
    static const int idLen = 20;
    static const int prefixLen;
    static long numAccounts;
};
// . . .
const int Account::idLen;
const int Account::prefixLen = 4;
long Account::numAccounts = 0;
```

For constant integral and enum static members, initialization may take place within or outside the class but may occur only once. For constant integer values, it's often a reasonable alternative to use enumerators in place of initialized constant integers:

```
class Account {
    // . . .
  private:
    enum {
        idLen = 20,
        prefixLen = 4
    };
    static long numAccounts;
};
// . . .
long Account::numAccounts = 0;
```

The enumerators may generally be used in place of constant integers. However, they occupy no storage and therefore cannot be pointed to. They have a different type from int and therefore may affect function matching if they're used as actual arguments in the call of an overloaded function. Note also that while the definition of numAccounts outside the class was necessary, its explicit initialization was not. In that case, it would be initialized by default to "all zeros" or zero. However, the explicit initialization to zero is still a good idea, because it tends to forestall a maintainer's decision to initialize it to something else (1 and −1 are popular choices, for some reason). See also Gotcha #25.

Runtime static initialization of static class members is a tremendously bad idea. The static member may be uninitialized at the time a static object of the class is itself initialized by a runtime static initialization:

```
class Account {
  public:
    Account() {
        . . . calculateCount()  . . .
    }
    // . . .
    static long numAccounts;
    static const int fudgeFactor;
    int calculateCount()
        { return numAccounts+fudgeFactor; }
};
// . . .
static Account myAcct; // oops!
// . . .
long Account::numAccounts = 0;
const int Account::fudgeFactor = atoi(getenv("FUDGE"));
```

The Account object myAcct is defined before the static data member fudgeFactor, so the constructor for myAcct will use an uninitialized fudgeFactor when it calls calculateCount (see Gotcha #55). The value of fudgeFactor will be zero, due to the default "all zeros" initialization of static data. If zero is a valid value for fudge-Factor, this bug may be difficult to detect.

Some programmers try to circumvent this problem by "initializing" static data members within each of the class's constructors. This is impossible, since a static data member may not be present on a constructor's member initialization list, and once execution passes into the body of the constructor, initialization is no longer possible, only assignment:

```
Account::Account() {
    // . . .
    fudgeFactor = atoi( getenv( "FUDGE" ) ); // error!
}
```

The only alternative is to make `fudgeFactor` non-constant, write the code for "lazy initialization" (see Gotcha #3) in each of the class's constructors, and hope that any maintenance on the initialization code will be performed in parallel on all the constructors.

It's best to treat static data members like other statics. Avoid them, if possible. If you must have them, initialize them, but avoid runtime static initialization, if possible.

6 | Memory and Resource Management

C++ offers tremendous flexibility in managing memory, but few C++ programmers fully understand the available mechanisms. In this area of the language, overloading, name hiding, constructors and destructors, exceptions, static and virtual functions, operator and non-operator functions all come together to provide great flexibility and customizability of memory management. Unfortunately, and perhaps unavoidably, things can also get a bit complex.

In this chapter, we'll look at how the various features of C++ are used together in memory management, how they sometimes interact in surprising ways, and how to simplify their interactions.

Inasmuch as memory is just one of many resources a program manages, we'll also look at how to bind other resources to memory so we can use C++'s sophisticated memory management facilities to manage other resources as well.

Gotcha #60: Failure to Distinguish Scalar and Array Allocation

Is a `Widget` the same thing as an array of `Widgets`? Of course not. Then why are so many C++ programmers surprised to find that different operators are used to allocate and free arrays and non-arrays?

We know how to allocate and free a single `Widget`. We use the `new` and `delete` operators:

```
Widget *w = new Widget( arg );
// . . .
delete w;
```

Unlike most operators in C++, the behavior of the `new` operator can't be modified by overloading. The `new` operator always calls a function named `operator` new to (presumably) obtain some storage, then may initialize that storage. In the case of `Widget`, above, use of the `new` operator will cause a call to an `operator new` function that takes a single argument of type `size_t`, then will invoke a `Widget` constructor on the uninitialized storage returned by `operator new` to produce a `Widget` object.

The `delete` operator invokes a destructor on the `Widget` and then calls a function named `operator delete` to (presumably) deallocate the storage formerly occupied by the now deceased `Widget` object.

Variation in behavior of memory allocation and deallocation is obtained by overloading, replacing, or hiding the functions `operator new` and `operator delete`, not by modifying the behavior of the `new` and `delete` operators.

We also know how to allocate and free arrays of `Widgets`. But we don't use the `new` and `delete` operators:

```
w = new Widget[n];
// . . .
delete [] w;
```

We instead use the `new []` and `delete []` operators (pronounced "array new" and "array delete"). Like `new` and `delete`, the behavior of the array new and array delete operators cannot be modified. Array new first invokes a function called `operator new[]` to obtain some storage, then (if necessary) performs a default initialization of each allocated array element from the first element to the last. Array delete destroys each element of the array in the reverse order of its initialization, then invokes a function called `operator delete[]` to reclaim the storage.

As an aside, note that it's often better design to use a standard library `vector` rather than an array. A `vector` is nearly as efficient as an array and is typically safer and more flexible. A `vector` can generally be considered a "smart" array, with similar semantics. However, when a `vector` is destroyed, its elements are destroyed from first to last: the opposite order in which they would be destroyed in an array.

Memory management functions must be properly paired. If `new` is used to obtain storage, `delete` should be used to free it. If `malloc` is used to obtain storage, `free` should be used to free it. Sometimes, using `free` with `new` or `malloc` with `delete` will "work" for a limited set of types on a particular platform, but there is no guarantee the code will continue to work:

```
int *ip = new int(12);
// . . .
```

```
free( ip ); // wrong!
ip = static_cast<int *>(malloc( sizeof(int) ));
*ip = 12;
// . . .
delete ip; // wrong!
```

The same requirement holds for array allocation and deletion. A common error is to allocate an array with array new and free it with scalar delete. As with mismatched `new` and `free`, this code may work by chance in a particular situation but is nevertheless incorrect and is likely to fail in the future:

```
double *dp = new double[1];
// . . .
delete dp; // wrong!
```

Note that the compiler can't warn of an incorrect scalar deletion of an array, since it can't distinguish between a pointer to an array and a pointer to a single element. Typically, array new will insert information adjacent to the memory allocated for an array that indicates not only the size of the block of storage but also the number of elements in the allocated array. This information is examined and acted upon by array delete when the array is deleted.

The format of this information is probably different from that of the information stored with a block of storage obtained through scalar new. If scalar delete is invoked upon storage allocated by array new, the information about size and element count—which are intended to be interpreted by an array delete—will probably be misinterpreted by the scalar delete, with undefined results. It's also possible that scalar and array allocation employ different memory pools. Use of a scalar deletion to return array storage allocated from the array pool to the scalar pool is likely to end in disaster.

```
delete [] dp; // correct
```

This imprecision regarding the concepts of array and scalar allocation also show up in the design of member memory-management functions:

```
class Widget {
 public:
   void *operator new( size_t );
   void operator delete( void *, size_t );
   // . . .
};
```

The author of the Widget class has decided to customize memory management of Widgets but has failed to take into account that array operator new and delete functions have different names from their scalar counterparts and are therefore not hidden by the member versions:

```
Widget *w = new Widget( arg ); // OK
// . . .
delete w; // OK
w = new Widget[n];  // oops!
// . . .
delete [] w; // oops!
```

Because the Widget class declares no operator new[] or operator delete[] functions, memory management of arrays of Widgets will use the global versions of these functions. This is probably incorrect behavior, and the author of the Widget class should provide member versions of the array new and delete functions.

If, to the contrary, this is correct behavior, the author of the class should clearly indicate that fact to future maintainers of the Widget class, since otherwise they're likely to "fix" the problem by providing the "missing" functions. The best way to document this design decision is not with a comment but with code:

```
class Widget {
 public:
    void *operator new( size_t );
    void operator delete( void *, size_t );
    void *operator new[]( size_t n )
        { return ::operator new[](n); }
    void operator delete[]( void *p, size_t )
        { ::operator delete[](p); }
    // . . .
};
```

The inline member versions of these functions cost nothing at runtime and should convince even the most inattentive maintainer not to second-guess the author's decision to invoke the global versions of array new and delete functions for Widgets.

Gotcha #61: Checking for Allocation Failure

Some questions should just not be asked, and whether a particular memory allocation has succeeded is one of them.

Let's look at how life used to be in C++ when allocating memory. Here's some code that's careful to check that every memory allocation succeeds:

```
bool error = false;
String **array = new String *[n];
if( array ) {
    for( String **p = array; p < array+n; ++p ) {
        String *tmp = new String;
        if( tmp )
            *p = tmp;
        else {
            error = true;
            break;
        }
    }
}
else
    error = true;
if( error )
    handleError();
```

This style of coding is a lot of trouble, but it might be worth the effort if it were able to detect all possible memory allocation failures. It won't. Unfortunately, the String constructor itself may encounter a memory allocation error, and there is no easy way to propagate that error out of the constructor. It's possible, but not a pleasant prospect, to have the String constructor put the String object in some sort of acceptable error state and set a flag that can be checked by users of the class. Even assuming we have access to the implementation of String to implement this behavior, this approach gives both the original author of the code and all future maintainers yet another condition to test.

Or neglect to test. Error-checking code that's this involved is rarely entirely correct initially and is almost never correct after a period of maintenance. A better approach is not to check at all:

```
String **array = new String *[n];
for( String **p = array; p < array+n; ++p )
    *p = new String;
```

This code is shorter, clearer, faster, and correct. The standard behavior of new is to throw a bad_alloc exception in the event of allocation failure. This allows us to encapsulate error-handling code for allocation failure from the rest of the program, resulting in a cleaner, clearer, and generally more efficient design.

In any case, an attempt to check the result of a standard use of new will never indicate a failure, since the use of new will either succeed or throw an exception:

```
int *ip = new int;
if( ip ) { // condition always true
    // . . .
}
else {
    // will never execute
}
```

It's possible to employ the standard "nothrow" version of operator new that will return a null pointer on failure:

```
int *ip = new (nothrow) int;
if( ip ) { // condition almost always true
    // . . .
}
else {
    // will almost never execute
}
```

However, this simply brings back the problems associated with the old semantics of new, with the added detriment of hideous syntax. It's better to avoid this clumsy backward compatibility hack and simply design and code for the exception-throwing new.

The runtime system will also handle automatically a particularly nasty problem in allocation failure. Recall that the new operator actually specifies two function calls: a call to an operator new function to allocate storage, followed by an invocation of a constructor to initialize the storage:

```
Thing *tp = new Thing( arg );
```

If we catch a bad_alloc exception, we know there was a memory allocation error, but where? The error could have occurred in the original allocation of the storage for Thing, or it could have occurred within the constructor for Thing. In the first case we have no memory to deallocate, since tp was never set to anything. In the second case, we should return the (uninitialized) memory to which tp refers to the heap. However, it can be difficult or impossible to determine which is the case.

Fortunately, the runtime system handles this situation for us. If the original allocation of storage for the Thing object succeeds but the Thing constructor fails and throws any exception, the runtime system will call an appropriate operator delete (see Gotcha #62) to reclaim the storage.

Gotcha #62: Replacing Global New and Delete

It's almost never a good idea to replace the standard, global versions of operator new, operator delete, array new, or array delete, even though the standard permits it. The standard versions are typically highly optimized for general-purpose storage management, and user-defined replacements are unlikely to do better. (However, it's often reasonable to employ member memory-management operations to customize memory management for a specific class or hierarchy.)

Special-purpose versions of operator new and operator delete that implement different behavior from the standard versions will probably introduce bugs, since the correctness of much of the standard library and many third-party libraries depends on the default standard implementations of these functions.

A safer approach is to overload the global operator new rather than replace it. Suppose we'd like to fill newly allocated storage with a particular character pattern:

```
void *operator new( size_t n, const string &pat ) {
    char *p = static_cast<char *>(::operator new( n ));
    const char *pattern = pat.c_str();
    if( !pattern[0] )
        pattern = "\0"; // note: two null chars
    const char *f = pattern;
    for( int i = 0; i < n; ++i ) {
        if( !*f )
            f = pattern;
        p[i] = *f++;
    }
    return p;
}
```

This version of `operator new` accepts a `string` pattern argument that is copied into the newly allocated storage. The compiler distinguishes between the standard `operator new` and our two-argument version through overload resolution.

```
string fill( "<garbage>" );
string *string1 = new string( "Hello" ); // standard version
string *string2 =
    new (fill) string( "World!" ); // overloaded version
```

The standard also defines an overloaded `operator new` that takes, in addition to the required `size_t` first argument, a second argument of type `void *`. The implementation simply returns the second argument. (The `throw()` syntax is an exception-specification indicating that this function will not propagate any exceptions. It may be safely ignored in the following discussion, and in general.)

```
void *operator new( size_t, void *p ) throw()
    { return p; }
```

This is the standard "placement new," used to construct an object at a specific location. (Unlike with the standard, single-argument `operator new`, however, attempting to replace placement new is illegal.) Essentially, we use it to trick the compiler into calling a constructor for us. For example, for an embedded application, we may want to construct a "status register" object at a particular hardware address:

```
class StatusRegister {
    // . . .
};
void *regAddr = reinterpret_cast<void *>(0XFE0000);
// . . .
// place register object at regAddr
StatusRegister *sr = new (regAddr) StatusRegister;
```

Naturally, objects created with placement new must be destroyed at some point. However, since no memory is actually allocated by placement new, it's important to ensure that no memory is deleted. Recall that the behavior of the `delete` operator is to first activate the destructor of the object being deleted before calling an `operator delete` function to reclaim the storage. In the case of an object "allocated" with placement new, we must resort to an explicit destructor call to avoid any attempt to reclaim memory:

```
sr->~StatusRegister(); // explicit dtor call, no operator delete
```

Placement new and explicit destruction are clearly useful features, but they're just as clearly dangerous if not used sparingly and with caution. (See Gotcha #47 for one example from the standard library.)

Note that while we can overload operator delete, these overloaded versions will never be invoked by a standard delete-expression:

```
void *operator new( size_t n, Buffer &buffer ); // overloaded new
void operator delete( void *p,
   Buffer &buffer ); // corresponding delete
// . . .
Thing *thing1 = new Thing; // use standard operator new
Buffer buf;
Thing *thing2 = new (buf) Thing; // use overloaded operator new
delete thing2; // incorrect, should have used overloaded delete
delete thing1; // correct, uses standard operator delete
```

Instead, as with an object created with placement new, we're forced to call the object's destructor explicitly, then explicitly deallocate the former object's storage with a direct call to the appropriate operator delete function:

```
thing2->~Thing(); // correct, destroy Thing
operator delete( thing2, buf ); // correct, use overloaded delete
```

In practice, storage allocated by an overloaded global operator new is often erroneously deallocated by the standard global operator delete. One way to avoid this error is to ensure that any storage allocated by an overloaded global operator new obtains that storage from the standard global operator new. This is what we've done with the first overloaded implementation above, and our first version works correctly with standard global operator delete:

```
string fill( "<garbage>" );
string *string2 = new (fill) string( "World!" );
// . . .
delete string2; // works
```

Overloaded versions of global operator new should, in general, either not allocate any storage or should be simple wrappers around the standard global operator new.

Often, the best approach is to avoid doing anything at all with global scope memory-management operator functions, but instead customize memory management on a class or hierarchy basis through the use of member operators new, delete, array new, and array delete.

We noted at the end of Gotcha #61 that an "appropriate" operator delete would be invoked by the runtime system in the event of an exception propagating out of an initialization in a new-expression:

```
Thing *tp = new Thing( arg );
```

If the allocation of Thing succeeds but the constructor for Thing throws an exception, the runtime system will invoke an appropriate operator delete to reclaim the uninitialized memory referred to by tp. In the case above, the appropriate operator delete would be either the global operator delete(void *) or a member operator delete with the same signature. However, a different operator new would imply a different operator delete:

```
Thing *tp = new (buf) Thing( arg );
```

In this case, the appropriate operator delete is the two-argument version corresponding to the overloaded operator new used for the allocation of Thing; operator delete(void *, Buffer &), and this is the version the runtime system will invoke.

C++ permits much flexibility in defining the behavior of memory management, but this flexibility comes at the cost of complexity. The standard, global versions of operator new and operator delete are sufficient for most needs. Employ more complex approaches only if they are clearly necessary.

Gotcha #63: Confusing Scope and Activation of Member new and delete

Member operator new and operator delete are invoked when objects of the class declaring them are created and destroyed. The actual scope in which the allocation expression occurs is immaterial:

```
class String {
  public:
    void *operator new( size_t ); // member operator new
    void operator delete( void * ); // member operator delete
    void *operator new[]( size_t ); // member operator new[]
    void operator delete [] ( void * ); // member operator delete[]
    String( const char * = "" );
    // . . .
};
```

```
void f() {
    String *sp = new String( "Heap" ); // uses String::operator new
    int *ip = new int( 12 ); // uses ::operator new
    delete ip; // uses :: operator delete
    delete sp; // uses String::delete
}
```

Again: the scope of the allocation doesn't matter; it's the type being allocated that determines the function called:

```
String::String( const char *s )
    : s_( strcpy( new char[strlen(s)+1], s ) )
    {}
```

The array of characters is allocated in the scope of class String, but the allocation uses the global array new, not String's array new; a char is not a String. Explicit qualification can help:

```
String::String( const char *s )
    : s_( strcpy( reinterpret_cast<char *>
        (String::operator new[](strlen(s)+1 )),s ) )
    {}
```

It would be nice if we could say something like String::new char[strlen(s)+1] to access String's operator new[] through the new operator (parse that!), but that's illegal syntax. (Although we can use ::new to access a global operator new and operator new[] and ::delete to access a global operator delete or operator delete[].)

Gotcha #64: Throwing String Literals

Many authors of C++ programming texts demonstrate exceptions by throwing character string literals:

```
throw "Stack underflow!";
```

They know this is a reprehensible practice, but they do it anyway, because it's a "pedagogic example." Unfortunately, these authors often neglect to mention to their readers that actually following the implicit advice to imitate the example will spell mayhem and doom.

Never throw exception objects that are string literals. The principal reason is that these exception objects should eventually be caught, and they're caught based on their type, not on their value:

```
try {
    // . . .
}
catch( const char *msg ) {
    string m( msg );
    if( m == "stack underflow" ) // . . .
    else if( m == "connection timeout" ) // . . .
    else if( m == "security violation" ) // . . .
    else throw;
}
```

The practical effect of throwing and catching string literals is that almost no information about the exception is encoded in the type of the exception object. This imprecision requires that a catch clause intercept every such exception and examine its value to see if it applies. Worse, the value comparison is also highly subject to imprecision, and it often breaks under maintenance when the capitalization or formatting of an "error message" is modified. In our example above, we'll never recognize that a stack underflow has occurred.

These comments also apply to exceptions of other predefined and standard types. Throwing integers, floating point numbers, `strings`, or (on a really bad day) `sets` of `vectors` of `floats` will give rise to similar problems. Simply stated, the problem with throwing exception objects of predefined types is that once we've caught one, we don't know what it represents, and therefore how to respond to it. The thrower of the exception is taunting us: "Something really, really bad happened. Guess what!" And we have no choice but to submit to a contrived guessing game at which we're likely to lose.

An exception type is an abstract data type that represents an exception. The guidelines for its design are no different from those for the design of any abstract data type: identify and name a concept, decide on an abstract set of operations for the concept, and implement it. During implementation, consider initialization, copying, and conversions. Simple. Use of a string literal to represent an exception makes about as much sense as using a string literal as a complex number. Theoretically it might work, but practically it's going to be tedious and buggy.

What abstract concept are we trying to represent when we throw an exception that represents a stack underflow? Oh. Right.

```
class StackUnderflow {};
```

Often, the type of an exception object communicates all the required information about an exception, and it's not uncommon for exception types to dispense with explicitly declared member functions. However, the ability to provide some descriptive text is often handy. Less commonly, other information about the exception may also be recorded in the exception object:

```
class StackUnderflow {
 public:
    StackUnderflow( const char *msg = "stack underflow" );
    virtual ~StackUnderflow();
    virtual const char *what() const;
    // . . .
};
```

If provided, the function that returns the descriptive text should be a virtual member function named what, with the above signature. This is for orthogonality with the standard exception types, all of which provide such a function. In fact, it's often a good idea to derive an exception type from one of the standard exception types:

```
class StackUnderflow : public std::runtime_error {
 public:
    explicit StackUnderflow( const char *msg = "stack underflow" )
        : std::runtime_error( msg ) {}
};
```

This allows the exception to be caught either as a StackUnderflow, as a more general runtime_error, or as a very general standard exception (runtime_error's public base class). It's also often a good idea to provide a more general, but non-standard, exception type. Typically, such a type would serve as a base class for all exception types that may be thrown from a particular module or library:

```
class ContainerFault {
 public:
    virtual ~ContainerFault();
    virtual const char *what() const = 0;
    // . . .
};
```

```
class StackUnderflow
    : public std::runtime_error, public ContainerFault {
  public:
    explicit StackUnderflow( const char *msg = "stack underflow" )
        : std::runtime_error( msg ) {}
    const char *what() const
        { return std::runtime_error::what(); }
};
```

Finally, it's also necessary to provide proper copy and destruction semantics for exception types. In particular, the throwing of an exception implies that it must be legal to copy construct objects of the exception type, since this is what the runtime exception mechanism does when an exception is thrown (see Gotcha #65), and the copied exception must be destroyed after it has been handled. Often, we can allow the compiler to write these operations for us (see Gotcha #49):

```
class StackUnderflow
    : public std::runtime_error, public ContainerFault {
  public:
    explicit StackUnderflow( const char *msg = "stack underflow" )
        : std::runtime_error( msg ) {}
    // StackUnderflow( const StackUnderflow & );
    // StackUnderflow &operator =( const StackUnderflow & );
    const char *what() const
        { return std::runtime_error::what(); }
};
```

Now, users of our stack type can choose to detect a stack underflow as a Stack-Underflow (they know they're using our stack type and are keeping close watch), as a more general ContainerFault (they know they're using our container library and are on the qui vive for any container error), as a runtime_error (they know nothing about our container library but want to handle any sort of standard runtime error), or as an exception (they're prepared to handle any standard exception).

Gotcha #65: Improper Exception Mechanics

Issues of general exception-handling policy and architecture are still subject to debate. However, lower-level guidelines concerning how exceptions should be thrown and caught are both well understood and commonly violated.

When a throw-expression is executed, the runtime exception-handling mechanism copies the exception object to a temporary in a "safe" location. The location of the temporary is highly platform dependent, but the temporary is guaranteed to persist until the exception has been handled. This means that the temporary will be usable until the last catch clause that uses the temporary has completed, even if several different catch clauses are executed for that temporary exception object. This is an important property because, to put it bluntly, when you throw an exception, all hell breaks loose. That temporary is the calm in the eye of the exception-handling maelstrom.

This is why it's not a good idea to throw a pointer.

```
throw new StackUnderflow( "operator stack" );
```

The address of the `StackUnderflow` object on the heap is copied to a safe location, but the heap memory to which it refers is unprotected. This approach also leaves open the possibility that the pointer may refer to a location that's on the runtime stack:

```
StackUnderflow e( "arg stack" );
throw &e;
```

Here, the storage to which the pointer exception object (remember, the pointer is what's being thrown, not what it points to) is referring to storage that may not exist when the exception is caught. (By the way, when a string literal is thrown, the entire array of characters is copied to the temporary, not just the address of the first character. This information is of little practical use, because we should never throw string literals. See Gotcha #64.) Additionally, a pointer may be null. Who needs this additional complexity? Don't throw pointers, throw objects:

```
StackUnderflow e( "arg stack" );
throw e;
```

The exception object is immediately copied to a temporary by the exception-handling mechanism, so the declaration of e is really not necessary. Conventionally, we throw anonymous temporaries:

```
throw StackUnderflow( "arg stack" );
```

Use of an anonymous temporary clearly states that the `StackUnderflow` object is for use only as an exception object, since its lifetime is restricted to the throw-expression. While the explicitly declared variable e will also be destroyed when the throw-expression executes, it is in scope, and accessible, until the end of the block containing its declaration. Use of an anonymous temporary also helps to stem some of the more "creative" attempts to handle exceptions:

```
static StackUnderflow e( "arg stack" );
extern StackUnderflow *argstackerr;
argstackerr = &e;
throw e;
```

Here, our clever coder has decided to stash the address of the exception object for use later, probably in some upstream catch clause. Unfortunately, the argstackerr pointer doesn't refer to the exception object (which is a temporary in an undisclosed location) but to the now destroyed object used to initialize it. Exception-handling code is not the best location for the introduction of obscure bugs. Keep it simple.

What's the best way to catch an exception object? Not by value:

```
try {
    // . . .
}
catch( ContainerFault fault ) {
    // . . .
}
```

Consider what would happen if this catch clause successfully caught a thrown StackUnderflow object. Slice. Since a StackUnderflow is-a ContainerFault, we could initialize fault with the thrown exception object, but we'd slice off all the derived class's data and behavior. (See Gotcha #30.)

In this particular case, however, we won't have a slicing problem, because ContainerFault is, as is proper in a base class, abstract (see Gotcha #93). The catch clause is therefore illegal. It's not possible to catch an exception object, by value, as a ContainerFault.

Catching by value allows us to expose ourselves to even more obscure problems:

```
catch( StackUnderflow fault ) {
    // do partial recovery . . .
    fault.modifyState(); // my fault
    throw; // re-throw current exception
}
```

It's not uncommon for a catch clause to perform a partial recovery, record the state of the recovery in the exception object, and re-throw the exception object for additional processing. Unfortunately, that's not what's happening here. This catch clause has performed a partial recovery, recorded the state of the recovery in a local copy of the exception object, and re-thrown the (unchanged) exception object.

For simplicity, and to avoid all these difficulties, we always throw anonymous temporary objects, and we catch them by reference.

Be careful not to reintroduce value copy problems into a handler. This occurs most commonly when a new exception is thrown from a handler rather than a re-throw of the existing exception:

```
catch( ContainerFault &fault ) {
    // do partial recovery . . .
    if( condition )
        throw; // re-throw
    else {
        ContainerFault myFault( fault );
        myFault.modifyState(); // still my fault
        throw myFault; // new exception object
    }
}
```

In this case, the recorded changes will not be lost, but the original type of the exception will be. Suppose the original thrown exception was of type StackUnderflow. When it's caught as a reference to ContainerFault, the dynamic type of the exception object is still StackUnderflow, so a re-thrown object has the opportunity to be caught subsequently by a StackUnderflow catch clause as well as a ContainerFault clause. However, the new exception object myFault is of type ContainerFault and cannot be caught by a StackUnderflow clause. It's generally better to re-throw an existing exception object rather than handle the original exception and throw a new one:

```
catch( ContainerFault &fault ) {
    // do partial recovery . . .
    if( !condition )
        fault.modifyState();
    throw;
}
```

Fortunately, the `ContainerFault` base class is abstract, so this particular manifestation of the error is not possible; in general, base classes should be abstract. Obviously, this advice doesn't apply if you must throw an entirely different type of exception:

```
catch( ContainerFault &fault ) {
    // do partial recovery . . .
    if( out_of_memory )
        throw bad_alloc(); // throw new exception
    fault.modifyState();
    throw; // re-throw
}
```

Another common problem concerns the ordering of the catch clauses. Because the catch clauses are tested in sequence (like the conditions of an if-elseif, rather than a switch-statement) the types should, in general, be ordered from most specific to most general. For exception types that admit to no ordering, decide on a logical ordering:

```
catch( ContainerFault &fault ) {
    // do partial recovery . . .
    fault.modifyState(); // not my fault
    throw;
}
catch( StackUnderflow &fault ) {
    // . . .
}
catch( exception & ) {
    // . . .
}
```

The handler-sequence above will never catch a `StackUnderflow` exception, because the more general `ContainerFault` exception occurs first in the sequence.

The mechanics of exception handling offer much opportunity for complexity, but it's not necessary to accept the offer. When throwing and catching exceptions, keep things simple.

Gotcha #66: Abusing Local Addresses

Don't return a pointer or reference to a local variable. Most compilers will warn about this situation; take the warning seriously.

Disappearing Stack Frames

If the variable is an automatic, the storage to which it refers will disappear on return:

```
char *newLabel1() {
    static int labNo = 0;
    char buffer[16]; // see Gotcha #2
    sprintf( buffer, "label%d", labNo++ );
    return buffer;
}
```

This function has the annoying property of working on occasion. After return, the stack frame for the newLabel1 function is popped off the execution stack, releasing its storage (including the storage for buffer) for use by a subsequent function call. However, if the value is copied before another function is called, the returned pointer, though invalid, may still be usable:

```
char *uniqueLab = newLabel1();
char mybuf[16], *pmybuf = mybuf;
while( *pmybuf++ = *uniqueLab++ );
```

This is not the kind of code a maintainer will put up with for very long. The maintainer might decide to allocate the buffer off the heap:

```
char *pmybuf = new char[16];
```

The maintainer might decide not to hand-code the buffer copy:

```
strcpy( pmybuf, uniqueLab );
```

The maintainer might decide to use a more abstract type than a character buffer:

```
std::string mybuf( uniqueLab );
```

Any of these modifications may cause the local storage referred to by uniqueLab to be modified.

Static Interference

If the variable is static, a later call to the same function will affect the results of earlier calls:

```
char *newLabel2() {
    static int labNo = 0;
    static char buffer[16];
    sprintf( buffer, "label%d", labNo++ );
    return buffer;
}
```

The storage for the buffer is available after the function returns, but any other use of the function can affect the result:

```
//case 1
cout << "first: " << newLabel2() << ' ';
cout << "second: " << newLabel2() << endl;

// case 2
cout << "first: " << newLabel2() << ' '
    << "second: " << newLabel2() << endl;
```

In the first case, we'll print different labels. In the second case, we'll probably (but not necessarily) print the same label twice. Presumably, someone who was intimately aware of the unusual implementation of the newLabel2 function wrote case 1 to break up the label output into separate statements, to take that flawed implementation into account. A later maintainer is unlikely to be as familiar with the implementation vagaries of newLabel2 and is likely to merge the separate output statements into one, causing a bug. Worse, the merged output statement could continue to exhibit the same behavior as the separate statements and change unpredictably in the future. (See Gotcha #14.)

Idiomatic Difficulties

Another danger is lurking as well. Keep in mind that users of a function generally do not have access to its implementation and therefore have to determine how to handle a function's return value from a reading of the function declaration. While a comment may provide this information (see Gotcha #1), it's also important that the function be designed to encourage proper use.

Avoid returning a reference that refers to memory allocated within the function. Users of the function will invariably neglect to delete the storage, causing memory leaks:

```
int &f()
    { return *new int( 5 ); }
// . . .
int i = f(); // memory leak!
```

The correct code has to convert the reference to an address or copy the result and free the memory. Not on my shift, buddy:

```
int *ip = &f(); // one horrible way
int &tmp = f(); // another
int i = tmp;
delete &tmp;
```

This is a particularly bad idea for overloaded operator functions:

```
Complex &operator +( const Complex &a, const Complex &b )
    { return *new Complex( a.re+b.re, a.im+b.im ); }
// . . .
Complex a, b, c;
a = b + c + a + b; // lots of leaks!
```

Return a pointer to the storage instead, or don't allocate storage and return by value:

```
int *f() { return new int(5); }
Complex operator +( Complex a, Complex b )
    { return Complex( a.re+b.re, a.im+b.im ); }
```

Idiomatically, users of a function that returns a pointer expect that they might be responsible for the eventual deletion of the storage referred to by the pointer and will make some effort to determine whether this is actually the case (say, by reading a comment). Users of a function that returns a reference rarely do.

Local Scope Problems

The problems we encounter with lifetimes of local variables can occur not only on the boundaries between functions but also within the nested scopes of an individual function:

```
void localScope( int x ) {
    char *cp = 0;
    if( x ) {
        char buf1[] = "asdf";
        cp = buf1; // bad idea!
        char buf2[] = "qwerty";
        char *cp1 = buf2;
        // . . .
    }
    if( x-1 ) {
        char *cp2 = 0; // overlays buf1?
        // . . .
    }
    if( cp )
        printf( cp ); // error, maybe . . .
}
```

Compilers have a lot of flexibility in how they lay out the storage for local variables. Depending on the platform and compiler options, the compiler may overlay the storage for `buf1` and `cp2`. This is legal, because `buf1` and `cp2` have disjoint scope and lifetime. If the overlay does occur, `buf1` will be corrupted, and the behavior of the `printf` may be affected (it probably just won't print anything). For the sake of portability, it's best not to depend on a particular stack frame layout.

The Static Fix

When faced with a difficult bug, sometimes the problem "goes away" with an application of the `static` storage class specifier:

```
// . . .
char buf[MAX];
long count = 0;
// . . .
```

```
int i = 0;
while( i++ <= MAX )
    if( buf[i] == '\0' ) {
        buf[i] = '*';
        ++count;
    }
assert( count <= i );
// . . .
```

This code has a poorly written loop that will sometimes write past the end of the buf array into count, causing the assertion to fail. In the wild thrashing that sometimes accompanies attempts to bug fix, the programmer may declare count to be a local static, and the code will then work:

```
char buf[MAX];
static long count;
// . . .
count = 0;
int i = 0;
while( i++ <= MAX )
    if( buf[i] == '\0' ) {
        buf[i] = '*';
        ++count;
    }
assert( count <= i );
```

Many programmers, not willing to question their good luck in fixing the problem so easily, will leave it at that. Unfortunately, the problem has not gone away; it has just been moved somewhere else. It's lying in wait, ready to strike at a future time.

Making the local variable count static has the effect of moving its storage out of the stack frame of the function and into an entirely different region of memory, where static objects are located. Because it has moved, it will no longer be overwritten. However, not only is count now subject to the problems mentioned under "Static Interference" above; it's also likely that another local variable—or a future local variable—is being overwritten. The proper solution is, as usual, to fix the bug rather than hide it:

```
char buf[MAX];
long count = 0;
// . . .
```

```
for( int i = 1; i < MAX; ++i )
    if( buf[i] == '\0' ) {
        buf[i] = '*';
        ++count;
    }
// . . .
```

Gotcha #67: Failure to Employ Resource Acquisition Is Initialization

It's a shame that many newer C++ programmers don't appreciate the wonderful symmetry of constructors and destructors. For the most part, these are programmers who were reared on languages that tried to keep them safe from the vagaries of pointers and memory management. Safe and controlled. Ignorant and happy. Programming precisely the way the designer of the language has decreed that one should program. The one, true way. Their way.

Happily, C++ has more respect for its practitioners and provides much flexibility as to how the language may be applied. This is not to say we don't have general principles and guiding idioms (see Gotcha #10). One of the most important of these idioms is the "resource acquisition is initialization" idiom. That's quite a mouthful, but it's a simple and extensible technique for binding resources to memory and managing both efficiently and predictably.

The order of execution of construction and destruction are mirror images of each other. When a class is constructed, the order of initialization is always the same: the virtual base class subobjects first ("in the order they appear on a depth-first left-to-right traversal of the directed acyclic graph of base classes," according to the standard), followed by the immediate base classes in the order of their appearance on the base-list in the class's definition, followed by the non-static data members of the class, in the order of their declaration, followed by the body of the constructor. The destructor implements the reverse order: destructor body, members in the reverse order of their declarations, immediate base classes in the inverse order of their appearance, and virtual base classes. It's helpful to think of construction as pushing a sequence onto a stack and destruction as popping the stack to implement the reverse sequence. The symmetry of construction and destruction is considered so important that all of a class's constructors perform their initializations in the same sequence, even if their member initialization lists are written in different orders (see Gotcha #52).

As a side effect or result of initialization, a constructor gathers resources for the object's use as the object is constructed. Often, the order in which these resources are seized is essential (for example, you have to lock the database before you write it; you have to get a file handle before you write to the file), and typically, the destructor has the job of releasing these resources in the inverse order in which they were seized. That there may be many constructors but only a single destructor implies that all constructors must execute their component initializations in the same sequence.

(This wasn't always the case, by the way. In the very early days of the language, the order of initializations in constructors was not fixed, which caused much difficulty for projects of any level of complexity. Like most language rules in C++, this one is the result of thoughtful design coupled with production experience.)

This symmetry of construction and destruction persists even as we move from the object structure itself to the uses of multiple objects. Consider a simple trace class:

➤➤ gotcha67/trace.h

```
class Trace {
 public:
   Trace( const char *msg )
       : m_( msg ) { cout << "Entering " << m_ << endl; }
   ~Trace()
       { cout << "Exiting " << m_ << endl; }
 private:
   const char *m_;
};
```

This trace class is perhaps a little too simple, in that it makes the assumption that its initializer is valid and will have a lifetime at least as long as the Trace object, but it's adequate for our purposes. A Trace object prints out a message when it's created and again when it's destroyed, so it can be used to trace flow of execution:

➤➤ gotcha67/trace.cpp

```
Trace a( "global" );
void loopy( int cond1, int cond2 ) {
   Trace b( "function body" );
it: Trace c( "later in body" );
   if( cond1 == cond2 )
       return;
```

```
    if( cond1-1 ) {
        Trace d( "if" );
        static Trace stat( "local static" );
        while( --cond1 ) {
            Trace e( "loop" );
            if( cond1 == cond2 )
                goto it;
        }
        Trace f( "after loop" );
    }
    Trace g( "after if" );
}
```

Calling the function loopy with the arguments 4 and 2 produces the following:

```
Entering global
Entering function body
Entering later in body
Entering if
Entering local static
Entering loop
Exiting loop
Entering loop
Exiting loop
Exiting if
Exiting later in body
Entering later in body
Exiting later in body
Exiting function body
Exiting local static
Exiting global
```

The messages show clearly how the lifetime of a Trace object is associated with the current scope of execution. In particular, note the effect the goto and return have on the lifetimes of the active Trace objects. Neither of these branches is exemplary coding practice, but they're the kinds of constructs that tend to appear as code is maintained.

```
void doDB() {
    lockDB();
    // do stuff with database . . .
    unlockDB();
}
```

In the code above, we've been careful to lock the database before access and unlock it when we've finished accessing it. Unfortunately, this is the kind of careful code that breaks under maintenance, particularly if the section of code between the lock and unlock is lengthy:

```
void doDB() {
    lockDB();
    // . . .
    if( i_feel_like_it )
        return;
    // . . .
    unlockDB();
}
```

Now we have a bug whenever the doDB function feels like it; the database will remain locked, and this will no doubt cause much difficulty elsewhere. Actually, even the original code was not properly written, because an exception might have been thrown after the database was locked but before it was unlocked. This would have the same effect as any branch past the call to unlockDB: the database would remain locked.

We could try to fix the problem by taking exceptions explicitly into account and by giving stern lectures to maintainers:

```
void doDB() {
    lockDB();
    try {
        // do stuff with database . . .
    }
    catch(  . . .  ) {
        unlockDB();
        throw;
    }
    unlockDB();
}
```

This approach is wordy, low-tech, slow, hard to maintain, and will cause you to be mistaken for a member of the Department of Redundancy Department. Properly written, exception-safe code usually employs few try blocks. Instead, it uses resource acquisition is initialization:

```
class DBLock {
 public:
    DBLock() { lockDB(); }
    ~DBLock() { unlockDB(); }
};

void doDB() {
    DBLock lock;
    // do stuff with database . . .
}
```

The creation of a DBLock object causes the database lock resource to be seized. When the DBLock object goes out of scope for whatever reason, the destructor will reclaim the resource and unlock the database. This idiom is so commonly used in C++, it often passes unnoticed. But any time you use a standard string, vector, list, or a host of other types, you're employing resource acquisition is initialization.

By the way, be wary of two common problems often associated with the use of resource handle classes like DBLock:

```
void doDB() {
    DBLock lock1; // correct
    DBLock lock2(); // oops!
    DBLock(); // oops!
    // do stuff with database . . .
}
```

The declaration of lock1 is correct; it's a DBLock object that comes into scope just before the terminating semicolon of the declaration and goes out of scope at the end of the block that contains its declaration (in this case, at the end of the function). The declaration of lock2 declares it to be a function that takes no argument and returns a DBLock (see Gotcha #19). It's not an error, but it's probably not what was intended, since no locking or unlocking will be performed.

The following line is an expression-statement that creates an anonymous temporary `DBLock` object. This will indeed lock the database, but because the anonymous temporary goes out of scope at the end of the expression (just before the semicolon), the database will be immediately unlocked. Probably not what you want.

The standard `auto_ptr` template is a useful general-purpose resource handle for objects allocated on the heap. See Gotchas #10 and #68.

Gotcha #68: Improper Use of `auto_ptr`

The standard `auto_ptr` template is a simple and useful resource handle with unusual copy semantics (see Gotcha #10). Most uses of `auto_ptr` are straightforward:

```
template <typename T>
void print( Container<T> &c ) {
    auto_ptr< Iter<T> > i( c.genIter() );
    for( i->reset(); !i->done(); i->next() ) {
        cout << i->get() << endl;
        examine( c );
    }
    // implicit cleanup . . .
}
```

This is a common use of `auto_ptr` to ensure that the storage and resources of a heap-allocated object are freed when the pointer that refers to it goes out of scope. (See Gotcha #90 for a more complete rendering of the `Container` hierarchy.) The assumption above is that the memory for the `Iter<T>` returned by genIter has been allocated from the heap. The `auto_ptr< Iter<T> >` will therefore invoke the `delete` operator to reclaim the object when the `auto_ptr` goes out of scope.

However, there are two common errors in the use of `auto_ptr`. The first is the assumption that an `auto_ptr` can refer to an array.

```
void calc( double src[], int len ) {
    double *tmp = new double[len];
    // . . .
    delete [] tmp;
}
```

The `calc` function is fragile, in that the allocated `tmp` array will not be recovered in the event that an exception occurs during execution of the function or if improper maintenance causes an early exit from the function. A resource handle is what's required, and `auto_ptr` is our standard resource handle:

```
void calc( double src[], int len ) {
    auto_ptr<double> tmp( new double[len] );
    // . . .
}
```

However, an `auto_ptr` is a standard resource handle to a single object, not to an array of objects. When `tmp` goes out of scope and its destructor is activated, a scalar deletion will be performed on the array of `double`s that was allocated with an array new (see Gotcha #60), because, unfortunately, the compiler can't tell the difference between a pointer to an array and a pointer to a single object. Even more unfortunately, this code may occasionally work on some platforms, and the problem may be detected only when porting to a new platform or when upgrading to a new version of an existing platform.

A better solution is to use a standard `vector` to hold the array of `double`s. A standard `vector` is essentially a resource handle for an array, a kind of "auto_array," but with many additional facilities. At the same time, it's probably a good idea to get rid of the primitive and dangerous use of a pointer formal argument masquerading as an array:

```
void calc( vector<double> &src ) {
    vector<double> tmp( src.size() );
    // . . .
}
```

The other common error is to use an `auto_ptr` as the element type of an STL container. STL containers don't make many demands on their elements, but they do require conventional copy semantics.

In fact, the standard defines `auto_ptr` in such a way that it's illegal to instantiate an STL container with an `auto_ptr` element type; such usage should produce a compile-time error (and probably a cryptic one, at that). However, many current implementations lag behind the standard.

In one common outdated implementation of `auto_ptr`, its copy semantics are actually suitable for use as the element type of a container, and they can be used successfully. That is, until you get a different or newer version of the standard library, at which time your code will fail to compile. Very annoying, but usually a straightforward fix.

A worse situation occurs when the implementation of `auto_ptr` is not fully standard, so that it's possible to use it to instantiate an STL container, but the copy semantics are not what is required by the STL. As described in Gotcha #10, copying an `auto_ptr` transfers control of the pointed-to object and sets the source of the copy to null:

```
auto_ptr<Employee> e1( new Hourly );
auto_ptr<Employee> e2( e1 );  // e1 is null
e1 = e2; // e2 is null
```

This property is quite useful in many contexts but isn't what is required of an STL container element:

```
vector< auto_ptr<Employee> > payroll;
// . . .
list< auto_ptr<Employee> > temp;
copy( payroll.begin(), payroll.end(), back_inserter(temp) );
```

On some platforms this code may compile and run, but it probably won't do what it should. The `vector` of `Employee` pointers will be copied into the `list`, but after the copy is complete, the `vector` will contain all null pointers!

Avoid the use of `auto_ptr` as an STL container element, even if your current platform allows you to get away with it.

7 | Polymorphism

Along with data abstraction, inheritance and polymorphism form the basic set of tools necessary for object-oriented programming. The implementation of polymorphism in C++ is efficient and flexible but complex.

In this chapter, we'll see how the flexibility offered by C++'s implementation of polymorphism is often abused, and we'll offer guidelines for taming its complexity. Along the way, we'll examine how inheritance and virtual functions are implemented and how that implementation reflects in turn on the C++ language itself.

Gotcha #69: Type Codes

One of the surest signs of "my first C++ program" is the presence of a type code as a class data member. (I used them in my first C++ program, and they caused me no end of misery.) In object-oriented programming, the type of an object is represented by the way it behaves, not by its state. Only rarely is a specific type code necessary in a well-designed C++ program, and it's never necessary to store the type code as a data member.

```
class Base {
 public:
    enum Tcode { DER1, DER2, DER3 };
    Base( Tcode c ) : code_( c ) {}
    virtual ~Base();
    int tcode() const
        { return code_; }
    virtual void f() = 0;
 private:
    Tcode code_;
};
```

```
class Der1 : public Base {
 public:
   Der1() : Base( DER1 ) {}
   void f();
};
```

The code above is a pretty typical manifestation of this problem. The problem is that the designer is not yet confident enough to commit fully to an object-oriented design that employs dynamic binding consistently in a well-designed hierarchy. The type code is there in case (the designer thinks) a switch (that comfortingly pathological old C construct) is ever needed or if it's necessary to find out exactly what type of Base we're dealing with. Wrong. Using a type code in an object-oriented design is like trying to dive while keeping one foot on the diving board: it's not going to work, and the landing is going to be painful.

In C++, we never switch on type codes in the object-oriented segments of our design. Never. The major problem is obvious from the enum Tcode in Base. A source code change is required to add a new derived class, and the base class effectively knows about, and is coupled to, its derived classes. There is no guarantee that all the existing code that examines the Tcode enumerators is going to be properly updated. A common problem in the maintenance of C programs is updating only 98% of the statements that switch over a modified set of type codes. This is a problem that simply does not occur with virtual functions, and it's a problem a designer should not expend effort to reintroduce.

Type codes stored as data members cause subtler problems as well. It's possible that the type code may be copied from one type of Base to another. In a large and complex program that employs type codes, it's likely:

```
Base *bp1 = new Der1;
Base *bp2 = new Der2;
*bp2 = *bp1; // disaster!
```

Note that the type of the Der2 object hasn't changed. Type is defined by behavior, and much of the behavior of the Der2 object is determined by the mechanism that the constructor for the Der2 object set up when the object was initialized. For example, the virtual function table pointer, which is implicitly inserted by the compiler and determines what implementation an object's functions will use in dynamic binding, will not be changed by the code above, though the explicitly declared Base data members will be. (See Gotchas #50 and #78.) In Figure 7–1, only the shaded areas of the object referred to by bp2 will be modified by the assignment.

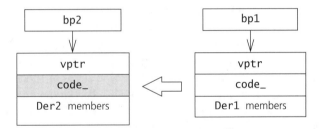

Figure 7–1 | Effect of assigning a base class subobject from one derived class object to another. Only the declared data members of the base class subobject are copied. Implicit, compiler-inserted class mechanism is not.

Once an object's type has been set during construction, it doesn't change. However, the `Der2` object referred to by `bp2` will claim to be a `Der1` object. Any switch-based code is going to believe the object's claim, and any (proper) dynamic-binding-based code will ignore it. A schizophrenic object.

If a particular rare design situation actually does require a type code, it's generally best to observe two implementation guidelines. First, don't store the code as a data member. Use a virtual function instead, because this has the effect of associating the type code more directly with the actual type (behavior) of the object and will avoid the schizophrenic problems inherent in a more casual association:

```cpp
class Base {
 public:
   enum Tcode { DER1, DER2, DER3 };
   Base();
   virtual ~Base();
   virtual int tcode() const = 0;
   virtual void f() = 0;
   // . . .
};
class Der1 : public Base {
 public:
   Der1() : Base() {}
   void f();
   int tcode() const
       { return DER1; }
};
```

Second, it's best if the base class can remain ignorant of its derived classes, since this reduces coupling within the hierarchy and facilitates the addition and removal of derived classes during maintenance. This generally implies that the set of type codes be maintained outside the program itself, perhaps as part of an official standard that maintains the lists of type codes or specifies an algorithm or procedure for generating the set of type codes. Each individual derived class may be aware of its own code, but this information should be hidden from the rest of the program.

One common situation that forces a designer to consider the use of a type code occurs when an object-oriented design must communicate with a non-object-oriented module. For example, a "message" of some sort may be read from an external source, and the type of the message is indicated by an initial integral code. The length and structure of the remainder of the message is determined by the code. What's a designer to do?

Generally, the best approach is to erect a design firewall. In this case, the portion of the design that communicates with the external representation of a message will switch on the integral code to generate a proper object that doesn't contain a type code. The bulk of the design can then safely ignore the type codes and employ dynamic binding. Note that it's trivial to regenerate the original message from the object, if necessary, since the object can be aware of its corresponding type code without actually storing it as a data member.

One drawback of this scheme is that it's necessary to modify and recompile that single switch-statement whenever the set of possible messages changes. However, because of the design firewall, any such modification is limited to the firewall code itself:

```
Msg *firewall( RawMsgSource &src ) {
    switch( src.msgcode ) {
    case MSG1:
        return new Msg1( src );
    case MSG2:
        return new Msg2( src );
    // etc.
    }
}
```

In some cases, even this limited recompilation is not acceptable. For example, it may be necessary to add new message types to an application while it's running. In cases like this, one can take advantage of the "fungible" nature of control structures and substitute an interpreted runtime data structure for compiled conditional code. In the case of our message example, we can get by with a simple sequence of objects, each of which represents a different type of message:

➤➤ gotcha69/firewall.h

```cpp
class MsgType {
 public:
   virtual ~MsgType() {}
   virtual int code() const = 0;
   virtual Msg *generate( RawMsgSource & ) const = 0;
};
class Firewall { // Monostate
 public:
   void addMsgType( const MsgType * );
   Msg *genMsg( RawMsgSource & );
 private:
   typedef std::vector<MsgType *> C;
   typedef C::iterator I;
   static C types_;
};
```

The interpreter is trivial in this case: we simply traverse the sequence looking for the message code of interest. If we find the code, we generate an object of the corresponding message type:

➤➤ gotcha69/firewall.cpp

```cpp
Msg *Firewall::genMsg( RawMsgSource &src ) {
   int code = src.msgcode;
   for( I i( types_.begin() ); i != types_.end(); ++i )
       if( code == i->code() )
           return i->generate( src );
   return 0;
}
```

The data structure is easily augmented to recognize new message types:

```cpp
void Firewall::addMsgType( const MsgType *mt )
   { types_.push_back(mt); }
```

The individual message types are trivial:

```cpp
class Msg1Type : public MsgType {
 public:
   Msg1Type()
       { Firewall::addMsgType( this ); }
```

```
    int code() const
        { return MSG1; }
    Msg *generate( RawMsgSource &src ) const
        { return new Msg1( src ); }
};
```

The list can be populated with `MsgTypes` in a number of ways. The simplest way is just to declare a static variable of the type. The constructor will have the side effect of adding the `MsgType` to the static `list` in `Firewall`:

```
static Msg1Type msg1type;
```

Note that the order of initialization of these static objects is not an issue. If it were, the provisos of Gotcha #55 would apply. New `MsgType` objects can be added to the list at runtime through the use of dynamic loading.

Speaking of static objects, note that the implementation of the `Firewall` class above contains only static data members but that these members are manipulated by non-static member functions. This is an instance of the Monostate pattern. Monostate is an alternative to Singleton as a way to avoid the use of global variables. Singleton forces its users to access the one-and-only object through the `instance` static member function. If `Firewall` had been implemented as a Singleton, we would have had to do just that:

```
Firewall::instance().addMessageType( mt );
```

A Monostate, on the other hand, permits an unbounded number of objects, but they all refer to the same static member data, and no special access protocol is required:

```
Firewall fw;
fw.genMsg( rawsource );
FireWall().genMsg( rawsource ); // different object, same state
```

Gotcha #70: Nonvirtual Base Class Destructor

This subject has been covered in almost every C++ programming text over the past fifteen years. First, there is no better documentation that a class is, or is not, intended for use as a base class than the virtualness of its destructor. If the destructor isn't virtual, chances are it's not a base class.

Undefined Behavior

Publication of the standard has made this advice even more compelling. First, destroying a derived class through its base class interface now results in undefined behavior if the base class destructor is not virtual:

```
class Base {
   Resource *br;
   // . . .
   ~Base() // note: nonvirtual
      { delete br; }
};
class Derived : public Base {
   OtherResource *dr;
   // . . .
   ~Derived()
      { delete dr; }
};
Base *bp = new Base;
// . . .
delete bp; // fine . . .
bp = new Derived;
// . . .
delete bp; // silent error!
```

Chances are you'll just get a call of the base class destructor for the derived class object: a bug. But the compiler may decide to do anything else it feels like (dump core? send nasty email to your boss? sign you up for a lifetime subscription to *This Week in Object-Oriented COBOL?*).

Virtual Static Member Functions

On the positive side, having a virtual destructor in a base class allows you to achieve the effect of a virtual static member function call. Virtual and static are mutually exclusive function-specifiers, and member memory-management operator functions (operators new, delete, new[], and delete[]) are static member functions. However, as with a virtual destructor, the most specialized member `operator delete` should be invoked during a deletion, particularly if there is a corresponding member `operator new` (see Gotcha #63):

```
class B {
 public:
    virtual ~B();
    void *operator new( size_t );
    void operator delete( void *, size_t );
};
class D : public B {
 public:
    ~D();
    void *operator new( size_t );
    void operator delete( void *, size_t );
};
// . . .
B *bp = getABofSomeSort();
// . . .
delete bp; // call derived delete!
```

Thanks to the virtual destructor in the base class, the standard promises that we'll invoke the member `operator delete` in "the scope of the dynamic type of the class." That is, we'll probably invoke the member `operator delete` from within the derived class destructor. Since the derived class's destructor is (of course) in the scope of the derived class, the call will be to the derived class's `operator delete`.

In sum, even though `operator delete` is a static member function, the presence of a virtual destructor in the base class ensures that the derived-class-specific `operator delete` will be called even when performing the deletion through a base class pointer. In the code above, for instance, the deletion of the bp pointer will invoke D's destructor, followed by D's `operator delete`, and the second argument to the `operator delete` will be sizeof(D), not sizeof(B). Neat. Virtual statics.

Leading Them On

Older C++ code is often written with the assumption that, under single inheritance, the address of a base class subobject is the same as that of the complete object. (See Gotcha #29.)

```
class B {
    int b1, b2;
};
class D : public B {
    int d1, d2;
};
D *dp = new D;
B *bp = dp;
```

While the standard makes no such promises, in this case the layout of a D object almost certainly starts with its B subobject, as in Figure 7–2.

However, if the derived class declares a virtual function, the object will probably contain a virtual function table pointer (vptr) inserted implicitly by the compiler (see Gotcha #78). Two common object layouts are used in this case, shown in Figure 7–3.

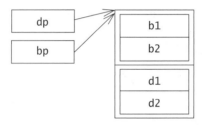

Figure 7–2 Likely layout under single inheritance of an object that contains no virtual function. In this implementation, both the D complete object and its B subobject share the same initial address.

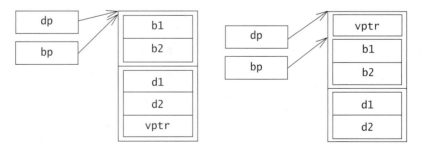

Figure 7–3 Two possible layouts for an object under single inheritance, in which the derived class declares a virtual function and the base class does not. The layout on the left locates the virtual function table pointer at the end of the complete object, whereas the layout on the right locates it at the beginning, causing the base class subobject to be offset within the complete object.

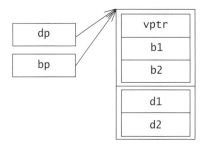

Figure 7–4 | Likely layout of an object under single inheritance, in which the base class declares a virtual function

In the first case, the tenuous assumption that the base subobject and derived object have the same address continues to hold, but it doesn't hold in the second case. Of course, the best way to deal with this problem is to rewrite any code that makes this nonstandard assumption. Typically, this means you have to stop using void * to hold class pointers (see Gotcha #29). Failing that, inserting a virtual function in the base class will make it more likely that an implementation will generate an object layout that will conform to the nonstandard assumption of address equivalence, as shown in Figure 7–4.

Usually, the best candidate for such a base class virtual function is a virtual destructor.

Exceptions

Even this most basic of idioms has exceptions. For instance, it's sometimes convenient to wrap a set of type names, static member functions, and static member data into a neat package:

```
namespace std {
   template <class Arg, class Res>
   struct unary_function {
      typedef Arg argument_type;
      typedef Res result_type;
   };
}
```

In this case, a virtual destructor is unnecessary, because classes generated from this template have no resources to reclaim. The class has also been carefully designed to have no storage or execution time impact when used as a base class:

```
struct Expired : public unary_function<Deal *, bool> {
    bool operator ()( const Deal *d ) const
        { return d->expired(); }
};
```

Finally, `unary_function` is part of the standard library. Experienced C++ programmers know not to treat it as a fully functional base class and will therefore not attempt to manipulate derived class objects through the `unary_function` interface. It's a special case.

Here's another example from a well-known but nonstandard library. The design constraints are the same in this case as for the standard base class above, but—because it's nonstandard—the author could not rely on the programmer's familiarity with the class:

```
namespace Loki {
    struct OpNewCreator {
        template <class T>
        static T *Create() { return new T; }
      protected:
        ~OpNewCreator() {}
    };
}
```

The author's solution in this case was to declare a protected, inline, nonvirtual destructor. This retains the required space and time efficiency, makes it difficult to misuse the destructor, and is an explicit reminder that the class is not intended for use except as a base class.

These are exceptional cases, however, and it's generally good design practice to ensure that a base class has a virtual destructor.

Gotcha #71: Hiding Nonvirtual Functions

A nonvirtual function specifies an invariant over the hierarchy (or subhierarchy) rooted at the base class. Derived class designers cannot override nonvirtual functions and should not hide them. (See Gotcha #77.) The rationale for this rule is basic and straightforward: to do otherwise would defeat polymorphism.

A polymorphic object has a single implementation (class) but many types. From our knowledge of abstract data types, we know that a type is a set of operations,

and these operations are represented in an accessible interface. For example, a
Circle is-a Shape and should work in an unsurprising and consistent fashion
with code written to either of its interfaces:

```
class Shape {
 public:
    virtual ~Shape();
    virtual void draw() const = 0;
    void move( Point );
    // . . .
};
class Circle : public Shape {
 public:
    Circle();
    ~Circle();
    void draw() const;
    void move( Point );
    // . . .
};
```

The designer of Circle has decided to hide the base class move function (perhaps
the base class assumes that the Point is an upper corner, but the version for Circle
uses the center). Now it's possible for the same Circle object to behave differently,
depending on the interface used to access it:

```
void doShape( Shape *s, void (Shape::*op)(Point), Point p )
    { (s->*op)( p ); }
Circle *c = new Circle;
Point pt( x, y );
c->move( pt );
doShape( c, &Shape::move, pt ); //oops!
```

Hiding a base class nonvirtual function raises the complexity of using a hierarchy
without providing any compensating merit:

```
class B {
 public:
    void f();
    void f( int );
};
```

```
class D : public B {
 public:
   void f(); // bad idea!
};


B *bp = new D;
bp->f();        // oops! called B::f() for D object
D *dp = new D;
dp->f( 123 ); // error! B::f(int) hidden
```

Virtual and pure virtual functions are the mechanisms used to specify type-variant implementations. With virtual functions, overriding in the derived class assures that only a single implementation—and therefore a single set of behaviors—will be available for a particular object at runtime. Therefore, the behavior of the object is not dependent on the interface used to access it.

As an aside, note that virtual functions can be called in a nonvirtual manner through use of the scope operator, but this is a property of the use of the interface, not its design. However, in this sense, an overridden base class virtual function is still available to its derived classes:

```
class Msg {
 public:
   virtual void send();
   // . . .
};
class XMsg : public Msg {
 public:
   void send();
   // . . .
};
// . . .
XMsg *xmsg = new XMsg;
xmsg->send(); // call XMsg::send
xmsg->Msg::send(); // call hidden/overridden Msg::send
```

This is a sometimes-necessary hack, not a design. However, the availability of a nonvirtual call to an overridden base class virtual function can rise to the level of a design. Such a call is commonly used to provide a shared, basic implementation in the base class for overriding derived class functions.

A standard implementation of the Decorator pattern is one common illustration of this approach. The Decorator pattern is used to augment, rather than replace, the existing functions of a hierarchy:

➤➤ gotcha71/msgdecorator.h

```
class MsgDecorator : public Msg {
 public:
    void send() = 0;
    // . . .
 private:
    Msg *decorated_;
};
inline void MsgDecorator::send() {
    decorated_->send(); // forward call
}
```

The class `MsgDecorator` is an abstract class, since it declares a pure virtual `send` function. Concrete classes derived from `MsgDecorator` must override the pure virtual `MsgDecorator::send`. However, even though it can't be called as a virtual function (except in unusual, nonstandard, and typically erroneous circumstances; see Gotcha #75), `MsgDecorator::send` may be invoked in a nonvirtual manner through use of the scope operator. The implementation of `MsgDecorator::send` provides a common, shared implementation that all overriding derived class `send`s must implement. They do this through a nonvirtual call:

➤➤ gotcha71/msgdecorator.cpp

```
void BeepDecorator::send() {
    MsgDecorator::send(); // do base class functionality
    cout << '\a' << flush; // additional behavior . . .
}
```

An alternative might be for the `MsgDecorator` class to declare a protected non-virtual function containing the common functionality, but the use of a defined pure virtual function more clearly indicates its intended use by derived class functions.

Gotcha #72: Making Template Methods Too Flexible

The Template Method pattern partitions an algorithm into invariant and variant parts. We specify an invariant algorithm as a nonvirtual member in the base class. However, this nonvirtual function allows customization of certain steps of its algorithm by derived classes. Typically, the algorithm invokes protected virtual functions that may be overridden in derived classes. (Note that the Template Method pattern has nothing whatever to do with C++ templates.)

This allows a base class designer the ability to guarantee the overall structure of an algorithm for every derived class while allowing an appropriate level of customizability of the algorithm:

```
class Base {
 public:
    // . . .
    void algorithm();
 protected:
    virtual bool hook1() const;
    virtual void hook2() = 0;
};
void Base::algorithm() {
    // . . .
    if( hook1() ) {
        // . . .
        hook2();
    }
    // . . .
}
```

A Template Method gives us a level of control between that of nonvirtual and virtual functions. Taking our base class design idioms together, it's instructive to see how much design constraint we can communicate to derived class designers through idiom alone:

```
class Base {
 public:
    virtual ~Base(); // I'm a base class
    virtual bool verify() const = 0; // you must verify yourself
    virtual void doit(); // you can do it your way or mine
    long id() const; // live with this function or go elsewhere
    void jump(); // when I say "jump," all you can ask is . . .
 protected:
    virtual double howHigh() const; //  . . . how high, and . . .
    virtual int howManyTimes() const = 0; //  . . . how many times.
};
```

Many novice designers erroneously assume that a design should be maximally flexible. These designers often make the mistake of declaring the algorithm of a template method to be virtual, assuming that the additional flexibility would benefit derived class designers. Wrong. Designers of derived classes are helped most by an unambiguous contract in the base class. If generic code is expecting a particular general behavior from a template method, then that must be respected and implemented by derived classes.

Gotcha #73: Overloading Virtual Functions

What's wrong with the following base class fragment?

```
class Thing {
 public:
     // . . .
         virtual void update( int );
         virtual void update( double );
};
```

Consider a derived class produced by a designer who has determined that only the integer version of update requires different behavior in the derived class:

```
class MyThing : public Thing {
 public:
         // . . .
         void update( int );
};
```

Here we have an unhappy confluence of overloading and overriding—which have nothing to do with each other. The result is similar to that of hiding a base class nonvirtual: the behavior of a MyThing object will vary depending on the interface used to access it:

```
MyThing *mt = new MyThing;
Thing *t = mt;
t->update( 12.3 ); // OK, base
mt->update( 12.3 ); // oops, derived!
```

The call `mt->update( 12.3 )` will find the name `update` in the derived class and then perform a successful match by converting the `double` argument to an `int`. This is probably not what the programmer intended. Even if it is the intent of a programmer with an unusual worldview, such code does not benefit future maintainers of the code of a more conventional mind-set.

Rather than argue against the overloading of virtual functions, we could, as is often suggested in substandard C++ texts, demand that derived class designers override every member of a set of overloaded virtual functions. This approach is impractical, because it requires every derived class designer to follow a particular rule. Many derived classes, such as those used to extend a framework, are developed in environments remote from that of the base class and the coding and design conventions under which it was developed.

In any case, avoiding the overloading of virtual functions does not impose any severe restriction on the base class interface. If the overloading is essential to the usability of the base class, it's perfectly reasonable to overload nonvirtual functions that kick down to differently named virtual functions:

```
class Thing {
 public:
   // . . .
   void update( int );
   void update( double );
 protected:
   virtual void updateInt( int );
   virtual void updateDouble( double );
};
inline void Thing::update( int a )
   { updateInt( a ); }
inline void Thing::update( double d )
   { updateDouble( d ); }
```

The derived class may now override either virtual function independently without defeating polymorphism. Of course, the derived class should not declare a member called `update`; the ban on hiding base class nonvirtuals is still in effect!

This rule has exceptions, but they're relatively uncommon. One exception arises in a common implementation of the Visitor pattern (see Gotcha #77).

Gotcha #74: Virtual Functions with Default Argument Initializers

This is really the same problem as overloading virtual functions. Like overloading, default argument initializers are basically syntactic sugar, used to change the interface of a function without adding new behavior:

```
class Thing {
    // . . .
    virtual void doitNtimes( int numTimes = 12 );
};
class MyThing : public Thing {
    // . . .
    void doitNtimes( int numTimes = 10 );
};
```

The problems that arise result from a mismatch between the static and dynamic behavior of an object and are often difficult to track down:

```
Thing *t = new MyThing;
t->doitNtimes();
```

The assumption is that it's important to do it, by default, ten times for a MyThing versus twelve times for other types of Thing. Unfortunately, the default argument initializer is applied statically, and the statically determined base class default of 12 is passed to the dynamically bound derived class function.

We could attempt to circumvent this problem by demanding that all derived class designers duplicate precisely a base class function's default initializers when overriding. However, this is a bad approach, for a number of reasons.

First, developers being the way they are, some of them won't follow this advice. (They may have lost confidence in the base class design when they saw the default argument initializer, and decided to strike out on their own.)

Second, such advice renders the derived classes unnecessarily vulnerable to changes in the base class. If the default argument initializer should be modified in the base class, that would require a coordinated change to every derived class as well. Typically, this is not possible.

Third, the meaning of a default argument initializer can vary, according to where it appears in the source code. Syntactically identical initializers may have very different meanings between the base class and derived class contexts:

```
// In file thing.h . . .
const int minim = 12;
namespace SCI {
class Thing {
   // . . .
   virtual void doitNtimes( int numTimes = minim ); // uses ::minim
};
}

// In file mything.h . . .
namespace SCI {
const int minim = 10;
class MyThing : public Thing {
   // . . .
   void doitNtimes( int numTimes = minim ); // uses SCI::minim
};
}
```

It would be hard to blame the derived class designer for picking up the wrong minim, particularly if the declaration of SCI::minim were added after the MyThing class had been written.

The safest and simplest procedure is to avoid default argument initializers in virtual functions. As with overloaded virtual functions, we can achieve our interface goals with a little inline trickery:

```
class Thing {
   // . . .
   void doitNtimes( int numTimes = minim )
      { doitNtimesImpl( numTimes ); }
 protected:
   virtual void doitNtimesImpl( int numTimes );
};
```

Users of the Thing hierarchy will pick up the statically determined default from the base class interface, and derived classes can modify the behavior of the function without concerning themselves with a default initializer.

Gotcha #75: Calling Virtual Functions in Constructors and Destructors

Constructors are used to seize resources an object needs to perform its operations, and destructors are used to free those resources. Why don't we just make that architectural decision explicit in the design of our base class?

```
class B {
 public:
   B() { seize(); }
   virtual ~B() { release(); }
 protected:
   virtual void seize() {}
   virtual void release() {}
};
```

Derived classes can then override the base class `seize` and `release` functions to customize their resource-acquisition behavior:

```
class D : public B {
 public:
   D() {}
   ~D() {}
   void seize() {
       B::seize(); // get base resources
       // get derived resources . . .
   }
   void release() {
       // release derived resources . . .
       B::release(); // release base resources
   }
};
// . . .
D x; // no resources seized or released!
```

As the first step in the initialization of x, the derived class constructor invokes the base class constructor, which in turn makes a virtual function call to `seize`. As the last step in the destruction of x, the derived class destructor invokes the base class destructor, which in turn makes a virtual call to `release`. However, no resources are seized or released.

The problem is that, at the point the base class constructor is invoked from the derived class constructor, the object x is not yet of type D. The base class constructor initializes the B subobject within x to behave like a B object. Therefore, when the virtual `seize` function is called, it binds to `B::seize`. The same situation occurs in reverse on destruction. When the derived class destructor invokes the base class destructor, the object x is no longer of type D, and the B subobject of x will behave like a B object. The virtual function call of `release` will bind to `B::release`.

In this case, the simplest solution would be the built-in mechanism for implementing construction and destruction of complex objects. The code that seizes and releases resources for base class subobjects should be present in the constructors and destructors:

```cpp
class B {
 public:
   B() {
       // get base resources . . .
   }
   virtual ~B() {
       // release base resources . . .
   }
};
class D : public B {
 public:
   D() {
       // get derived resources . . .
   }
   ~D() {
       // release derived resources . . .
   }
};
// . . .
D x; // works!
```

By the way, this is one way it's sometimes possible to call a pure virtual function with a virtual, rather than static, calling sequence:

```
class Abstract {
 public:
   Abstract();
   Abstract( const Abstract & );
   virtual bool validate() const = 0;
   // . . .
};
bool Abstract::validate() const
   { return true; }
Abstract::Abstract() {
   if( validate() ) // attempt to call pure virtual
     // . . .
};
```

However, the standard specifies that the behavior of such a call is undefined. Typical observed behaviors on specific platforms include making a virtual call to a function that simply aborts, attempting to call a function through a null pointer to function, or (this is the dangerous one) actually calling `Abstract::validate`. Even if this is desired behavior, such code is fragile and unportable.

Note that this gotcha deals only with the invocation of a virtual function on an object currently under construction or destruction. It's perfectly reasonable for a constructor or destructor to call a virtual function of another, fully constructed object:

```
Abstract::Abstract( const Abstract &that ) {
   if( that.validate() ) // OK
     // . . .
}
```

Gotcha #76: Virtual Assignment

Assignment may be virtual, but use of virtual assignment is rarely justified. For example, we may have a container hierarchy that supports virtual assignment through the base class interface:

```
template <typename T>
class Container {
 public:
    virtual Container &operator =( const T & ) = 0;
    // . . .
};
template <typename T>
class List : public Container<T> {
    List &operator =( const T & );
    // . . .
};
template <typename T>
class Array : public Container<T> {
    Array &operator =( const T & );
    // . . .
};
// . . .
Container<int> &c( getCurrentContainer() );
c = 12; // is the meaning clear?
```

Note that this is not a copy assignment, since the argument type is not the same as the type of the container. (See Gotcha #77 for the reason why the return types of the overriding derived class assignment operators may differ from those of the base class assignment.) This assignment is intended to set all the elements of a `Container` to the same value. Unfortunately, experience shows that this use of assignment is sometimes misinterpreted, with some users assuming that the assignment changes the size of the container and some users assuming that the assignment sets the value of the first element only (see Gotcha #84). A safer interface would abandon operator overloading in favor of an unambiguous non-operator function:

```
template <typename T>
class Container {
 public:
    virtual void setAll( const T &newElementValue ) = 0;
    // . . .
};
```

```
// . . .
Container<int> &c( getCurrentContainer() );
c.setAll( 12 ); // meaning is clear
```

Copy assignment may also be virtual, but this is rarely a good idea, since the derived class copy assignment operator doesn't override the base class copy assignment:

```
template <typename T>
class Container {
 public:
    virtual Container &operator =( const Container & ) = 0;
    // . . .
};
template <typename T>
class List : public Container<T> {
    List &operator =( const List & ); // doesn't override!
    List &operator =( const Container<T> & ); // overrides . . .
    // . . .
};
// . . .
Container<int> &c1 = getMeAList();
Container<int> &c2 = getMeAnArray();
c1 = c2; // assign an array to a list?!?
```

Virtual copy assignment would permit the assignment of one derived class object to another derived class object of a different type! There are few circumstances where this makes sense. Avoid virtual copy assignment.

One might try to make a case for virtual copy assignment in the Container hierarchy above, since it *could* make sense to assign the content of one container (an array) to another container (a list). However, this assumes that each container type knows about all the others (which is usually a bad design practice) or that a rather involved framework is employed. A simpler and therefore better solution would be to employ a nonvirtual copyContent member or non-member function of Container written in terms of virtual functions or iterators that extract element values from the source of the copy and insert the values into the target of the copy:

```
Container<int> &c1 = getMeAList();
Container<int> &c2 = getMeAnArray();
c1.copyContent( c2 ); // copy content of array to list
```

One example of this approach is found in the standard library containers, where it's possible to initialize a container with a sequence obtained from an existing container of different type:

```
vector<int> v;
// . . .
list<int> el( v.begin(), v.end() );
```

Often, virtual copy construction is a better design approach than virtual assignment. Of course, C++ has no virtual constructors, but we do have a "virtual constructor" idiom, now more generally known as the Prototype pattern. Rather than assign an object of unknown type, we clone it. The base class provides a pure virtual `clone` operation that is overridden in derived classes to return an exact copy of themselves. Typically, the copy is generated with the derived class's copy constructor, and we can think of the `clone` operation as a kind of virtual copy construction:

➤➤ gotcha90/container.h

```
template <typename T>
class Container {
 public:
   virtual Container *clone() const = 0;
   // . . .
};
template <typename T>
class List : public Container<T> {
   List( const List & );
   List *clone() const
       { return new List( *this ); }
   // . . .
};
```

```
template <typename T>
class Array : public Container<T> {
   Array( const Array & );
   Array *clone() const
       { return new Array( *this ); }
   // . . .
};
// . . .
Container<int> *cp = getCurrentContainer();
Container<int> *cp2 = cp->clone();
```

Use of the Prototype pattern allows us to say, effectively, "I don't know precisely what I'm pointing to, but I want another one just like it!"

Gotcha #77: Failure to Distinguish among Overloading, Overriding, and Hiding

It's always a shock to discover, many minutes into a technical discussion, that your interlocutor doesn't know the difference between overloading and overriding. Add a poor appreciation for block-structured hiding and you've got the makings of some really murky communication. Things don't have to be that way, however, and it's a cinch to distinguish among these concepts.

In C++, overloading is simply the use of the same function identifier for different functions declared in the same scope. That last proviso is important:

```
bool process( Credit & );
bool process( Acceptance & );
bool process( OrderForm & );
```

These three global functions are clearly overloaded. They share the process identifier and are declared in the same scope. The compiler will distinguish among them by the actual argument used in the call to process. That makes sense. If I ask to process an Acceptance, I'd expect the call to resolve to the second process function above, not the first or third. In C++, the name of a function is composed of a combination of the function's identifier (in this case, process) and the types of the formal arguments in the function's declaration. Let's embed these three functions in a class:

```
class Processor {
 public:
    virtual ~Processor();
    bool process( Credit & );
    bool process( Acceptance & );
    bool process( OrderForm & );
    // . . .
 };
```

They're still overloaded, and the compiler will still be able to perform the proper resolution based on the actual argument to the member function. The virtual destructor in the Processor class indicates that its designer intended it to be used as a base class, so we should feel free to extend its functionality through derivation:

```
class MyProcessor : public Processor {
 public:
    bool process( Rejection & );
    // . . .
 };
```

But not like this. The derived class process function doesn't additionally overload the base class process functions. It hides them:

```
Acceptance a;
MyProcessor p;
p.process( a ); // error!
```

When the compiler looks up the name process in the scope of the derived class, it finds a single candidate function. This function is declared to take a Rejection formal argument, so we have an argument mismatch (unless there is some way to convert an Acceptance into a Rejection). End of discussion. The compiler will not continue its search for candidate process functions into enclosing scopes. The derived class process is declared in the scope of the derived class, not of the base class, and therefore can't overload the base class functions.

It's possible to import the base class declarations into the derived class scope with a using-declaration:

```
class MyProcessor : public Processor {
 public:
    using Processor::process;
    bool process( Rejection & );
    // . . .
};
```

Now all four names are present in the same scope, and the derived class `process` function additionally overloads the three functions explicitly imported into the derived class scope. Note that this is not necessarily an exemplary design practice, because it's complex, and a complex design is always inferior to a simple design unless it has some compensating merit.

In this case, a `Rejection` can be processed only through the `MyProcessor` interface, and a compile-time error will result if we attempt to process a `Rejection` with the base class `Processor` interface. If a `Rejection` can be converted to an `Acceptance`, `OrderForm`, or `Credit`, however, the call will succeed under either interface but will exhibit different behavior.

Overriding can occur only in the presence of a base class virtual function. Period. Overriding has nothing whatsoever to do with overloading. A nonvirtual base class function cannot be overridden, only hidden:

```
class Doer {
 public:
    virtual ~Doer();
    bool doit( Credit & );
    virtual bool doit( Acceptance & );
    virtual bool doit( OrderForm & );
    virtual bool doit( Rejection & );
    // . . .
};
class MyDoer : public Doer {
 private:
    bool doit( Credit & ); // #1, hides
    bool doit( Acceptance & ); // #2, overrides
    virtual bool doit( Rejection & ) const; // #3, doesn't override
    double doit( OrderForm & ); // #4, an error
    // . . .
};
```

(Please note that the Doer classes above are for illustration only and are not intended to exemplify good design practice. In particular, it's only rarely acceptable to overload virtual functions. See Gotcha #73.)

The doit function labeled #1 above does not override the corresponding base class function, because the base class function is not virtual. It does, however, hide all four base class doit functions.

The function labeled #2 does override the corresponding base class function. Note that access level has no effect on overriding. It doesn't matter that the base class function is public and the derived class function is private or vice versa. Conventionally, an overriding derived class function has the same access level as the corresponding base class function. In some cases, however, it may be desirable to depart from this standard practice:

```cpp
class Visitor {
 public:
    virtual void visit( Acceptance & );
    virtual void visit( Credit & );
    virtual void visit( OrderForm & );
    virtual int numHits();
};
class ValidVisitor : public Visitor {
    void visit( Acceptance & ); // overrides
    void visit( Credit & ); // overrides
    int numHits( int ); // #5, nonvirtual
};
```

In this case, the hierarchy designer has decided to allow customization of the base class behavior but would still like to require users of the hierarchy to employ the base class interface. The designer does this by declaring the base class member functions public but overriding them with private derived class functions.

Note also that the use of the keyword virtual in the derived class is purely optional when overriding a base class function. The meaning of the derived class function declaration is precisely the same with or without the presence of the keyword:

```cpp
class MyValidVisitor : public ValidVisitor {
    void visit( Credit & ); // overrides
    void visit( OrderForm & ); // overrides
    int numHits(); // #6, virtual, overrides Visitor::numHits
};
```

A common misconception is that the absence of the `virtual` keyword in an overriding derived class function will prevent that function from being over-ridden itself in more derived classes. That is not the case, and `MyValid-Visitor::visit( Credit & )` overrides the corresponding functions in `ValidVisitor` and `Visitor`.

It's also perfectly valid for a derived class to override remote base class functions. `MyValidVisitor::visit( OrderForm & )` overrides the corresponding function in `Visitor`.

It's even legal for a derived class to override a remote base class function that isn't visible in the scope of the derived class. For example, the function labeled #5, `Valid-Visitor::numHits`, doesn't override the base class function `Visitor::numHits`, but it does hide the base class function from more derived classes. In spite of this hiding, the function `MyValidVisitor::numHits` does override `Visitor::numHits`.

The member function of `MyDoer` labeled #3 is subtle. It is virtual, but only because it's so declared. It doesn't actually override a base class virtual because it's a const member function, and the base class has no corresponding virtual const member function. Constness is part of the function signature (see Gotcha #82).

The member function of `MyDoer` labeled #4 above is in error. It overrides the cor-responding base class virtual function, but it doesn't have a compatible return type; the base class function returns `bool`, and the derived class version returns `double`. This is a compile-time error.

In general, if a derived class function overrides a base class function, it must have the same return type. This is to ensure static type safety during runtime binding. A derived class virtual function is usually invoked through the base class func-tion's interface (that's why we have virtual functions, after all). The compiler must generate code that assumes that the type of value returned from the function call—whether it's actually bound at runtime to the base class function or to an overriding derived class function—is the one declared in the base class.

In the case of the illegal function declaration labeled #4, the derived class function would attempt to copy an object that is `sizeof(double)` bytes into a location reserved for the return value of `sizeof(bool)` bytes. Even if the sizes are compat-ible (that is, `bool`s are at least as big as `double`s) it is unlikely a `double`, when interpreted as a `bool`, would give a consistently reasonable result.

This rule has an exception for what are known as "covariant return types." (Don't confuse covariance with contravariance. See Gotcha #46.) The return types of a base class member function and an overriding derived class function are covari-ant if they are pointers or references to classes and the class type in the derived class function return has an is-a relationship to the class type in the base class function return. That's a mouthful, so let's look at two canonical examples of covariant return types:

```
class B {
    virtual B *clone() const = 0;
    virtual Visitor *genVisitor() const;
    // . . .
};
class D : public B {
    D *clone() const;
    ValidVisitor *genVisitor() const;
};
```

The clone function returns a pointer to a duplicate of the object making the clone request (this is an instance of the Prototype pattern; see Gotcha #76). Typically, the request is made through the base class interface, and the precise type of the cloned object is not known:

```
B *aB = getAnObjectDerivedFromB();
B *anotherLikeThat = aB->clone();
```

On occasion, however, we'll have more precise information about the type, and we'd like to avoid losing that information or forcing a downcast:

```
D *aD = getAnObjectThatIsAtLeastD();
D *anotherLikeThatD = aD->clone();
```

Without the covariant return, we'd be forced to downcast the return value from B * to D *:

```
D *anotherLikeThatD = static_cast<D *>(aD->clone());
```

Note that, in this case, we're able to use the efficient static_cast operator in preference to dynamic_cast, because we know that D's clone operation returns a D object. In other contexts the use of dynamic_cast (or avoiding a cast entirely) would be safer and preferable.

The genVisitor function (an instance of the Factory Method pattern; see Gotcha #90) illustrates that the classes in the covariant returns don't have to be related to the hierarchy in which the functions occur.

The overriding mechanism in C++ is a flexible and useful tool. However, this utility comes at the cost of some complexity. Other items in this chapter provide advice on how to tame the overriding mechanism's complexity while retaining the ability to exploit it as the need arises.

Gotcha #78: Failure to Grok Virtual Functions and Overriding

Many novice C++ programmers have only a superficial understanding of the mechanics of overriding as it's implemented in C++. Sometimes an illustration of the mechanics of the implementation of overriding helps to clarify things. There are a number of different effective mechanisms for implementing virtual functions and overriding in C++. The treatment below describes one common approach.

Let's look first at a simple implementation for single inheritance.

```
class B {
  public:
    virtual int f1();
    virtual void f2( int );
    virtual int f3( int );
};
```

In this implementation of virtual functions, each virtual function contained within a class is assigned an index by the compiler. For example, B::f1 is assigned index 0, B::f2 is assigned index 1, and so on. These indexes are used to access a table of pointers to functions. The table element at index 0 contains the address of B::f1, the element at index 1 contains the address of B::f2, and so on. Each object of the class contains a pointer, inserted implicitly by the compiler, to the table of function pointers. An object of type B might be laid out as in Figure 7–5.

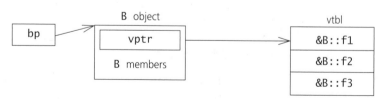

Figure 7–5 | A simple implementation of virtual functions under single inheritance

Colloquially, the table of function pointers is called the "vtbl," pronounced "vee table," and the pointer to vtbl is called the "vptr," pronounced "vee pointer." The constructors for class B initialize the vptr to refer to the appropriate vtbl (see Gotcha #75). Calling a virtual function involves indirection through the vtbl. The function call

```
B *bp = new B;
bp->f3(12);
```

is translated something like this:

```
(*(bp->vptr)[2])(bp, 12)
```

We get the address of the function to call by indexing the vtbl with that function's index. We then make an indirect call, passing the address of the object as the implicit "this" argument to the function. The virtual function mechanism in C++ is efficient. The indirect function call is generally highly optimized for each hardware architecture, and all objects of the same type typically share a single vtbl. Under single inheritance, each object has a single vptr, no matter how many virtual functions are declared in the class.

Let's look at the implementation of a derived class that overrides some of its base class's virtual functions:

```
class B {
 public:
   virtual int f1();
   virtual void f2( int );
   virtual int f3( int );
};
class D : public B {
   int f1();
   virtual void f4();
   int f3( int );
};
```

An object of type D contains a subobject of type B. Typically, but not universally (see Gotcha #70), the base class subobject is located at the start of the derived class object (that is, at offset 0), and any additional derived class data members are appended after the base class part, as in Figure 7–6.

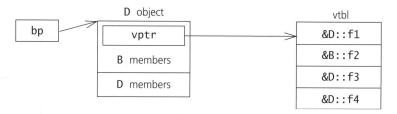

Figure 7–6 | A simple implementation of virtual functions under single inheritance for a derived class object. The base class subobject still contains a vptr, but it refers to a table customized for the derived class.

Let's look at the same virtual member function call we saw earlier, but this time we'll use a D object rather than a B object:

```
B *bp = new D;
bp->f3(12);
```

The compiler will generate the same calling sequence, but this time we'll bind at runtime to the function D::f3 rather than B::f3:

```
(*(bp->vptr)[2])(bp, 12)
```

The utility of the virtual function mechanism is more obvious in truly polymorphic code, where the precise type of object being manipulated is unknown:

```
B *bp = getSomeSortOfB();
bp->f3(12);
```

The virtual calling sequence generated by the compiler is capable of calling, without recompilation, the f3 function of any class derived from B, even of classes that do not yet exist.

Mechanically speaking, overriding is the process of replacing the address of a base class member function with the address of a derived class member function when constructing a virtual function table for a derived class. In our example above, class D has overridden the base class virtual functions f1 and f3, inherited the implementation of f2, and added a new virtual function f4. This is reflected precisely in the structure of the virtual table for class D.

The mechanics of virtual functions under multiple inheritance are more complex in their details but employ essentially the same approach. The additional complexity is the result of a single object's having more than one base class subobject and therefore more than one valid address. Consider the following hierarchy:

```
class B1 { /* . . . */ };
class B2 { /* . . . */ };
class D : public B1, public B2 { /* . . . */ };
```

A derived class object can be manipulated through the interface of any of its public base classes; this is the meaning of the is-a relationship. Therefore, an object of type D can be referred to through pointers or references to D, B1, or B2:

```
D *dp = new D;
B1 *b1p = dp;
B2 *b2p = dp;
```

Only one base class subobject can be located at offset 0 in a derived class object, so base class subobjects are typically allocated in the order in which they appear on the base class list in the derived class definition. In the case of D, the storage for B1 will come first, followed by that for B2, as in Figure 7–7 (see Gotcha #38).

Let's flesh out this simple multiple-inheritance hierarchy with some virtual functions:

```
class B1 {
 public:
   virtual void f1();
   virtual void f2();
};
class B2 {
 public:
   virtual void f2();
   virtual void f3( int );
   virtual void f4();
};
```

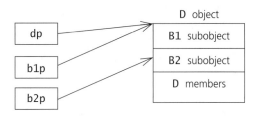

Figure 7–7 Likely layout of an object under multiple inheritance

The B1 and B2 classes each have virtual functions, so objects of these types will each contain a vptr to a class-specific vtbl, as in Figure 7–8.

A D object is-a B1 and is-a B2, so it will have two vptrs and two associated vtbls (see Figure 7–9):

```
class D : public B1, public B2 {
 public:
   void f2();
   void f3( int );
   virtual void f5();
};
```

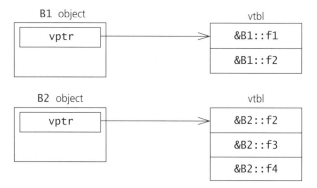

Figure 7–8 | Two potential base classes

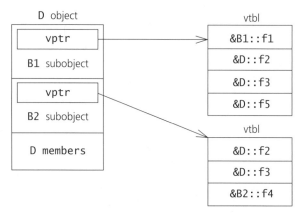

Figure 7–9 | Possible implementation of virtual functions under multiple inheritance. The complete object overrides virtual functions for both of its base class subobjects.

Notice that D::f2 overrides the f2 in both of its base classes. An overriding derived class function will override every base class virtual function with the same name and signature (number and type of formal arguments), whether the base class is a direct base class or a base class of a base class (of a base class . . .). Note that even though D adds a new virtual function (D::f5), the compiler doesn't insert a vtpr into the D-specific part of the object. Typically, new derived class virtual functions will be appended to one of the base class virtual function tables.

We do have a problem, though. Let's look at some possible code:

```
B2 *b2p = new D;
b2p->f3(12);
```

We're going to engage in the common practice of manipulating a derived class object through one of its base class interfaces. However, if we generate the same calling sequence we did under the single-inheritance model we examined earlier, we'll wind up with a bad value for the this pointer:

```
(*(b2p->vptr)[1])(b2p,12)
```

The reason is that the call is dynamically bound to D::f3, which is expecting an implicit this argument that refers to the start of a D object. Unfortunately, b2p refers to the start of a B2 (sub)object, which is offset some number of bytes into the D object in which it's embedded. (Refer to Figure 7–7.) It's necessary to "fix up" the value of this passed in the call by adjusting the value of b2p to refer to the start of the D object.

Fortunately, when it's constructing the vtbl for a derived class, the compiler knows precisely what these fix-up values are, since it knows precisely the class for which it's constructing the vtbl and the offsets of the various base class subobjects within the derived class. There are several common ways to apply this fix-up information, from small sections of code (misnamed "thunks") executed before the actual function is attained, to member functions with multiple entry points. Conceptually, the cleanest way to represent the operation is simply to record the required offset value in the vtbl and modify the calling sequence to take the offset into account, as in Figure 7–10.

The vtbl entries are now small structures containing the member function address (fptr) and an offset (delta) to add to the this value, and the calling sequence becomes

```
(*(b2p->vptr)[1].fptr)(b2p+(b2p->vptr)[1].delta,12)
```

This code can be heavily optimized, so it's not as expensive as it might look.

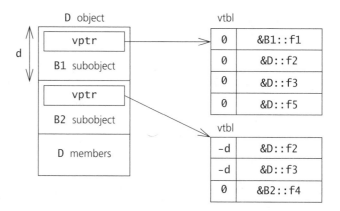

Figure 7–10 | One of many possible implementations of virtual functions under multiple inheritance. This implementation records the fix-up values for the **this** pointer in the virtual function table itself.

Gotcha #79: Dominance Issues

You may wonder how you ended up programming in a language that includes concepts like friends, private parts, bound friends, and dominance. In this item we'll examine the concept of dominance in hierarchy design, why it's weird, and why it's sometimes necessary. Oh, it's easy enough to claim that you lead your life in such a way that this manner of issue is never a concern, but sooner or later most expert C++ programmers find themselves face to face with a dominance situation—whether their own or one of their colleagues'—and it's best to be prepared. Forewarned is forearmed.

Dominance becomes an issue only in the context of virtual inheritance and is best illustrated graphically. In Figure 7–11, the identifier B::name dominates A::name if A is a base class of B. Note that this dominance extends to other lookup paths. For example, if the compiler looks up the identifer name in the scope of class D, it will find both B::name and, through a different path, A::name. However, because of dominance, no ambiguity arises. The identifier B::name dominates.

Note that the analogous case without virtual inheritance will result in an ambiguity. In Figure 7–12, the lookup of name in the scope of D is ambiguous, because B::name doesn't dominate the A::name in the base class of C.

This may seem like an odd language rule, but, without dominance, it would be impossible in many cases to construct virtual function tables for classes that use virtual inheritance. In short, the combination of dynamic binding and virtual inheritance implies the dominance rule.

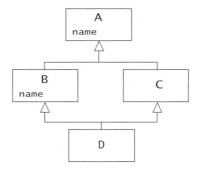

Figure 7–11 The identifier `B::name` dominates `A::name`.

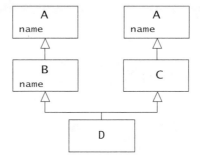

Figure 7–12 No dominance here. The identifier `B::name` hides `A::name` on one path but not on the other.

Let's look at a simple virtual-inheritance hierarchy, as in Figure 7–13. We can represent the storage layout of a D object as containing three base class subobjects, with pointers providing access to the shared V subobject, as shown in Figure 7–14. (Many implementations are possible. This one is a bit dated but is easy to draw and is logically equivalent to other approaches.)

As one might expect, the declaration of the member function D::f, shown in Figure 7–13, overrides both B1::f and V::f:

```
B2 *b2p = new D;
b2p->f();  // calls D::f
```

Let's examine another case, shown in Figure 7–15. This case is simply illegal, because either B1::f and B2::f could be used to override V::f in D. It's ambiguous and results in a compile-time error.

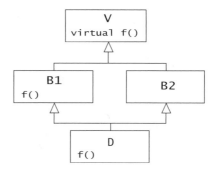

Figure 7–13 | The function D::f overrides both B1::f and V::f. Virtual tables for B1 and V subobjects contain information to call D::f.

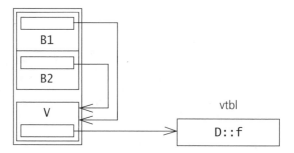

Figure 7–14 | Possible layout of a D complete object, showing the virtual function table for the V subobject.

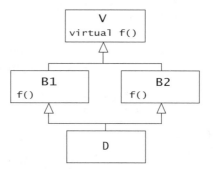

Figure 7–15 | An ambiguity. Either B1::f or B2::f could override V::f in the V subobject's virtual table.

Finally, let's examine a case where dominance comes into play:

```
B2 *b2p = new D;
b2p->f(); // calls B1::f()!
```

As Figure 7–16 shows, the identifier B1::f dominates the identifier V::f on all paths, and the virtual table for the V subobject of a D object will be set to B1::f. Without the dominance rule, this case would also be ambiguous, since the implementation of V::f in a D object could be either V::f or B1::f. Dominance settles the ambiguity in favor of B1::f.

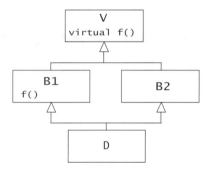

Figure 7–16 | Dominance disambiguates virtual table construction. B1::f dominates V::f, so the V subobject's virtual table contains information to call B1::f.

8 | Class Design

The design of effective abstract data types is as much art as science. The production of good interfaces involves equal parts technical knowledge, social psychology, and experience. Yet nothing is more important than clear, intuitive interfaces in assuring that code will be readily understood and correctly maintained.

In this chapter, we'll examine a number of common mistakes in the design of class interfaces and offer suggestions on how to circumvent them. We'll also examine several implementation issues that affect class interfaces.

Gotcha #80: Get/Set Interfaces

In an abstract data type, all member data should be private. However, a class that's just a collection of private data members with public get/set functions for access is not much of an abstract data type.

Recall that the purpose of data abstraction is to raise the level of discourse above a particular implementation of a type and enable readers and writers of code to communicate directly in the language of the problem domain. To accomplish this, an abstract data type is defined purely as a set of operations, and those operations correspond to our abstract view of what the type is. Consider a stack:

```
template <class T>
class UnusableStack {
 public:
    UnusableStack();
    ~UnusableStack();
    T *getStack();
    void setStack( T * );
    int getTop();
    void setTop( int );
```

```
  private:
    T *s_;
    int top_;
};
```

The only positive thing one can say about this template is that it's properly named. There is no abstraction here, just a thinly disguised collection of data. The public interface doesn't provide an effective abstraction of a stack for the users of the type and doesn't even provide insulation against changes in the stack's implementation. A proper stack implementation provides a clear abstraction as well as implementation independence:

```
template <class T>
class Stack {
  public:
    Stack();
    ~Stack();
    void push( const T & );
    T &top();
    void pop();
    bool empty() const;
  private:
    T *s_;
    int top_;
};
```

Now, in point of fact, no designer would actually produce a stack interface as flawed as that of UnusableStack. Every competent programmer knows what operations are required of a stack, and production of an effective interface is almost automatic. This is not the case for all abstract data types, however, particularly in the case where we're designing in domains where we're not domain experts. In these situations, it's essential to work closely with domain experts to determine not only what abstract data types are required but also what their operations should be. One of the surest ways to identify a project with inadequate domain expertise is by the large percentage of classes with get/set interfaces.

That said, it's often the case that some portion of a class's interface may properly consist of accessor, or get/set, functions. What is the proper form for rendering these functions? We have several common possibilities:

```
class C {
public:
    int getValue1() const            // get/set style 1
        { return value_; }
    void setValue1( int value )
        { value_ = value; }
    int &value2()              // get/set style 2
        { return value_; }
    int setValue3( int value )// get/set style 3
        { return value_ = value; }
    int value4( int value ) { // get/set style 4
        int old = value_;
        value_ = value;
        return old;
    }
private:
    int value_;
};
```

The second style is the tersest and most flexible but also the most dangerous. In returning a handle to the private implementation of the class, the value2 function is hardly an improvement over public data. Users of the class can develop dependencies on the current implementation and access the internals of the class directly. This form is problematic even if only read access is provided. Consider a class implemented with a standard library container:

```
class Users {
public:
    const std::map<std::string,User> &getUserContainer() const
        { return users_; }
    // . . .
private:
    std::map<std::string,User> users_;
};
```

The "get" function has exposed the rather private information that the user container is implemented with a standard map. Any code that calls that public function now can (and most probably will) develop a dependency on that particular implementation of Users. In the likely case that profiling reveals a vector to be a more efficient implementation, all users of the Users class will have to be rewritten. This kind of accessor function should simply not exist.

The third style is a bit unusual, in that it doesn't actually provide access to the current value of the data member but both sets and returns the newly set value. (You're supposed to remember the old value. After all, you set it, right? No?) This allows users of the class to write expressions like a += setValue3(12) rather than the two short statements setValue1(12); a +=getValue1();. The real problem is that many users of the interface will assume that the value returned is the previous value, which can lead to some difficult-to-locate bugs.

Our fourth alternative is attractive in that it provides the ability to both get the current value and to set a new value with a single function. However, just getting the current value requires a little finesse:

```
int current = c.value4( 0 ); // get and set
c.value4( current ); // restore
```

To get the current value, we must provide a "dummy" new value to value4. This bogus new value must then be reset to the previous value. This may seem a little loopy, but the technique does have a distinguished C++ pedigree and is used by the standard library facilities set_new_handler, set_unexpected, and set_terminate to register callback functions for memory management and exception handling. Typically, these functions are used to implement a stack discipline of callback functions without employing a stack specifically:

```
typedef void (*new_handler)(); // the type of a callback
// . . .
new_handler old_handler = set_new_handler( handler ); // push
// do something . . .
set_new_handler( old_handler ); // pop
```

Using this mechanism to access the current handler can be involved. The following usage is a C++ coding idiom for doing so:

```
new_handler handler = set_new_handler( 0 ); // get current
set_new_handler( handler ); // restore
```

However, outside its use in setting standard callbacks, avoid this approach as a general get/set mechanism. It raises the cost and complexity of simple read access to a data member, complicates exception safety and multithreaded code, and may be confused with get/set style number 3, described earlier.

The first get/set style is the preferred one. It's the simplest available mechanism, it's efficient, and, most important, it's unambiguous to all readers of the code:

```
int a = c.getValue1(); // get, of course
c.setValue1( 12 ); // set, of course
```

If your class design must include get/set access, use style number 1.

Gotcha #81: Const and Reference Data Members

One good piece of general advice is "Anything that can be const should be const." A related piece of good advice is "If something is not always used as a const, don't declare it to be const." Taken together, these pieces of advice imply that one should examine the current and expected future uses of a construct and make it "as const as possible, but no more so."

In this item, I'll attempt to convince you that it rarely makes sense to declare const or reference data members in a class. Const and reference data members tend to make classes harder to work with, require unnatural copy semantics, and encourage maintainers to introduce dangerous changes.

Let's look at a simple class with const and reference data members:

```
class C {
  public:
    C();
    // . . .
  private:
    int a_;
    const int b_;
    int &ra_;
};
```

The constructor must initialize const and reference data members:

```
C::C()
    : a_( 12 ), b_( 12 ), ra_( a_ )
    {}
```

So far, so good. We can declare objects of type C and initialize them:

```
C x; // default ctor
C y( x ); // copy ctor
```

Oops! Where did that copy constructor come from? The compiler wrote it for us, and by default, that copy constructor will perform a member-by-member initialization of the members of y with the corresponding members of x (see Gotcha #49). Unfortunately, this default implementation will set the ra_ reference in y to the a_ in x. Since we're on the subject of good, general advice, another such piece of advice is "Consider writing copy operations for any class that contains a handle (generally a pointer or reference) to other data":

```
C::C( const C &that )
    : a_( that.a_ ), b_( that.b_ ), ra_( a_ )
    {}
```

Let's continue to use our C objects:

```
x = y; // error!
```

The problem here is that the compiler is unable to generate an assignment operation for us. By default, it will attempt to generate an assignment operation that simply assigns each data member of y to the corresponding data member of x. For objects of type C, that isn't possible, since the b_ and ra_ members can't be assigned. This is just as well, really, since such an assignment operation would exhibit the same incorrect behavior as that of the default copy constructor.

The problem is, it's not a simple task to write the assignment operator. Consider a first attempt:

```
C &C::operator =( const C &that ) {
    a_ = that.a_; // OK
    b_ = that.b_; // error!
    return *this;
}
```

It's not legal to assign to a constant. The danger here is that a "creative" maintainer of our code will attempt to perform the assignment anyway. Usually, the first recourse is to a cast:

```
int *pb = const_cast<int *>(&b_);
*pb = that.b_;
```

Now, in point of fact, this code will probably not cause any runtime problems, since it's unlikely that the b_ member will be in a read-only segment when it's part of a non-constant C object. However, one can hardly call this a natural implementation, and this trick won't work on a reference member. (Note that in this particular assignment operator, it was not necessary to attempt to rebind the reference data member of C, since it was already referring to the a_ member of its own object.)

Some excessively creative maintainers might take a different tack. Rather than assign y to x, they'll destroy x entirely and reinitialize it with y:

```
C &C::operator =( const C &that ) {
    if( this != &that ) {
        this->~C(); // call dtor
        new (this) C(that); // copy ctor
    }
    return *this;
}
```

A lot of ink has been expended over the years in proposing and, ultimately, rejecting this approach. Even though it may work in this limited case—for a time—it's complex, doesn't scale, and is likely to cause problems in the future. Consider what would happen if C ultimately became a base class. It's likely that a derived class assignment operator would call C's assignment operator. The destructor call, if virtual, will destroy the entire object, not just the C part. The destructor call, if nonvirtual, will have undefined behavior. Avoid this approach.

The easiest and most straightforward approach is to simply avoid const and reference data members. Since all our data members are private (they *are* private, aren't they?), we already have adequate protection from accidental modification. If, on the other hand, the intent of using const or reference data members is to keep the compiler from generating a default assignment operator, a more idiomatic way will achieve that (see Gotcha #49):

```
class C {
    // . . .
  private:
    int a_;
    int b_;
    int *pa_;
    C( const C & ); // disallow copy construction
    C &operator =( const C & ); // disallow assignment
};
```

Const or reference data members are rarely needed. Avoid them.

Gotcha #82: Not Understanding the Meaning of Const Member Functions

Syntax

One of the first things one notices about const member functions is the rather unnerving syntax used to specify them. That const stuck onto the end of the declaration just looks like a hack. It isn't. Like the rest of the declaration syntax C++ inherits from C, the syntax for declaring a const member function is both logically consistent and confusing:

```
class BoundedString {
  public:
    explicit BoundedString( int len );
    // . . .
    size_t length() const;
    void set( char c );
    void wipe() const;
  private:
    char * const buf_;
    int len_;
    size_t maxLen_;
};
```

Let's look first at the declaration of the private data member buf_, which is declared to be a constant pointer to character (this is an illustrative example; see Gotcha #81). The pointer is constant, not the characters it points to, so the const type-qualifier follows the pointer modifier. If we had put const before the asterisk, it would refer to the char base type, and we'd have declared a non-const pointer to constant characters.

The same is true of the const member function length. If we had put the const before the name of the function, we would have declared a member function that takes no argument and returns a constant size_t. The appearance of const after the function modifier indicates that the function is const, not its return value.

Simple Semantics and Mechanics

What does it mean for a member function to be const? The usual answer to this question is simply that a const member function doesn't change its object. That's a simple statement, and it's simple for the compiler to implement.

Every non-static member function has an implicit argument that is a pointer to the object used to call the member function. Within the function, the `this` keyword gives the value of the pointer:

```
BoundedString bs( 12 );
cout << bs.length(); // "this" is &bs
BoundedString *bsp = &bs;
cout << bsp->length(); // "this" is bsp
```

For a non-const member function of a class X, the type of the `this` pointer is X `*` `const`; that is, it's a constant pointer to a non-constant X. The pointer itself may not be modified (and therefore `this` will always refer to the same X object), but the members of X may be modified. Within a non-const member function, any access to a non-static class member is accomplished through a pointer to non-const:

```
void BoundedString::set( char c ) {
    for( int i = 0; i < maxLen_; ++i )
        buf_[i] = c;
    buf_[maxLen_] = '\0';
}
```

For a const member function of a class X, the type of the `this` pointer is `const` X `*` `const`; it's a constant pointer to a constant X. Neither the pointer nor the object it points to can be changed:

```
size_t BoundedString::length() const
    { return strlen( buf_ ); }
```

Essentially, a const member function gives us a way to specify the constness of the implicit `this` argument of a member function. For example, consider the declaration of a non-member equality operator for `BoundedString`:

```
bool operator ==( const BoundedString &lhs,
                   const BoundedString &rhs );
```

The function doesn't change its arguments—it only examines them—and therefore both the left and right arguments are declared to be reference to const. The same should be the case for an analogous member function:

```
class BoundedString {
    // . . .
    bool operator <( const BoundedString &rhs );
    bool operator >=( const BoundedString &rhs ) const;
};
```

Remember that the left argument of an overloaded binary member operator function is passed implicitly to the function as the `this` pointer. The right argument is used to initialize the explicitly declared formal argument (named `rhs` in the two member operator functions above). The greater-than-or-equal-to operator is properly declared, and the function makes guarantees not to change either the left or right arguments. However, the less-than operator is improper, in that it guarantees the safety of the right argument without making any such promise for the left argument. This impropriety will probably show up when we try to implement >= in the most straightforward way:

```
bool BoundedString::operator >=( const BoundedString &rhs ) const
    { return !(*this < rhs); }
```

We'll get a compile-time error in the call to `operator` <. When we pass the expression `*this` as the first argument to `operator` <, we're attempting to initialize the `this` pointer of a non-const member function with the address of a constant object.

The Meaning of a Const Member Function

We've described the mechanics of const member functions above, but the meaning of const member functions is, to a large extent, socially determined by the community of competent C++ programmers. Consider an implementation of the `wipe` member of `BoundedString`:

```
void BoundedString::wipe() const
    { buf_[0] = '\0'; }
```

This is legal, but just because something is legal doesn't mean it's either morally permissible or expected. The `wipe` function doesn't change its object; that is, it doesn't modify any of BoundedString's data members. However, it does change data outside the object that affects the behavior of the object. The logical state of the BoundedString object will have changed after a call to wipe. The constness of the this pointer affects access only to the data members within the Bounded-String object itself. Data outside the object are not included in this protection, but the data are nevertheless part of the logical state of the BoundedString object.

Most users of BoundedString would be unpleasantly surprised to find that the behavior of their object had been modified by a call to a const member function. Because wipe changes the logical state of its object, it should not be declared to be const. That's why our earlier definition of the set member was declared to be non-const, even though the compiler would have permitted it to be declared const.

Conversely, let's look at the implementation of the length member function. This is a function that clearly should be const, since determining the length of a BoundedString doesn't change its logical state. The most straightforward implementation would employ the standard library function strlen, as we did above. This is probably the best implementation, since it's simple, reasonably fast, and gives the correct result. However, suppose we observe that many strings never have their lengths taken, many others have their lengths taken repeatedly, and that strings tend to be long. In that case, a different implementation might be preferable:

```
size_t BoundedString::length() const {
    if( len_ < 0 )
        len_ = strlen( buf_ );
    return len_;
}
```

In this case, we've decided to store the current string length within the Bounded-String object and to perform a "lazy evaluation" of the string length. Therefore there is little runtime cost in the event that the string length is never taken and minimal for repeated calls to length. Unfortunately, the compiler will issue an error when we attempt to assign a value to len_. This is a const member function and is not allowed to change its object.

We could deal with this problem by making length non-const, but this defeats the logical intent of the function and wouldn't allow us to determine the length of a BoundedString declared to be const (whether it's actually const or not; see Gotchas #6 and #31). We'd be making length non-const due to an implementation issue, but, to the extent practical, implementation issues shouldn't affect the interface of an abstract data type.

A common and reprehensible practice in a situation like this is to "cast away const" in the const member function:

```
size_t BoundedString::length() const {
    if( len_ < 0 )
        const_cast<int &>(len_) = strlen( buf_ );
    return len_;
}
// . . .
BoundedString a(12);
int alen = a.length(); // will work . . .
const BoundedString b(12);
int blen = b.length(); // undefined!
```

Any attempt to modify a constant object outside its constructors or destructor results in undefined behavior. Therefore, calling the `length` member function on b may work—or may fail mysteriously long after the code has been tested and delivered. That the cast is a newfangled `const_cast` doesn't help in the least.

The proper solution is to declare the `len_` data member to be `mutable`. The `mutable` storage-class-specifier may be applied to a non-static, non-const, non-reference data member to indicate that it may be safely modified by const (as well as non-const) member functions.

```
class BoundedString {
  // . . .
 private:
   char * const buf_;
   mutable int len_;
   size_t maxLen_;
};
```

For the community of C++ programmers, a const member function implements "logical" constness. That is, the observable state of an object is not changed by a call to a const member function, even though its physical state may be.

Gotcha #83: Failure to Distinguish Aggregation and Acquaintance

It isn't possible to distinguish ownership (aggregation) and uses (acquaintance) relationships in the C++ language itself. This can result in a variety of bugs, including memory leaks and aliasing:

```
class Employee {
 public:
    virtual ~Employee();
    void setRole( Role *newRole );
    const Role *getRole() const;
    // . . .
 private:
    Role *role_;
    // . . .
};
```

It's not clear from the above interface whether an Employee object owns its Role or simply refers to a Role that may be shared by other Employee objects. The problems occur when a user of the Employee class makes an assumption about ownership that differs from what the designer of the Employee class implemented:

```
Employee *e1 = getMeAnEmployee();
Employee *e2 = getMeAnEmployee();
Role *r = getMeSomethingToDo();
e1->setRole( r );
e2->setRole( r ); // bug #1!
delete r; // bug #2!
```

In the case where the designer of the Employee class has decided that the Employee owns its Role, the line marked bug #1 will result in two Employee objects aliasing the same Role object. At a minimum, a double deletion of the Role object will occur when e2 and e1 are deleted and their destructors each delete the unintentionally shared Role object.

The line marked bug #2 is more problematic. Here, the user of the Employee class is assuming that setRole makes a copy of its Role argument and the allocated Role object must be cleaned up. If this is not the case, both e1 and e2 will contain dangling pointers.

An experienced developer might look at the implementation of the setRole function for a clue and be confronted with one of the following implementations:

```
void Employee::setRole( Role *newRole ) // version #1
    { role_ = newRole; }


void Employee::setRole( Role *newRole ) { // version #2
    delete role_;
    role_ = newRole;
}


void Employee::setRole( Role *newRole ) { // version #3
    delete role_;
    role_ = newRole->clone();
}
```

Version #1 of the setRole function indicates that the Employee object doesn't own its Role object, since no attempt is made to clean up the existing Role object before setting a pointer to the new one. (We're making the assumption that this is a reflection of the intent of the designer of the Employee class and not a simple bug.)

Version #2 indicates that the Employee owns its Role object and is taking over ownership of the Role referred to by the argument. Version #3 also indicates that the Employee object owns its Role. However, it makes a copy of its Role argument rather than simply taking control of it. Note that it would be better, in the case of version #3, to declare the argument to be const Role * rather than Role *. Cloning is invariably a const operation, since it doesn't modify its object but simply makes a copy of it. It would also be unusual for a shared Role object, such as version #1 implies, to be passed as a pointer to non-const.

However, users of an abstract data type don't generally have access to its implementation, since such access would tend to defeat data hiding and promote dependency on a particular implementation. For example, the fact that version #1 of setRole above doesn't delete the existing Role does not necessarily indicate that the designer of the Employee class intended to share the Role object; it might simply have been a bug. However, after a significant amount of client code has made the assumption that Roles are shared, it's no longer a bug. It's a feature.

Since it's not possible to specify ownership issues directly in C++ language, we have to resort to naming conventions, formal argument types, and (yes, in this case) comments:

```
class Employee {
 public:
    virtual ~Employee();
    void adoptRole( Role *newRole ); // take ownership
    void shareRole( const Role *sharedRole ); // does not own
    void copyRole( const Role *roleToCopy ); // set role to clone
    const Role *getRole() const;
    // . . .
};
```

The names `adoptRole`, `shareRole`, and `copyRole` are unusual enough to encourage users of the `Employee` class to read the comments. If the comments are short and clear, they may even be maintained. (See Gotcha #1.)

One common source of ownership miscommunication occurs with containers of pointers. Consider a list of pointers type:

➤➤ gotcha83/ptrlist.h

```
template <class T> class PtrList;
template <> class PtrList<void> {
    // . . .
};
template <class T>
class PtrList : private PtrList<void> {
 public:
    PtrList();
    ~PtrList();
    void append( T *newElem );
    // . . .
};
```

The problem is, once again, the likelihood of miscommunication between the designer and users of the container:

```
PtrList<Employee> staff;
staff.append( new Techie );
```

In the code above, the user of `PtrList` is probably assuming that the container is taking ownership of the object referred to by the argument to append—that is, that the `PtrList` destructor is going to delete all the objects its pointer elements refer to. If the container doesn't perform such a cleanup, there will be a memory leak. The author of the code below makes a different assumption:

```
PtrList<Employee> management;
Manager theBoss;
management.append( &theBoss );
```

In this case, the user of the `PtrList` container is assuming that the container will not attempt to delete the objects to which its elements refer. If this isn't the case, the `PtrList` will attempt to delete unallocated storage.

The best way to avoid miscommunication of ownership in containers is to use standard containers. Because these containers are part of the C++ standard, all experienced C++ programmers have shared understanding of their behavior. For pointer elements, the standard containers will clean up the pointers but not the objects to which they refer:

```
std::list<Employee *> management;
Manager theBoss;
management.push_back( &theBoss ); // correct
```

In the case where we'd like the container to clean up the objects to which its elements refer, we have a couple of choices. The most straightforward approach is to perform the cleanup manually:

```
template <class Container>
void releaseElems( Container &c ) {
   typedef typename Container::iterator I;
   for( I i = c.begin(); i != c.end(); ++i )
      delete *i;
}
// . . .
std::list<Employee *> staff;
staff.push_back( new Techie );
// . . .
releaseElems( staff ); // clean up
```

Unfortunately, manual cleanup code is easily forgotten, often removed or misplaced during maintenance, and generally fragile in the presence of exceptions. Often, a better choice is to use a smart pointer element in place of a raw pointer.

(Note that the standard `auto_ptr` template should not be used as a container element, due to the inappropriate semantics of its copy operations. See Gotcha #68.) A simple example of such a pointer might look like this:

➤➤ gotcha83/cptr.h

```cpp
template <class T>
class Cptr {
 public:
    Cptr( T *p ) : p_( p ), c_( new long( 1 ) ) {}
    ~Cptr() { if( !--*c_ ) { delete c_; delete p_; } }
    Cptr( const Cptr &init )
        : p_( init.p_ ), c_( init.c_ ) { ++*c_; }
    Cptr &operator =( const Cptr &rhs ) {
        if( this != &rhs ) {
            if( !--*c_ ) { delete c_; delete p_; }
            p_ = rhs.p_;
            ++*(c_ = rhs.c_);
        }
        return *this;
    }
    T &operator *() const
        { return *p_; }
    T *operator ->() const
        { return p_; }
 private:
    T *p_;
    long *c_;
};
```

The container is instantiated to contain smart pointers rather than raw pointers (see Gotcha #24). When the container deletes its elements, the smart pointer semantics clean up the objects to which they refer:

```cpp
std::vector< Cptr<Employee> > staff;
staff.push_back( new Techie );
staff.push_back( new Temp );
staff.push_back( new Consultant );
// no explicit cleanup necessary . . .
```

The utility of this smart pointer extends to more complex cases as well:

```
std::list< Cptr<Employee> > expendable;
expendable.push_back( staff[2] );
expendable.push_back( new Temp );
expendable.push_back( staff[1] );
```

When the `expendable` container goes out of scope, it will correctly delete its second, `Temp` element and decrement the reference counts of its first and third elements, which it shares with the `staff` container. When `staff` goes out of scope, it will delete all three of its elements.

Gotcha #84: Improper Operator Overloading

It's possible to get by without operator overloading:

```
class Complex {
 public:
    Complex( double real = 0.0, double imag = 0.0 );
    friend Complex add( const Complex &, const Complex & );
    friend Complex div( const Complex &, const Complex & );
    friend Complex mul( const Complex &, const Complex & );
    // . . .
};
// . . .
Z = add( add( R, mul( mul( j, omega ), L ) ),
    div( 1, mul( j, omega ), C ) ) );
```

Operator overloading is often just "syntactic sugar," but it makes reading and writing code more palatable and eases the communication of a design's meaning:

```
class Complex {
 public:
    Complex( double real = 0.0, double imag = 0.0 );
    friend Complex operator +( const Complex &, const Complex & );
    friend Complex operator *( const Complex &, const Complex & );
    friend Complex operator /( const Complex &, const Complex & );
    // . . .
};
```

```
// . . .
Z = R + j*omega*L + 1/(j*omega*C);
```

The version of the formula for AC impedance using infix operators is correct, but the earlier version that employed function call syntax is not. However, the error is harder to see and correct without the use of operator overloading.

Operator overloading is also justified when extending an existing syntactic framework, like the iostream and standard template libraries:

```
ostream &operator <<( ostream &os, const Complex &c )
    { return os << '(' << c.r_ << ", " << c.i_ << ')'; }
```

These successful uses often encourage novice designers to overuse operator overloading:

```
template <typename T>
class Stack {
 public:
    Stack();
    ~Stack();
    void operator +( const T & ); // push
    T &operator *(); // top
    void operator -(); // pop
    operator bool() const; // not empty?
    // . . .
};
// . . .
Stack<int> s;
s + 12;
s + 13;
if( s ) {
    int a = *s;
    -s;
    // . . .
```

Clever? No, it's puerile nonsense. Operator overloading exists largely to make code radically and universally clearer to its readers, not so the designer can show off. Use of an overloaded operator should appeal to readers' existing prejudices, so any reasonable assumption an experienced reader makes about an operator's meaning will be correct. A proper implementation of a stack would employ the universally recognized, non-operator names for the stack's operations:

```
template <typename T>
class Stack {
 public:
    Stack();
    ~Stack();
    void push( const T & );
    T &top();
    void pop();
    bool isEmpty() const;
    // . . .
};
// . . .
Stack<int> s;
s.push( 12 );
s.push( 13 );
if( !s.isEmpty() ) {
    int a = s.top();
    s.pop();
    // . . .
```

Note that the meaning of an overloaded operator must be universally understood to be valid. Even if the meaning of an overloaded operator is obvious to you and 75% of your colleagues, a 25% rate of misunderstanding and misapplication is unacceptable, and overloading the operator will cause more problems than it solves.

A personal example brought this home to me. I was designing a simple array template:

>> gotcha05/array.h

```
template <class T, int n>
class Array {
 public:
    Array();
    explicit Array( const T &val );
    Array &operator =( const T &val ); // universally obvious?
    // . . .
```

```
  private:
    T a_[n];
  };
  // . . .
  Array<float,100> ary( 0 );
  ary = 123; // obvious?
```

I was absolutely convinced that the effect of the assignment was obvious. Clearly, it means that I want to assign the value 123 to every element of the array. Right? Not according to significant percentages of users of the `Array` template. Some experienced programmers thought it meant to resize the array to have 123 elements. Some thought it meant to assign 123 to the first element. I knew I was right and that everyone who thought differently was wrong, but practicality forced me to back off and use an unambiguous non-operator function for that operation:

```
  ary.setAll( 123 ); // boring, but clear
```

Unless overloading an operator is clearly better than the alternative of a non-operator function, don't overload the operator.

Gotcha #85: Precedence and Overloading

The precedence of an operator is part of the user's set of expectations about the operator's behavior, and if these expectations are not met, the operator will be misused. Consider a nonstandard complex number implementation:

```
  class Complex {
   public:
    Complex( double = 0, double = 0 );
    friend Complex operator +( const Complex &, const Complex & );
    friend Complex operator *( const Complex &, const Complex & );
    friend Complex operator ^( const Complex &, const Complex & );
    // . . .
  };
```

We'd like to have an exponentiation operator for complex numbers, but C++ doesn't have an exponentiation operator. Since we can't introduce any new operators, we decide to press an existing operator into service that has no pre-defined meaning for complex numbers: exclusive-or.

In fact, we already have a problem, since an experienced C or C++ programmer will (properly) read an expression like a^b as a exclusive-ored with b rather than as a raised to the b power. However, there's also a more insidious problem:

```
a = -1 + e ^ (i*pi);
```

In mathematical notation and in most programming languages that support exponentiation, the exponentiation operator has very high precedence. It's likely that the author of this code is expecting the expression to be parsed with the exponentiation binding more tightly than the addition:

```
a = -1 + (e ^ (i*pi));
```

In actuality, the compiler knows nothing about anyone's expectation of precedence of exponentiation. It sees an exclusive-or and parses the expression appropriately:

```
a = (-1 + e) ^ (i*pi);
```

In this case, it's better to abandon operator overloading for the clearer use of a simple non-operator function:

```
a = -1 + pow( e, (i*pi) );
```

The precedence of an operator is part of its interface. Make sure an overloaded operator has a precedence that satisfies its users' expectations.

Gotcha #86: Friend versus Member Operators

An overloaded operator should allow application of any conversions its argument types support:

```
class Complex {
  public:
    Complex( double re = 0.0, double im = 0.0 );
    // . . .
};
```

For example, the Complex constructor permits a conversion from the predefined numeric types to a Complex. The non-member add function allows this conversion to be performed implicitly on either of its arguments:

```
Complex add( const Complex &, const Complex & );
Complex c1, c2;
double d;

add(c1,c2);
add(c1,d); // add( c1, Complex(d,0.0) )
add(d,c1); // add( Complex(d,0.0), c1 )
```

The non-member operator + function below permits the same implicit conversions:

```
Complex operator +( const Complex &, const Complex & );
c1 + c2;
operator +(c1,c2); // same as above
c1 + d;
operator +(c1,d); // same as above
d + c1;
operator +(d,c1); // same as above
```

However, if we implement the binary addition of Complex with a member function, we introduce an asymmetry with respect to implicit conversion:

```
class Complex {
 public:
   // member operators
   Complex operator +( const Complex & ) const; // binary
   Complex operator -( const Complex & ) const; // binary
   Complex operator -() const; // unary
   // . . .
};
// . . .
c1 + c2; // fine.
c1.operator +(c2); // fine.
c1 + d; // fine.
c1.operator +(d); // fine.
d + c1; // error!
d.operator +(c1); // error!
```

The compiler cannot apply an implicit, user-defined conversion to the first argument of a member function. If such a conversion is part of the desired interface, this implies that a member implementation of the binary operator is inappropriate. Non-member friends allow conversions on their first argument. Members allow only is-a conversion. (See also Gotcha #42.)

Gotcha #87: Problems with Increment and Decrement

Even the best C programmers tend to use prefix and postfix increment and decrement interchangeably when either will do:

```
int j;
for( j = 0; j < max; j++ ) /* OK, in C. */
```

However, this is now considered démodé in C++, and prefix increment and decrement are always to be preferred over the postfix versions of the operators when either will do. The reason has to do with operator overloading.

Increment and decrement operators are often overloaded to support operations on iterators or smart pointers. These may be member or non-member operators but are commonly implemented as members for class types:

```
class Iter {
 public:
    Iter &operator ++(); // prefix
    Iter operator ++(int); // postfix
    Iter &operator --(); // prefix
    Iter operator --(int); // postfix
    // . . .
};
```

The prefix forms should return a modifiable lvalue, to mimic the behavior of the predefined operators. Effectively, this is a requirement that the operator return a reference to its object:

```
Iter &Iter::operator ++() {
    // increment *this . . .
    return *this;
}
```

```
// . . .
int j = 0;
++++j; // OK, but j+=2 might be better
Iter i;
++++++++i; // OK, but odd
```

The postfix forms are distinguished from the prefix forms by the addition of an unused integer argument. The compiler simply passes a zero actual argument to distinguish postfix from prefix:

```
Iter i;
++i; // same as i.operator ++();
i++; // same as i.operator ++(0);
i.operator ++(1024); // legal, but strange
```

Typically, the implementations of the postfix operators ignore the integer argument. To mimic the behavior of the predefined postfix increment and decrement operators, an overloaded version must return a copy of its object containing the object's value before the increment operation. The postfix operator is commonly implemented in terms of the corresponding prefix operator:

```
Iter Iter::operator ++(int) {
    Iter temp( *this );
    ++*this;
    return temp;
}
```

Effectively, this is a requirement that the postfix operator return by value. Even with the possible application of common program transformations like the named return value optimization (see Gotcha #58), use of a postfix increment or decrement operator is likely to be slower than that of the corresponding prefix version if the argument is of class type. Consider a common use within the standard template library:

```
vector<T> v;
// . . .
vector<T>::iterator end( v.end() );
for( vector<T>::iterator vi( v.begin() ); vi != end;
    vi++ ) { // gauche!
    // . . .
```

The implementation of the `vector`'s iterator could be a simple pointer, in which case the runtime effect of postfix increment is nonexistent, or the iterator could be of class type, in which case the effect could be significant. For this reason, it's considered better form in C++ to always prefer prefix forms to postfix forms. Many implementations of generic algorithms take this advice even further (perhaps too far), and avoid the use of postfix increment and decrement at any cost:

```
template <typename In, typename Out>
Out myCopy( In b, In e, Out r ) {
    while( b != e ) {
        // rather than *r++ = *b++
        *r = *b;
        ++r;
        ++b;
    }
    return r;
}
```

Note that the predefined postfix increment and decrement operators return an rvalue; that is, the result of the operation has no address and can't be used with operators that require an lvalue (see Gotcha #6):

```
int a = 12;
++a = 10; // OK
++++a; // OK
a++ = 10; // error!
a++++; // error!
```

Unfortunately, our earlier implementation of postfix ++ returns an anonymous temporary class object generated by the compiler. According to the standard it's not an lvalue, but we can still call the member functions of such an object, which means it can be incremented and assigned. But the incremented and assigned temporary is destroyed at the end of the expression!

```
Iter i;
Iter j;
++i = j; // OK
i++ = j; // legal, but should be an error!
```

The value of i is unaffected by the assignment from j, since the assignment is to an anonymous temporary that (presumably) contains the value of i before it was post-incremented. A safer implementation of a user-defined postfix increment or decrement would return a constant:

```
class Iter {
 public:
   Iter &operator ++(); // prefix
   const Iter operator ++(int); // postfix
   Iter &operator --(); // prefix
   const Iter operator --(int); // postfix
   // . . .
};
// . . .
i++ = j; // error!
i++++; // error!
```

This will prevent most accidental misuses of the return value of postfix increment and decrement but will not protect against willful abuse. The return value is not modifiable, but it still has an address:

```
const Iter *ip = &i++;
```

This clever programmer has managed to take the address not of i but of a compiler-generated temporary that's destroyed immediately after the pointer is initialized. This is an act of programming fraud with malice aforethought and will be punished appropriately (see Gotcha #11).

We mentioned above that most user-defined increment and decrement operators are implemented as member functions. This is not the case, of course, for increment and decrement for enum types, since they can have no member functions:

```
enum Sin { pride, covetousness, lust, anger,
           gluttony, envy, sloth, future_use, num_sins };

inline Sin &operator ++( Sin &s )
   { return s = static_cast<Sin>(s+1); }

inline const Sin operator ++( Sin &s, int ) {
   Sin ret( s );
   s = ++s;
   return ret;
}
```

Note the absence of range checking in these functions. A programmer who has chosen to represent a concept as an enum rather than as a more sophisticated class type is probably doing so for reasons of efficiency. Any attempt to perform range checking on such a type is likely to defeat the original intent of using the type. It will also probably result in a lot of unnecessary double-checking of end conditions:

```
for( Sin s = pride; s != num_sins; ++s ) // . . .
```

Gotcha #88: Misunderstanding Templated Copy Operations

A common use of template member functions is to implement constructors. For example, many standard containers have a template constructor that allows initialization of the container by a sequence:

```
template <typename T>
class Cont {
 public:
    template <typename In>
        Cont( In b, In e );
    // . . .
};
```

Use of the template constructor allows the container to be initialized by an input sequence derived from any source and renders the container much more useful than it would be otherwise. The standard `auto_ptr` template uses template member functions as well:

```
template <class X>
class auto_ptr {
 public:
    auto_ptr( auto_ptr & ); // copy ctor
    template <class Y>
        auto_ptr( auto_ptr<Y> & );
    auto_ptr &operator =( auto_ptr & ); // copy assignment
    template <class Y>
        auto_ptr &operator =( auto_ptr<Y> & );
    // . . .
};
```

Notice, however, that `auto_ptr`, in addition to its template constructor and assignment operator, has explicitly declared its copy operations. This is necessary for correct behavior, since template member functions are never instantiated for use as copy operations. As always, in the absence of an explicitly declared copy constructor or copy assignment operator, the compiler will still generate one as necessary. This often-overlooked exception to template instantiation is an occasional source of problems:

➤➤ gotcha88/money.h

```cpp
enum Currency { CAD, DM, USD, Yen };


template <Currency currency>
class Money {
 public:
   Money( double amt );
   template <Currency otherCurrency>
       Money( const Money<otherCurrency> & );
   template <Currency otherCurrency>
       Money &operator =( const Money<otherCurrency> & );
   ~Money();
   double get_amount() const
       { return amt_; }
   // . . .
 private:
   Curve *myCurve_;
   double amt_;
};
// . . .
Money<Yen> acct1( 1000000.00 );
Money<DM> acct2( 123.45 );
Money<Yen> acct3( acct2 ); // template ctor
Money<Yen> acct4( acct1 ); // compiler-generated copy ctor!
acct3 = acct2; // template assignment
acct4 = acct1; // compiler-generated assignment!
```

This is simply a new version of a very old problem in C++ class design. Whenever a class contains a pointer or other resource handle that doesn't manage itself, it's important to control the class's copy operations carefully, so as to avoid leaking or aliasing the resource. Consider a fragment of the implementation of the template assignment above:

➤➤ gotcha88/money.h

```
template <Currency currency>
template <Currency otherCurrency>
Money<currency> &
Money<currency>::operator =( const Money<otherCurrency> &rhs ) {
    amt_ = myCurve_->
        convert( currency, otherCurrency, rhs.get_amount() );
}
```

Clearly, it's important to the implementation of Money that the Curve referred to by myCurve_ not be modified or shared during assignment. However, this is exactly what the compiler-generated copy operations will do, and will do silently:

```
template <Currency currency>
Money<currency> &
Money<currency>::operator =( const Money<currency> &that ) {
    myCurve_ = that.myCurve_; // leak, alias, and change of curve!
    amt_ = rhs.amt_;
}
```

The Money template should implement its copy operations explicitly.

Copy operations are never implemented by template member functions. Always consider copy operations in the design of any class (see Gotcha #49).

9 | Hierarchy Design

Hierarchy design is hard. Class hierarchies must be flexible enough to allow reasonable extension but concrete enough to actually state a design. They must be as simple as possible while still representing an effective abstraction of the problem domain. Unlike the design of most other program components, class hierarchies will be extended and modified long after their initial developers have designed, compiled, and distributed them. The designer of a class hierarchy must, therefore, also determine the extent and kind of customization its users should be permitted and design accordingly.

Hierarchy design comes down to balancing the various forces on a design to achieve an optimal solution, but, like an analogous problem in linear programming, a particular design situation may have many optimal solutions. Effective hierarchy design is often more a matter of experience and clairvoyance than the application of specific rules; as a result, the advice parceled out in this chapter is perhaps a bit softer and more opinionated than that of previous chapters.

However, there are some common pitfalls in hierarchy design. Some result from importing design practices from other languages into C++, where they don't apply. Others are the commonly observed results of inexperience. Still others are simply new, bad ideas that somehow caught on. We'll dispose of them here.

Gotcha #89: Arrays of Class Objects

Be wary of arrays of class types, especially of base class types. Consider an "applicator" function that applies a function to each element of an array:

➤➤ gotcha89/apply.cpp

```
void apply( B array[], int length, void (*f)( B & ) ) {
    for( int i = 0; i < length; ++i )
        f( array[i] );
}
```

```
// . . .
D *dp = new D[3];
apply( dp, 3, somefunc ); // disaster!
```

The trouble is that the type of the first formal argument to `apply` is "pointer to B," not "array of B." As far as the compiler is concerned, we're initializing a B `*` with a D `*`. This is legal if B is a public base class of D, since a D is-a B. However, an array of D is not an array of B, and the code will fail badly when we attempt pointer arithmetic using B offsets on an array of D objects.

Figure 9–1 illustrates the situation. The `apply` function expects the `array` pointer to refer to an array of B (on the left of the diagram), but it actually refers to an array of D (on the right). Recall that indexing is really just shorthand for pointer arithmetic (see Gotcha #7), so the expression `array[i]` is equivalent to `*(array+i)`. Unfortunately, the compiler will perform the pointer addition with the assumption that `array` refers to a base class object. If a derived class object is larger than or has a different layout from a base class object, the index operation will result in an incorrect address.

Incremental attempts to make the array behave sensibly fail. If the base class B were declared to be abstract (a good idea in general), that would prevent any arrays of B from being created, but the `apply` function would still be legal (if incorrect), since it deals with pointers to B rather than B objects. Declaring the formal argument to be a reference to an array (as in B (&array)[3]) is effective but not practical, as we must then fix the size of the array to a given bound (in this case, 3) and cannot pass a pointer (to an allocated array, for instance) as an actual argument.

Arrays of base class objects are just plain inadvisable, and arrays of class objects in general have to be watched closely.

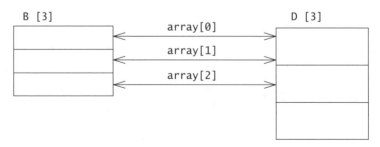

Figure 9–1 | Pointer arithmetic used to access the elements of an array of base class objects usually doesn't work for an array of derived objects.

Using a generic algorithm in place of a function hard-coded to a specific type can be an improvement:

```
for_each( dp, dp+3, somefunc );
```

The use of the standard `for_each` algorithm allows the compiler to perform argument type deduction on the arguments to the function template. The implicit conversion from derived class to public base is not a problem, because no such conversion is performed. The compiler will instantiate a version of `for_each` for the derived class D. Unfortunately, this is a different solution from our original design, in that we've swapped a runtime polymorphic approach for a compile-time one.

A better approach is to use an array of pointers to class objects rather than using an array of objects. This allows polymorphic use of the array without the associated pointer arithmetic issues:

```
void apply_prime( B *array[], int length, void (*f)( B * ) ) {
    for( int i = 0; i < length; ++i )
        f( array[i] );
}
```

Often, an even better approach is to dispense with arrays entirely and employ instead one of the standard containers, generally a `vector`. The use of a strongly typed container avoids the possibility of pointer arithmetic problems for containers of class objects, and a container of pointers to a base class allows polymorphic use:

```
vector<B> vb; // no Ds allowed!
vector<B *> vbp; // polymorphic
```

Gotcha #90: Improper Container Substitutability

The STL containers are the default containers of choice for C++ programmers. However, STL containers don't answer all needs, in part because their strengths also imply some limitations. One of the nice things about the STL containers is that, because they're implemented with templates, most of the decisions about their structure and behavior are made at compile time. This results in small and efficient implementations precisely tuned to the static context of their use.

However, all relevant information may not be present at compile time. For example, consider a simplified framework-oriented structure that supports the "open-closed principle," in that it may be modified and extended without recompilation of the framework. This simple framework contains a hierarchy of containers and a parallel hierarchy of iterators:

➤➤ gotcha90/container.h

```
template <typename T>
class Container {
 public:
   virtual ~Container();
   virtual Iter<T> *genIter() const = 0; // Factory Method
   virtual void insert( const T & ) = 0;
   // . . .
};
template <typename T>
class Iter {
 public:
   virtual ~Iter();
   virtual void reset() = 0;
   virtual void next() = 0;
   virtual bool done() const = 0;
   virtual T &get() const = 0;
};
```

We can write code in terms of these abstract base classes, compile it, and later augment it by adding new derived container and iterator classes:

➤➤ gotcha90/main.cpp

```
template <typename T>
void print( Container<T> &c ) {
   auto_ptr< Iter<T> > i( c.genIter() );
   for( i->reset(); !i->done(); i->next() )
       cout << i->get() << endl;
}
```

The use of parallel hierarchies in a design is, in general, problematic, because a change to one hierarchy requires coordinated change in the other. We would prefer to be able to have a single point of change. However, use of the Factory Method pattern in the implementation of Container helps mitigate this problem in our Container/Iter parallel hierarchy.

A Factory Method provides a mechanism for the user of an abstract base class interface to generate an object appropriate to the actual type of the derived object while remaining ignorant of the object's type. In the case of the `Container` abstract base class, a user of `Container`'s `genIter` Factory Method is saying, "Generate an `Iter` of the appropriate type to yourself, but spare me the details." Often, use of a Factory Method is an alternative to the ill-advised use of type-based conditional code (see Gotcha #96). In other words, we never want to write code that says, essentially, "`Container`, if you're actually an `Array`, give me an `ArrayIter`. Otherwise, if you're a `Set`, give me a `SetIter`. Otherwise ..."

It's fairly easy to design substitutable derived `Container` types. A `Set<T>` would then be substitutable for a `Container<T>`, and the usual conversions from `Set<T> *` to `Container<T> *` would hold. The presence of the pure virtual `genIter` Factory Method in the `Container` base class is an explicit reminder for the designer of a concrete container type to perform the corresponding maintenance on the `Iter` hierarchy:

```
template <typename T>
SetIter<T> *Set<T>::genIter() const
    { return new SetIter<T>( *this ); } // better write SetIter!
```

However, there is an unfortunate and common tendency to assume that substitutability of container elements implies substitutability of the containers of these elements. We know that this relationship doesn't hold for arrays, C++'s predefined container. An array of derived class objects may not be reliably substituted for an array of base class objects (see Gotcha #89). The same warning applies to user-defined containers of substitutable elements. Consider the following simple container hierarchy in support of a financial-instrument-pricing framework:

➤➤ gotcha90/bondlist.h

```
class Object
    { public: virtual ~Object(); };
class Instrument : public Object
    { public: virtual double pv() const = 0; };
class Bond : public Instrument
    { public: double pv() const; };
class ObjectList {
 public:
    void insert( Object * );
    Object *get();
    // . . .
};
```

```
class BondList : public ObjectList { // bad idea!!!
 public:
   void insert( Bond *b )
       { ObjectList::insert( b ); }
   Bond *get()
       { return static_cast<Bond *>(ObjectList::get()); }
   // . . .
};
```

➤➤ gotcha90/bondlist.cpp

```
double bondPortfolioPV( BondList &bonds ) {
       double sumpv = 0.0;
       for( each bond in list ) {
               Bond *b = current bond;
               sumpv += b->pv();
       }
       return sumpv;
}
```

Now, nothing is wrong with implementing a list of Bond pointers with a list of Object pointers (although a better design would have employed a list of void * and drop-kicked the entire notion of an Object class into the bit bucket; see Gotcha #97). The error is in using public inheritance, rather than private inheritance or membership, to force an is-a relationship on types that are not substitutable. In essence, when we wrapped access to our substitutable pointers in a container, we rendered them unsubstitutable. However, unlike the case in which we have a pointer to a pointer (or an array of pointers) the compiler can no longer warn us of our folly (see Gotcha #33):

➤➤ gotcha90/bondlist.cpp

```
class UnderpaidMinion : public Object {
 public:
   virtual double pay()
       { /* deposit $1M in minion's account */ }
};
void sneaky( ObjectList &list )
   { list.insert( new UnderpaidMinion ); }
```

```
void victimize() {
   BondList &blist = getBondList();
   sneaky( blist );
   bondPortfolioPV( blist ); //done!
}
```

Here, we've managed to substitute one sibling class object for another; we've plugged in an `UnderpaidMinion` where the pricing framework is expecting a `Bond`. Under most environments, the result will be an invocation of `UnderpaidMinion::pay` rather than `Bond::pv`; an undetectable runtime type error. Just as an array of substitutable derived objects is not substitutable for an array of base objects or pointers, a user-defined container of substitutable derived objects or pointers is not substitutable for a user-defined container of base objects or pointers.

Container substitutability, if present at all, should focus on the structure of the container and not that of the contained elements.

Gotcha #91: Failure to Understand Protected Access

The legality of access to a class's members is sometimes a matter of perspective. For example, a base class's public members are private when viewed through the perspective of a privately derived class:

```
class Inst {
 public:
   int units() const
       { return units_; }
   // . . .
 private:
   int units_;
   // . . .
};
```

```
class Sbond : private Inst {
   // . . .
};
// . . .
```

```
void doUnits() {
    Sbond *bp = getNextBond();
    Inst *ip = (Inst *)bp; // old-style cast necessary . . .
    bp->units(); // error!
    ip->units(); // legal
}
```

This particular situation, while amusing, doesn't arise often. More conventionally, we would have employed public inheritance if we'd wanted to expose the base class interface through the derived class. Private inheritance is employed almost exclusively to inherit an implementation. The necessity of using a cast to convert the derived class pointer to a base class pointer is a strong indicator of a bad design practice.

As an aside, note the required use of an old-style cast for the conversion of the derived class pointer to private base class pointer. We would generally prefer to use a safer static_cast, but we can't in this case. A static_cast can't cast from a derived class to an inaccessible base class. Unfortunately, using an old-style cast will tend to mask errors that may occur if the relationship between Sbond and Inst should later change (see Gotchas #40 and #41). My own position is that the cast should go entirely and the hierarchy should be redesigned.

So let's give the base class a virtual destructor, make the accessor function protected, and derive some proper, substitutable derived classes:

```
class Inst {
 public:
    virtual ~Inst();
    // . . .
 protected:
    int units() const
        { return units_; }
 private:
    int units_;
};
class Bond : public Inst {
 public:
    double notional() const
        { return units() * faceval_; }
    // . . .
```

```
  private:
    double faceval_;
};


class Equity : public Inst {
 public:
    double notional() const
        { return units() * shareval_; }
    bool compare( Bond * ) const;
    // . . .
 private:
    double shareval_;
};
```

The base class member function that returns the number of units for a financial instrument is now protected, indicating that it's intended for use by derived classes. The calculation of the notional amount for both bonds and equities uses this information in the calculation.

However, these days it's a good idea to compare an equity to a bond, so the Equity class has declared a compare function that does just that:

```
bool Equity::compare( Bond *bp ) const {
    int bunits = bp->units(); // error!
    return units() < bunits;
}
```

Many programmers are surprised to find that the first attempt to access the protected units member function results in an access violation. The reason for this is that access is being attempted from a member of the Equity derived class but is being made for a Bond object. For non-static members, protected access requires not only that the function making the access be a member or friend of the derived class, but also that the object being accessed have the same type as the class of which the function is a member (or, equivalently, is an object of a publicly derived class) or which is granting access to a non-member friend.

In this case, a member or friend of Equity can't be trusted to provide the proper interpretation of the meaning of units for a Bond object. The Inst base class has provided the units function to its derived classes, but it's up to each derived class to interpret it appropriately. In the case of the compare function above, the comparison of the raw number of units of each instrument type is unlikely to have any useful meaning without additional (and private) derived class-specific information on the face value of a bond or the price of a share. This additional access-checking rule for protected members has the beneficial effect of promoting the decoupling of derived classes.

An attempt to circumvent the access protection violation by passing a Bond as an Inst doesn't help:

```
bool Equity::compare( Inst *ip ) const {
    int bunits = ip->units(); // error!
    return units() < bunits;
}
```

Access to inherited protected members is restricted to objects of the derived class (and classes publicly derived from the derived class) making the call. The best placement for a function like compare, if it's necessary at all, is higher up in the hierarchy, where its presence won't promote coupling among derived classes:

```
bool Inst::unitCompare( const Inst *ip ) const
    { return units() < ip->units(); }
```

Failing that, and if you don't mind a little coupling between Equity and Bond (though you should mind), a mutual friend will do the trick:

```
class Bond : public Inst {
 public:
    friend bool compare( const Equity *, const Bond * );
    // . . .
};
class Equity : public Inst {
 public:
    friend bool compare( const Equity *, const Bond * );
    // . . .
};
bool compare( const Equity *eq, const Bond *bond )
    { return eq->units() < bond->units(); }
```

Gotcha #92: Public Inheritance for Code Reuse

Class hierarchies promote reuse in two ways. First, they permit code common to different derived class implementations to be placed in a shared base class. Second, they permit the base class interface to be shared by all publicly derived classes. Both code sharing and interface sharing are desirable goals in hierarchy design, but interface sharing is the more important of the two.

Use of public inheritance primarily for the purpose of reusing base class implementations in derived classes often results in unnatural, unmaintainable, and, ultimately, more inefficient designs. The reason is that a priori use of public inheritance for code reuse may constrain the base class interface to the extent that it may be difficult to design substitutable derived classes. This, in turn, may restrict the extent to which generic code written to the base class "contract" may be leveraged by derived classes. Typically, much more code reuse is achieved by leveraging large amounts of generic code than by sharing a modest amount in the base class.

The advantages of leveraging generic code written to a base class contract are so extensive that it often makes sense to facilitate this by designing a hierarchy with an interface class at its root. An "interface class" is a base class with no data, a virtual destructor, and typically all pure virtual member functions and no declared constructor. Interface classes are sometimes called "protocol classes," since they specify a protocol for using a hierarchy without any associated implementation. (A "mix-in" is similar to interface class, but a mix-in may contain some minimal data and implementation.)

Using an interface class at the root of a hierarchy eases later maintenance of the hierarchy by simplifying the application of patterns like Decorators, Composites, Proxies, and so on. (Using interface classes also mitigates technical problems associated with the use of virtual base classes; see Gotcha #53.)

The canonical example of an interface class is the use of the Command pattern to implement an abstract callback hierarchy. For instance, we may have a GUI Button class that executes a callback Action when pressed:

➤➤ gotcha92/button.h

```
class Action {
 public:
    virtual ~Action();
    virtual void operator ()() = 0;
    virtual Action *clone() const = 0;
};
```

```
class Button {
 public:
   Button( const char *label );
   ~Button();
   void press() const;
   void setAction( const Action * );
 private:
   string label_;
   Action *action_;
};
```

The Command pattern encapsulates an operation as an object so all the advantages of using an object may be leveraged for the operation. In particular, we'll see below that use of the Command pattern allows us to apply additional patterns to our design.

Note the use of an overloaded operator () in the implementation of Action. We could have used a non-operator member function named execute, but the use of an overloaded function call operator is a C++ coding idiom that indicates Action is an abstraction of a function, in the same way use of an overloaded operator -> in a class indicates that objects of the class are to be used as "smart pointers" (see Gotchas #24 and #83). The Action class also employs the Prototype pattern through the declaration of the clone member function, which is used to create a duplicate of an Action object without precise knowledge of its type (see Gotcha #76).

Our first concrete Action type employs the Null Object pattern to create an Action that does nothing in such a way that all the requirements of an Action are satisfied. A NullAction is-a Action:

➤➤ gotcha92/button.h

```
class NullAction : public Action {
 public:
   void operator ()()
       {}
   NullAction *clone() const
       { return new NullAction; }
};
```

With the `Action` framework in place, it's trivial to produce a safe and flexible `Button` implementation. Use of Null Object ensures that a `Button` will always do something if `pressed`, even if "doing something" means doing nothing (see Gotcha #96).

➤➤ gotcha92/button.cpp

```cpp
Button::Button( const char *label )
    : label_( label ), action_( new NullAction ) {}
void Button::press() const
    { (*action_)(); }
```

Use of Prototype allows a `Button` to have its own copy of an `Action` while remaining ignorant of the exact type of `Action` it copies:

➤➤ gotcha92/button.cpp

```cpp
void Button::setAction( const Action *action )
    { delete action_; action_ = action->clone(); }
```

This is the basis of our `Button/Action` framework, and, as in Figure 9–2, we can add concrete operations (that, unlike `NullAction`, actually do something) without the necessity of recompiling the framework.

The presence of an interface class at the root of the `Action` hierarchy allows us to additionally augment the hierarchy's capabilities. For example, we could apply the Composite pattern to allow a tree of `Action`s to be executed by a `Button`:

➤➤ gotcha92/moreactions.h

```cpp
class Macro : public Action {
 public:
   void add( const Action *a )
       { a_.push_back( a->clone() ); }
   void operator ()() {
       for( I i(a_.begin()); i != a_.end(); ++i )
           (**i)();
   }
   Macro *clone() const {
       Macro *m = new Macro;
       for( CI i(a_.begin()); i != a_.end(); ++i )
           m->add((*i).operator ->());
       return m;
   }
```

```
private:
    typedef list< Cptr<Action> > C;
    typedef C::iterator I;
    typedef C::const_iterator CI;
    C a_;
};
```

The presence of a lightweight interface class at the root of the Action hierarchy enabled us to apply the Null Object and Composite patterns, as shown in Figure 9–3. The presence of significant implementation in the Action base class would have forced all derived classes to inherit it and any side effects the initialization and destruction of the inherited implementation entailed. This would effectively prevent the application of Null Object, Composite, and other commonly used patterns.

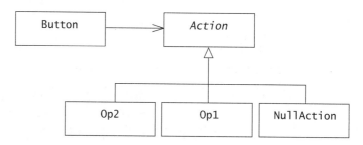

Figure 9–2 | Instances of the Command and Null Object patterns used for Button callback operations

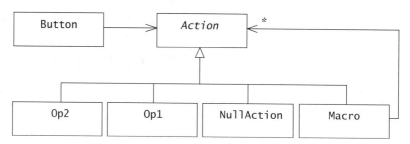

Figure 9–3 | Augmenting the Action hierarchy with an application of the Composite pattern

However, there is a tension between the flexibility of an interface class and the sharing and (often) marginally better performance that obtains with a more substantial base class. For example, it's possible that many of the concrete classes derived from `Action` have duplicate implementation that could be shared by placing the implementation in the `Action` base class. However, doing so would compromise our ability to add additional functionality to the hierarchy, as we did above with the application of the Composite pattern. In cases like this, it may be permissible to attempt to get the best of both worlds through the introduction of an artificial base class that is purely for implementation sharing, as in Figure 9–4.

However, overuse of this approach may result in hierarchies with many artificial classes that have no counterpart in the problem domain and are, as a result, hard to understand and maintain.

In general, it's best to concentrate on inheritance of interface. Proper and efficient code reuse will follow automatically.

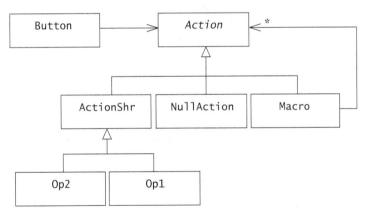

Figure 9–4 | Introduction of an artificial base class to allow both interface and implementation sharing

Gotcha #93: Concrete Public Base Classes

From the design point of view, public base classes should generally be abstract, because they represent abstract concepts from the problem domain. Just as we don't want or expect to see abstractions wandering around in our physical space (imagine, for example, what a generic employee, fruit, or I/O device might look like), we don't want objects of abstract interfaces wandering around in our program space.

In C++, we also have practical concerns related to implementation. We're primarily concerned with slicing and associated issues such as the implementation of copy operations (see Gotchas #30, #49, and #65). In general, public base classes should be abstract.

Gotcha #94: Failure to Employ Degenerate Hierarchies

The design heuristics for base classes and standalone classes are very different, and client code treats base classes very differently from standalone classes. It's therefore advisable to decide what kind of class you're trying to design before you design it.

Recognizing early in development that a class will become a base class in the future and transforming it into a simple, two-class hierarchy is an example of "designing for the future," in that it forces users of the hierarchy to write to an abstract interface and eases future augmentation of the hierarchy. The alternative of initially employing a concrete class and introducing derived types later would force us, or our users, to rewrite existing framework code. Such simple hierarchies may be termed "degenerate hierarchies" (which, no matter what one may hope, is a mathematical, not moral, use of the term "degenerate").

Standalone classes that later become base classes wreak havoc on using code. Standalone classes are often implemented with "value semantics"; that is, they're designed to be efficiently copied by value, and users are encouraged to pass such arguments by value, return them by value, and assign one such object to another.

When such a class later becomes a base class, every such copy becomes a potential slice (see Gotcha #30). Standalone classes may also encourage the declaration of arrays of class objects; this can later lead to errors in address arithmetic (see Gotcha #89). More obscure errors may also arise when generic code is written with the assumption that a particular type of object has a fixed size or fixed set of behaviors. Start a potential base class off as an abstract base class.

Conversely, many or perhaps most classes will never be base classes and should not be factored this way. Certainly, small types that must be maximally efficient should never be factored this way. Common examples of types that should rarely be part of a hierarchy are abstract numeric types, date types, strings, and the like. As designers, it's up to us to use our experience, judgment, and powers of clairvoyance to apply this advice appropriately.

Gotcha #95: Overuse of Inheritance

Wide or deep hierarchies may indicate poor design. Often, such hierarchies occur due to inappropriate factoring of the hierarchy's responsibilities. Consider a simple hierarchy of shapes, as in Figure 9–5.

As it turns out, these shapes are rendered in blue when drawn. Suppose a newly minted C++ programmer, fresh from a first exposure to inheritance, is given the task of extending this hierarchy of shapes to allow red shapes as well as blue. No problem.

As Figure 9–6 shows, we have a classic occurrence of an "exponentially" expanding hierarchy. To add a new color, we must augment the hierarchy with a new class for every shape. To add a new shape, we must augment the hierarchy with a new class for every color. This is silly, and the proper design is obvious. We should use composition instead, as in Figure 9–7.

A `Square` is-a `Shape` and a `Shape` has-a `Color`. Not all examples of overuse of inheritance are so obviously wrong. Consider a financial option hierarchy used to represent options on various types of financial instruments, as in Figure 9–8.

Here we employ a single option base class, and each concrete option type is a combination of the type of option and the type of financial instrument to which the option is applied. Once again we have an expanding hierarchy, in which the addition of a single new option type or financial instrument will result in many classes being added to the option hierarchy. Typically, the proper design involves composition of simple hierarchies, as in Figure 9–9, rather than a single, monolithic hierarchy.

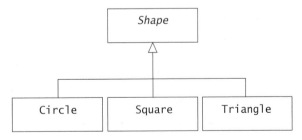

Figure 9–5 | A shape hierarchy

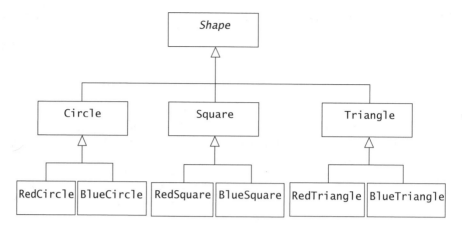

Figure 9–6 | An incorrect, exponentially expanding hierarchy

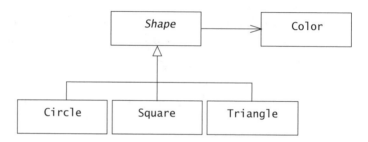

Figure 9–7 | A correct design that employs inheritance and composition properly

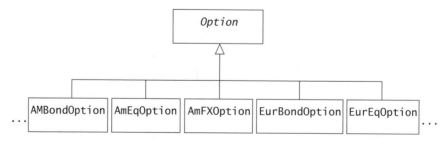

Figure 9–8 | A poorly designed, monolithic hierarchy

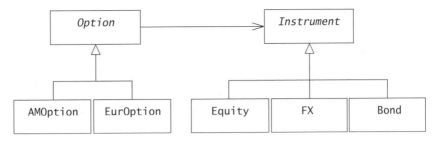

Figure 9–9 │ A correct design; composition of simple hierarchies

An Option has-a Instrument. These hierarchy difficulties are the result of poor domain analysis, but it's also common to produce an unwieldy hierarchy in spite of impeccable domain analysis. Continuing with our financial instruments, let's look at a simplified bond implementation:

```
class Bond {
 public:
    // . . .
    Money pv() const; // calculate present value
 };
```

The pv member function calculates the present value of a Bond. However, there may be several algorithms for performing the computation. One way to handle this would be to merge all the possible algorithms into a single function and select among them with a code:

```
class Bond {
 public:
    // . . .
    Money pv() const;
    enum Model { Official, My, Their };
    void setModel( Model );
 private:
    // . . .
    Model model_;
 };
```

```
Money Bond::pv() const {
    Money result;
    switch( model_ ) {
    case Official:
        // . . .
        return result;
    case My:
        // . . .
        return result;
    case Their:
        // . . .
        return result;
    }
}
```

However, this approach makes it hard to add new pricing models, since source change and recompilation are required. Standard object-oriented design practices tell us to employ inheritance and dynamic binding to implement variation in behavior, as in Figure 9–10.

Unfortunately, this approach fixes the behavior of the pv function when the Bond object is created, and it can't be changed later. Additionally, other aspects of a Bond's implementation may vary independently of the implementation of its pv function. This can lead to a combinatorial explosion in the number of derived classes.

For example, a Bond may have a member function to calculate the volatility of its price. If this algorithm is independent of that for calculating its present value, an additional pricing algorithm or volatility algorithm will require that new derived classes in every new combination of price/volatility calculation be added to the hierarchy. Generally, we use inheritance to implement variation of the entire behavior of an object, not just of a single operation.

As with our earlier example with colored shapes, the correct solution is to employ composition. In particular, we'll employ the Strategy pattern to reduce our monolithic Bond hierarchy to a composition of simple hierarchies, as in Figure 9–11.

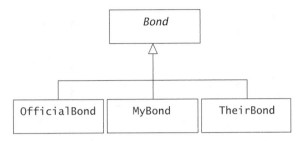

Figure 9–10 | Incorrect application of inheritance; use of inheritance to vary behavior of a single member function

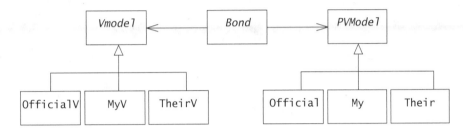

Figure 9–11 | Correct use of Strategy to express independent variation of behavior of two member functions

The Strategy pattern moves the implementation of an algorithm from the body of the function to a separate implementation hierarchy:

```
class PVModel { // Strategy
 public:
    virtual ~PVModel();
    virtual Money pv( const Bond * ) = 0;
};
class VModel { // Strategy
 public:
    virtual ~VModel();
    virtual double volatility( const Bond * ) = 0;
};
```

```
class Bond {
   // . . .
   Money pv() const
       { return pvmodel_->pv( this ); }
   double volatility() const
       { return vmodel_->volatility( this ); }
   void adoptPVModel( PVModel *m )
       { delete pvmodel_; pvmodel_ = m; }
   void adoptVModel( VModel *m )
       { delete vmodel_; vmodel_ = m; }
private:
   // . . .
   PVModel *pvmodel_;
   VModel *vmodel_;
};
```

Use of Strategy allows us to both simplify the structure of the Bond hierarchy and change the behavior of the pv and volatility functions easily at runtime.

Gotcha #96: Type-Based Control Structures

We never switch on type codes in object-oriented programs:

```
void process( Employee *e ) {
   switch( e->type() ) { // evil code!
   case SALARY: fireSalary( e ); break;
   case HOURLY: fireHourly( e ); break;
   case TEMP: fireTemp( e ); break;
   default: throw UnknownEmployeeType();
   }
}
```

The polymorphic approach is more appropriate:

```
void process( Employee *e )
   { e->fire(); }
```

The advantages of this approach are enormous. It's simpler. The code doesn't have to be recompiled as new employee types are added. It's impossible to have type-based runtime errors. And it's probably faster and smaller. Implement type-based decisions with dynamic binding, not with conditional control structures. (See also Gotchas #69, #90, and #98.)

The substitution of dynamic binding for conditional code is so effective that it often makes sense to recast a conditional as a type-based question to employ it. Consider code that simply wants to `process` a `Widget`. The `Widget` has a `process` function in its public interface, but, depending on where the `Widget` is located, additional work must be performed before the `process` function can be called:

```
if( Widget is in local memory )
   w->process();
else if( Widget is in shared memory )
   do horrible things to process it
else if( Widget is remote )
   do even worse things to process it
else
   error();
```

Not only can this conditional code fail ("I want to `process` the `Widget`, but I don't know where it is!") but it may be repeated many times in the source. All these independent sections of conditional code must be maintained in sync as the set of possible locations of `Widget`s grows or shrinks. A better approach might encode the location of a `Widget` in its type, as in Figure 9–12.

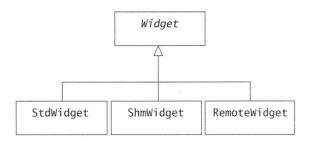

Figure 9–12 | Avoiding conditional code; use of the Proxy pattern to encode an object's access protocol as part of its type

This situation is so common that it has a name. This is an instance of the Proxy pattern. The different mechanisms for accessing `Widgets` according to location are now encoded in each `Widget`'s type, and a simple virtual function call is all that's required to distinguish them. Further, this code is not repeated, and the virtual call can't fail to know how to access the `Widget`:

```
Widget *w = getNextWidget();
w->process();
```

Another important benefit of avoiding conditional code is so obvious that it can be easily overlooked: one way to avoid making an incorrect decision is to avoid making any decision at all. Simply put, the less conditional code you write, the less likely it is you'll have incorrect conditional code.

One manifestation of this advice is the Null Object pattern. Consider a function that returns a pointer to a "device" that must be "handled":

```
class Device {
 public:
   virtual ~Device();
   virtual void handle() = 0;
};
// . . .
Device *getDevice();
```

The `Device` class is an abstract base class for a number of different device types. It's also possible that `getDevice` could fail to return a `Device`, so our code for getting and handling a `Device` looks like this:

```
if( Device *curDevice = getDevice() )
   curDevice->handle();
```

That's pretty simple code, but we're making a decision. In this case, we might worry about maintenance that neglects to check the return value of `getDevice` before attempting to `handle` it.

The Null Object pattern suggests that we create an artificial type of `Device` that satisfies all the constraints on a `Device` (it can be `handled`) but that does nothing. Essentially, it does nothing in exactly the right way:

```
class NullDevice : public Device {
 public:
    void handle() {}
};
// . . .
Device &getDevice();
```

Now `getDevice` can never fail, we can remove some conditional code, and we circumvent a potential future bug:

```
getDevice().handle();
```

Gotcha #97: Cosmic Hierarchies

More than a decade ago, the C++ community decided that the use of "cosmic" hierarchies (architectures in which every object type is derived from a root class, usually called `Object`) was not an effective design approach in C++. There were a number of reasons for rejecting this approach, both on the design level and on the implementation level.

From a design standpoint, cosmic hierarchies often give rise to generic containers of "objects." The content of these containers are often unpredictable and lead to unexpected runtime behavior. Bjarne Stroustrup's classic counterexample considered the possibility of putting a battleship in a pencil cup—something a cosmic hierarchy would allow but that would probably surprise a user of the pencil cup.

A pervasive and dangerous assumption among inexperienced designers is that an architecture should be as flexible as possible. Error. Rather, an architecture should be as close to the problem domain as possible while retaining sufficient flexibility to permit reasonable future extension. When "software entropy" sets in and new requirements are difficult to add within the existing structure, the code should be refactored into a new design. Attempts to create maximally flexible architectures a priori are similar to attempts to create maximally efficient code without profiling; there will be no useful architecture, and there will be a loss of efficiency. (See also Gotcha #72.)

This misapprehension of the goal of an architecture, coupled with an unwilling-ness to do the hard work of abstracting a complex problem domain, often results in the reintroduction of a particularly noxious form of cosmic hierarchy:

```
class Object {
 public:
   Object( void *, const type_info & );
   virtual ~Object();
   const type_info &type();
   void *object();
   // . . .
};
```

Here, the designer has abdicated all responsibility for understanding and properly abstracting the problem domain and has instead created a wrapper that can be used to effectively "cosmicize" otherwise unrelated types. An object of any type can be wrapped in an `Object`, and we can create containers of `Objects` into which we can put anything at all (and frequently do).

The designer may also provide the means to perform a type safe conversion of an `Object` wrapper to the object it wraps:

```
template <class T>
T *dynamicCast( Object *o ) {
   if( o && o->type() == typeid(T) )
       return reinterpret_cast<T *>(o->object());
   return 0;
}
```

At first glance, this approach may seem acceptable (if somewhat ungainly), but consider the problem of extracting and using the content of a container that can contain anything at all:

```
void process( list<Object *> &cup ) {
   typedef list<Object *>::iterator I;
   for( I i(cup.begin()); i != cup.end(); ++i ) {
       if( Pencil *p =
           dynamicCast<Pencil>(*i) )
           p->write();
```

```
        else if( Battleship *b =
            dynamicCast<Battleship>(*i) )
            b->anchorsAweigh();
        else
            throw InTheTowel();
    }
}
```

Any user of the cosmic hierarchy will be forced to engage in a silly and childish "guessing game," the object of which is to uncover type information that shouldn't have been lost in the first place. In other words, that a pencil cup can't contain a battleship doesn't indicate a design flaw in the pencil cup. The flaw may be found in the section of code that thinks it's reasonable to perform such an insertion. It's unlikely that the ability to put a battleship in a pencil cup corresponds to anything in the application domain, and this is not the type of coding we should encourage or submit to. A local requirement for a cosmic hierarchy generally indicates a design flaw elsewhere.

Since our design abstractions of pencil cups and battleships are simplified models of the real world (whatever "real" means in the context), it's worth considering the analogous real-world situation. Imagine that, as the designer of a (physical) pencil cup, you received a complaint from one of your users that his ship didn't fit in the cup. Would you offer to fix the pencil cup, or would you offer some other type of assistance?

The repercussions of this abdication of design responsibility are extensive and serious. Any use of a container of Objects is a potential source of an unbounded number of type-related errors. Any change to the set of object types that may be wrapped as Objects will require maintenance to an arbitrary amount of code, and that code may not be available for modification. Finally, because no effective architecture has been provided, every user of the container is faced with the problem of how to extract information about the anonymous objects.

Each of these acts of design will result in different and incompatible ways of detecting and reporting errors. For example, one user of the container may feel just a bit silly asking questions like "Are you a pencil? No? A battleship? No? . . ." and opt for a capability-query approach. The results are not much better (see Gotcha #99).

Often, the presence of an inappropriate cosmic hierarchy is not as obvious as it is in the case we just discussed. Consider a hierarchy of assets, as in Figure 9–13.

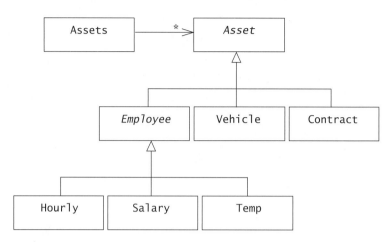

Figure 9–13 An iffy hierarchy. It's not clear whether the use of `Asset` is overly general or not.

It's not immediately clear whether the `Asset` hierarchy is overly general or not, especially in this high-level picture of the design. Often the suitability of a design choice is not clear until much lower-level design or coding has taken place. If the general nature of the hierarchy leads to certain disreputable coding practices (see Gotchas #98 and 99), it's probably a cosmic hierarchy and should be refactored out of existence. Otherwise, it may simply be an acceptably general hierarchy.

Sometimes, refactoring our perceptions can improve a hierarchy, even without source code changes. Many of the problems associated with cosmic hierarchies have to do with employing an overly general base class. If we reconceptualize the base class as an interface class and communicate this reconceptualization to the users of the hierarchy, as in Figure 9–14, we can avoid many of the damaging coding practices mentioned earlier.

Our design no longer expresses a cosmic hierarchy but three separate hierarchies that leverage independent subsystems through their corresponding interfaces. This is a conceptual change only, but an important one. Now employees, vehicles, and contracts may be manipulated as assets by an asset subsystem, but the subsystem, because it's ignorant of classes derived from `Asset`, won't attempt to uncover more precise information about the `Asset` objects it manipulates. The same reasoning applies to the other interface classes, and the possibility of a runtime type-related error is small.

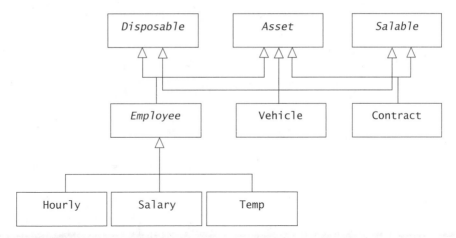

Figure 9–14 | An effective reconceptualization. The is-a relationship is appropriately weakened if we consider **Asset** to be a protocol rather than a base class.

Gotcha #98: Asking Personal Questions of an Object

This item considers a commonly abused capability in object-oriented design: runtime type information. The C++ language has standardized the form of runtime type queries, effectively legitimizing their use with an implicit seal of approval. But while it's true that runtime type queries have legitimate uses in C++ programming, these uses should be rare and should almost never form the basis for a design. Regrettably, much of the wisdom the C++ community has accumulated about proper and effective communication with hierarchies of types is often jettisoned in favor of underdesigned, overly general, complex, unmaintainable, and error-prone approaches using runtime type queries.

Consider the venerable employee base class below. Sometimes features must be added after a significantly large subsystem has been developed and tested. For instance, the **Employee** base class interface has a glaring omission:

```
class Employee {
  public:
    Employee( const Name &name, const Address &address );
    virtual ~Employee();
    void adoptRole( Role *newRole );
    const Role *getRole( int ) const;
    // . . .
};
```

That's right. We have to be able to rightsize these assets. (We also have to pay these assets, but that can wait until a future release.) Our management tells us to add the capability to fire an employee, given only a pointer to the employee base class and without recompiling or otherwise changing the Employee hierarchy. Clearly, salaried employees must be fired differently from hourly employees:

```
void terminate( Employee * );
void terminate( SalaryEmployee * );
void terminate( HourlyEmployee * );
```

The most straightforward way to accomplish this is to hack. We'll simply run down a list of questions about the precise type of employee:

```
void terminate( Employee *e ) {
    if( HourlyEmployee *h = dynamic_cast<HourlyEmployee *>(e) )
        terminate( h );
    else if( SalaryEmployee *s = dynamic_cast<SalaryEmployee *>(e) )
        terminate( s );
    else
        throw UnknownEmployeeType( e );
}
```

This approach has clear problems in terms of efficiency and the potential for runtime error in the case of an unknown employee type. Generally, because C++ is a statically typed language and because its dynamic binding mechanism (the virtual function) is statically checked, we should be able to avoid this class of runtime errors entirely. This is reason enough to recognize this implementation of the terminate function as a temporary hack rather than as the basis of an extensible design.

The poverty of the design is perhaps even more obvious if the code is back-translated into the problem domain it's supposedly modeling:

> The vice president of widgets storms into her office in a terrible rage. Her parking space has been occupied for the third time this month by the junk heap driven by that itinerant developer she hired the month before. "Get Dewhurst in here!" she roars into her intercom.

> Seconds later, she fixes the hapless developer with a gimlet eye and intones, "If you're an hourly employee, you're fired as an hourly employee. Otherwise, if you're a salaried employee, you're fired as a salaried employee. Otherwise, get out of my office and become someone else's problem."

I'm a consultant, and I've never lost a contract to a manager who used runtime type information to solve her problems. The correct solution is, of course, to put the appropriate operations in the `Employee` base class and use standard, type-safe, dynamic binding to resolve type-based questions at runtime:

```
class Employee {
  public:
    Employee( const Name &name, const Address &address );
    virtual ~Employee();
    void adoptRole( Role *newRole );
    const Role *getRole( int ) const;
    virtual bool isPayday() const = 0;
    virtual void pay() = 0;
    virtual void terminate() = 0;
    // . . .
};
```

. . . she fixes the hapless developer with a gimlet eye and intones, "You're fired!"

Runtime type queries are sometimes necessary or preferable to other design choices. As we've seen, they can be used as a convenient and temporary hack when one is faced with poorly designed third-party software. They can also be useful when one is faced with an otherwise impossible requirement to modify existing code without recompilation when that code wasn't designed to accommodate such modification. Runtime type queries are also handy in debugging code and have rare, scattered uses in specific problem domains like debuggers, browsers, and the like. Finally, if the problem domain being modeled has an intrinsic lack of orthogonality, that intrinsic glitch may well show up as a runtime type query glitch in the code.

Since the standardization of runtime typing mechanisms in C++, however, many designers have employed runtime typing in preference to simpler, more efficient, more maintainable design approaches. Typically, runtime type queries are used to compensate for bad architecture, which typically arises from compounded hacks, poor domain analysis, or the mistaken notion that an architecture should be maximally flexible.

In practice, it should rarely be necessary to ask an object personal questions about its type.

Gotcha #99: Capability Queries

In fact, abuse of runtime type information as obvious as that in the `terminate` function of the previous gotcha is usually the result of compounded hacks and poor project management rather than bad design. However, some "advanced" uses of dynamic casting with multiple inheritance are often pressed into service to form the basis of an architecture.

> The employee reports to the HR department on his first day of work and is told, "Get in line with the other assets." He's directed to a long line of other employees that also includes, strangely, a variety of office equipment, vehicles, furniture, and legal agreements.
>
> Finally reaching the head of the line, he's assaulted by a sequence of odd questions: "Do you consume gasoline?" "Can you program?" "Can I make copies with you?" Answering "no" to all the questions, he's eventually sent home, wondering why no one thought to ask him if he could mop floors, since that was what he was hired to do.

Sounds a little odd, doesn't it? (Perhaps not, if you've worked for a large corporation.) It should sound odd, because this is an example of improper use of capability queries.

Let's leave human resources for a while and head down the hall to finance, to look at a financial instrument hierarchy. Suppose we're trading securities. We have at our disposal a pricing subsystem and a persistence subsystem whose code we'd like to leverage in the implementation of our hierarchy. The requirements of each subsystem are clearly stated in an interface class from which the user of the subsystem must derive:

```
class Saveable { // persistence interface
  public:
    virtual ~Saveable();
    virtual void save() = 0;
    // . . .
};
class Priceable { // pricing interface
  public:
    virtual ~Priceable();
    virtual void price() = 0;
    // . . .
};
```

Some concrete classes of the Deal hierarchy fulfill the subsystem contracts and leverage the subsystem code. This is a standard, effective, and correct use of multiple inheritance:

```
class Deal {
 public:
    virtual void validate() = 0;
    // . . .
};
class Bond
  : public Deal, public Priceable
    {/* . . . */};
class Swap
  : public Deal, public Priceable, public Saveable
    {/* . . . */};
```

Now we have to add the ability to "process" a deal, given just a pointer to the Deal base class. A naïve approach would simply ask straightforward questions about the object's type, which is no better than our earlier attempt to terminate employees (see Gotcha #98):

```
void processDeal( Deal *d ) {
    d->validate();
    if( Bond *b = dynamic_cast<Bond *>(d) )
        b->price();
    else if( Swap *s = dynamic_cast<Swap *>(d) ) {
        s->price();
        s->save();
    }
    else
        throw UnknownDealType( d );
}
```

Another distressingly popular approach is not to ask the object what it is but rather what it can do. This is often called a "capability query":

```
void processDeal( Deal *d ) {
    d->validate();
    if( Priceable *p = dynamic_cast<Priceable *>(d) )
        p->price();
```

```
    if( Saveable *s = dynamic_cast<Saveable *>(d) )
        s->save();
}
```

Each base class represents a set of capabilities. A `dynamic_cast` across the hierarchy, or "cross-cast," is equivalent to asking whether an object can perform a particular function or set of functions, as in Figure 9–15. The second version of `processDeal` essentially says, "Deal, validate yourself. If you can be priced, price yourself. If you can be saved, save yourself."

This approach is a bit more sophisticated than the previous implementation of `processDeal`. It may also be somewhat less fragile, since it can handle new types of deals without throwing an exception. However, it still suffers from efficiency and maintenance problems. Consider what would happen if a new interface class should appear in the `Deal` hierarchy, as in Figure 9–16.

The appearance of a new capability in the hierarchy is not detected. Essentially, the code never thinks to ask if the deal is legal (which, on the other hand, is pretty realistic domain analysis). As with our earlier solution to the problem of terminating an employee, this capability-query-based approach to processing a deal is an ad hoc solution, not a basis for an architecture.

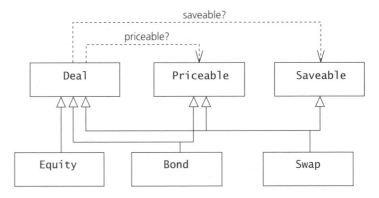

Figure 9–15 | Use of cross-casting to implement capability queries

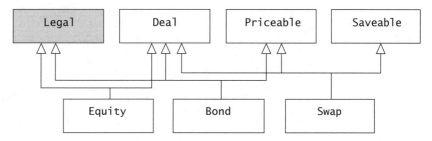

Figure 9–16 | The fragility of capability queries. What if we neglect to ask the right question?

The root problem with both identity-based and capability-based queries in object-oriented design is that some of the essential behavior of an object is determined externally to the object itself. This approach runs counter to the principle of data abstraction, perhaps the most basic of the foundations of object-oriented programming. With these approaches, the meaning of an abstract data type is no longer encapsulated within the class used to implement it but is distributed throughout the source code.

As with the Employee hierarchy, the safest and most efficient way to add a capability to the Deal hierarchy is also the simplest:

```
class Deal {
 public:
   virtual void validate() = 0;
   virtual void process() = 0;
   // . . .
};
class Bond : public Deal, public Priceable {
 public:
   void validate();
   void price();
   void process() {
       validate();
       price();
   }
};
```

```
class Swap : public Deal, public Priceable, public Saveable {
public:
  void validate();
  void price();
  void save();
  void process() {
      validate();
      price();
      save();
  }
};
// etc . . .
```

Other techniques can be used to improve on the capability query without modifying the hierarchy if the original design makes provision for them. The Visitor pattern allows new capabilities to be added to a hierarchy but is fragile when the hierarchy is maintained. The Acyclic Visitor pattern is less fragile than Visitor but requires a (single) capability query that may fail. Either of these approaches, however, is an improvement over systematic use of capability queries.

Generally, the necessity for capability queries is indicative of a bad design, and a simple, efficient, type-safe virtual function call that always succeeds is preferable.

The employee reports to the HR department on his first day of work. He's directed to a long line of other employees. Finally reaching the head of the line, he's told, "Get to work!" Since he was hired as a janitor, he grabs a mop and spends the rest of the day washing floors.

Bibliography

Andrei Alexandrescu. *Modern C++ Design*, Addison-Wesley, 2001.

Association for Computing Machinery. *ACM Code of Ethics and Professional Conduct*, www.acm.org/constitution/code.html.

————. *Software Engineering Code of Ethics and Professional Practice*, www.acm.org/serving/se/code.htm.

Marshall P. Cline, Greg A. Lomow, and Mike Girou. *C++ FAQs, Second Edition*, Addison-Wesley, 1999.

Erich Gamma, Richard Helm, Ralph Johnson, and John Vlissides. *Design Patterns*, Addison-Wesley, 1995.

Nicolai Josuttis. *The C++ Standard Library*, Addison-Wesley, 1999.

Robert Martin. *Agile Software Development*, 2nd ed., Prentice Hall, 2003.

Scott Meyers. *Effective C++*, 2nd ed. Addison-Wesley, 1998.

————. *Effective STL*, Addison-Wesley, 2001.

————. *More Effective C++*, Addison-Wesley, 1996.

Stephen C. Dewhurst and Kathy T. Stark. *Programming in C++*, 2nd ed., Prentice-Hall, 1995.

William Strunk and E. B. White. *The Elements of Style*, 3d ed., Macmillan, 1979.

Herb Sutter. *More Exceptional C++*, Addison-Wesley, 2002.

E. B. White. *Writings from* The New Yorker, HarperCollins, 1990.

Index

, (comma operator), 39–40
?: (conditional operator), 15–16, 40–41
[ ] (allocating and deleting arrays), 35, 36, 168
( ) (allocating arrays), 35
-> (arrow operator), 58–60, 257–258
[ ] (index operator), 16–17
&& (logical operator), 40
|| (logical operator), 40
<<< (Sergeant operator), 48–49

A

access protection
  Bridge pattern, 21–22
  vs. data abstraction, 241–242
  description, 19
  inheritance, 23, 277–280
  naming conventions, 23
  vs. visibility, 19–23
accessor functions. See get/set interfaces.
ACM Code of Ethics..., 32
acquaintance vs. aggregation, 253–258
acronyms, 25–26
Acyclic Visitor pattern, 306
addresses
  arithmetic errors, 77–78, 89, 101, 286
  base class subobjects, 206–208
  members. See pointers, to members.
  of a non-lvalue return, 267
adolescent behavior, 31–33

aggregation vs. acquaintance, 253–258
Alexandrescu, Andrei, xv
algorithms, variant and invariant, 212–214
aliases
  aggregation/acquaintance relationships, 253
  references as, 10–13, 112–115
allocation failure, 171–173
ampersands (&&) logical operator, 40
anonymous namespace, 55
anonymous temporaries
  function object for pass by value, 109, 111
  initialization of a reference formal argument, 107
  initialize reference to const, 112
  lifetime, 110–111
  result of a postfix ++ or --, 266
  as a result of copy initialization, 153–154
  throwing, 181–182
array names vs. constant pointers, 87
arrays
  of arrays, 52, 87–88
  of class objects, 271–273
  confused with initializers, 35–36
  freeing, 167–170
  migrating type-qualifiers, 52
  pointer-to-multidimensional array conversions, 87–88
  references to, 12
  vs. vectors, 168

arrow operator (->), 58–60, 257–258

`assert` macro, 72–74

assertions, side effects, 72–74

assignment *vs.* initialization, 125–129, 139–141

associativity

  and precedence, 42

  problems, 44–45

`auto_ptr` template, 28–29, 195–197

B

base class subobject

  addresses, 206–208

  initialization, 142–147, 147–150, 218–219

base class types, arrays of class objects, 271–273

base language. *See* C++ base language.

battleship, in pencil cup, 295

binding

  dynamic, 200

  reference to function, 13

  reference to lvalue, 11, 112–115

Bridge pattern, 21–22

C

C++ base language

  conditional operator, 15–16

  fallthrough, 17–19

  index operator, 16–17

  logical operators, 14–15

  switch-statements, 17

calling a pure virtual function, 212, 220

capability queries, 302–306

cast operators *vs.* conversion operators, 24–25

casting. *See also* `void *`.

  base class pointers to derived class pointers. *See* downcasting.

  incomplete types, 100–101

  under multiple inheritance, 98–100, 147

  non-dynamic casts. *See* static casts.

  old-style casts, 102–103

  to references, 12–13

  `reinterpret_cast`, 76, 100–101

  static casts, 103–105

casting away const, 252

casts, maintenance, 76, 84, 102, 103

catch clauses, ordering, 184

catching

  exceptions, 182–183

  string literals, 178–180

change logs, 2–3

Cheshire Cat technique. *See* Bridge pattern.

Clamage, Steve, xv

class design

  aggregation *vs.* acquaintance, 253–258

  const data members, 245–247

  const member functions

    casting away const, 252

    meaning of, 250–252

    semantics and mechanics, 249–250

    syntax, 248

  decrement operator, 264–268

  friend *vs.* member operators, 262–264

  get/set interfaces, 241–245

  increment operator, 264–268

  operator overloading, 258–264

  operator precedence, 261–262

  overloading, 258–262

  reference data members, 245–247

  templated copy operations, 268–270

class hierarchies. *See* hierarchy design.

class implementation, varying with #if, 70–71

class objects, bitwise copy, 136–138

classes
  access protection, 19–23
  interface, 145
  POD (Plain Old Data), 136
  pure virtual base, 24

cleverness, unnecessary, 29–31

Cline, Marshall, xvi

code reuse, 281–285

coders. *See* programmers.

coding, conciseness, 2

Comeau, Greg, xv

comma (,) operator, 39–40

Command pattern, 281–285

comments. *See also* maintenance; readability.
  avoiding, 2–4
  change logs, 2–3
  excessive, 1–4
  fallthrough, 18
  maintaining, 1–4
  self-documenting code, 2
  specifying ownership, 254–255

compilation, avoiding recompilation, 21, 202–203

compiler-generated assignment of virtual base subobjects, 145

component coupling
  defeating access protection, 280
  global variables, 6
  polymorphism, 202

Composite pattern, 281, 283–284

computational constructors, 161

concrete public base classes, 285–286

conditional operator (?:), 15–16, 40

const data members, 245–247

const member functions
  casting away const, 252
  meaning of, 250–252
  semantics and mechanics, 249–250
  syntax, 248

const objects *vs.* literals, 13–14

const pointers
  vs. array names, 87
  definition, 50
  vs. pointer to const, 81
  pointer-to-const conversion, 81–82

const type-qualifier
  migrating, 52
  references, 10–11

constant-expressions, 67

constants
  assigning to, 246
  vs. literals, 4–6, 13–14

const_cast operator, 103, 112, 246, 252

constructors
  calling virtual functions, 218–220
  computational, 161
  conversions, 95–98
  implementing with template member functions, 268–270
  initialization *vs.* assignment, 139–141
  initializing static members, 163–165
  virtual constructor idiom, 223

container substitutability, 273–277

containers of pointers, 255–258

contravariance, 120–123

conversion functions, explicit, 90, 136–138

conversion operators
  alternative to, 90
  ambiguous, 90–94
  diction, 24–25
  purpose of, 92

conversions
  array names *vs.* constant pointers, 87
  casting
    incomplete types, 100–101
    multiple inheritance, 98–100
    under multiple inheritance, 98–100
    old-style casts, 102–103
    reinterpret_cast, 76, 100–101
    static casts, 103–105
  const pointers
    vs. array names, 87
    pointer-to-const conversion, 81–82
  const_cast operator, 103–105, 112,
    246, 252
  contravariance, 120–123
  delta arithmetic
    casting incomplete types, 101
    class object addresses, 98–100
    correcting this value in virtual
      function call, 235–236
    downcasting, 89
  downcasting, 89
  dynamic_cast operator
    ambiguity, 116–120
    to ask a personal question of a
      type, 300
    for a capability query, 303–304
    of pointer to virtual base sub-
      object, 146
    in preference to static cast, 89
    static_cast in preference to, 146
  formal arguments
    passing by reference, 109
    passing by value, 108–109
    temporary initialization, 106–109
  functions for, 90–94
  implicit
    ambiguous results, 90–94

constructor conversions, 95–98
contravariance, 120–123
  from derived class to public base, 122
  initialization of formal arguments,
    106–109
  references, 112–115
initializing
  formal arguments, 106–109
  references, 112–115
Meyers, Scott, 105
objects, temporary lifetime, 110–111
old-style casts, 102–103
platform dependency, 76
pointer-to-const conversion, 81–82
pointer-to-multidimensional arrays,
  87–88
pointer-to-pointer-to-base conversion,
  86–87
pointer-to-pointer-to-const conversion,
  82–86
pointers
  converting, 82–86
  to incomplete class types, 100–101
  to members, converting, 120–123
  to pointers to derived classes, 86–87
qualification conversions, 82–86
references
  as aliases, 112–115
  conversions, 112–115
  to incomplete class types, 100–101
reinterpret_cast, 76, 100–101
slicing derived class objects, 79–81
static casts, 103–105
temporaries, 110–115. *See also*
  anonymous temporaries.
void *, 75–78
converting types. *See* casting; void *.
copy constructor base, initializing,
  147–150

copy operations
  denying, 135
  idiom, 27–29
  initialization, 132–136
  templated, 268–270
cosmic hierarchies, 295–299
coupling. *See* component coupling.
covariant return types, 228
cowpath simile for natural language, 26
cross-cast, 304
cv-qualifiers. *See* `const` type-qualifier;
    `volatile` type-qualifier.

D

dark corners (of the C++ language)
  address of a non-lvalue return, 267
  calling a pure virtual function, 212, 220
  compiler-generated assignment of
    virtual base subobjects, 145
  dynamic scope of invocation member
    `operator delete`, 206
  `dynamic_cast` to inaccessible base, 177
  guarantees associated with
    `reinterpret_cast`, 100
  ignoring qualifiers on reference type
    name, 10
  indexing an integer, 16
  lvalue result of conditional operator, 16
  overriding invisible functions, 228
  point of declaration of an
    enumerator, 54
  qualification of function typedef, 52
  string literal temporary for `throw`
    expression, 181
  switch-statement structure, 18

data abstraction
  for exception types, 178
  purpose of, 241
data hiding. *See* access protection.
debug code, in executable modules, 67
debugging
  `#if`, 66–69
  unreachable code, 67–69
declaration-specifiers, ordering, 50–51
Decorator pattern, 212, 281
decrement operator, 264–268
default argument initializer. *See* default
    initialization.
default initialization
  vs. overloading, 8–9
  uses for, 7, 9
  and virtual base objects, 244
`#define`, and namespace, 62
`#define` literals, 61–63
`#define` pseudofunctions, 64–66
degenerate hierarchies, 286
`delete []` operator, 168–170
  array allocation, 168–170
  replacing, 173–176
  scalar allocation, 168–170
  scope and activation, 176–177
delta arithmetic
  casting incomplete types, 101
  class object addresses, 98–100
  correcting `this` value in virtual
    function call, 235–236
  downcasting, 89
derived class objects, slicing, 79–81
derived classes, overriding functions,
    228–229
design firewalls, 202
destroyed *vs.* destructed, 24
destructors, calling virtual functions,
    218–220

developers. *See* programmers.
Dewhurst, David, xv
diction. *See also* idiom.
    acronyms, 25–26
    cast operators, 24–25
    conversion operators, 24–25
    destructed *vs.* destroyed, 24
    function calls, 24
    member functions, 24
    methods, 24
    null pointers, 25
    pure virtual base classes, 24
direct argument initialization, 156–158
dominance, 236–239
downcasting, 89
dynamic binding, 200
dynamic scope of invocation member
    `operator delete`, 206
`dynamic_cast` operator
    ambiguity, 116–120
    to ask a personal question of a type, 300
    for a capability query, 303–304
    conversions, 116–120
    of pointer to virtual base subobject, 146
    in preference to static cast, 89
    `static_cast` in preference to, 146
    virtual base default initialization, 146
`dynamic_cast` to inaccessible base, 177

E

Eiffel, 29
The Elements of Style, 26
enumerators
    `#define` literals, 63
    initializing static members, 163
    magic numbers, 5
    point of declaration, 54

ethics of programming, 32–33
evaluation order. *See* precedence.
examples, source code, xiv
exception handling, 172–173, 177–184,
    193–194
exception types, 178–180
extern types, 55

F

Factory Method pattern, 229, 274–275
fallthrough, 17–19
`for` statement
    variable scope restriction, 45–48
    vs. `while` statement, 47
formal arguments
    passing by reference, 109
    passing by value, 108–109
    specifying ownership, 254–255
    temporary initialization, 106–109
forward class declaration. *See* incomplete
    declaration.
`free` *vs.* `delete`, 168–169
freeing
    arrays and scalars, 167–170
    resources of heap-allocated objects, 195
friend *vs.* member operators, 262–264
function matching. *See* overloading.
function/object ambiguity, 51
function object idiom, 282
function typedef, qualification, 52
functions
    binding references to, 13
    for conversions, 90–94
    invisible, overriding, 228
    pointers to, 13
    references for return values, 11–12
    references to, 13

G

Gamma, Erich, xi
get/set interfaces, 241–245
global variables, 6–8
gotchas, definition, xi
Gschwind, Thomas, xv
guarantees associated with
    `reinterpret_cast`, 100

H

header files
  reference counting inclusions, 152–153
  Schwarz counter, 152–153
Hewins, Sarah, xv
hiding
  nonvirtual functions, 209–212
  vs. overloading and overriding, 224–230
hierarchy design
  address arithmetic errors, 286
  arrays of class objects, 271–273
  capability queries, 302–306
  code reuse, 281–285
  concrete public base classes, 285–286
  container substitutability, 273–277
  cosmic hierarchies, 295–299
  degenerate hierarchies, 286
  inheritance, 287–292
  interface classes, 281
  protected access, 277–280
  protocol classes, 281
  public inheritance, 281–285
  runtime type queries, 299–301
  slicing, 286
  switching on type codes, 292–295
  type-based control structures, 292–295
  value semantics, 286
hyphen angle bracket (->) operator,
    58–60

I

idiom. *See also* diction.
  `auto_ptr` template, 28–29
  copy operation, 27–29
  function object, 282
  natural language, as a cowpath, 26
  and natural selection, 27
  resource acquisition is initialization, 28
  rules of natural language, 26
  smart pointer, 59, 282
  virtual constructor, 223. *See also*
    Prototype pattern.
`#if`
  debugging, 66–69
  platform independence, 69
  portability, 69–70
  in the real world, 71–72
  varying class implementation, 70–71
ignoring qualifiers on reference type
    name, 10
implicit conversions
  ambiguous results, 90–94
  constructor conversions, 95–98
  contravariance, 120–123
  from derived class to public base, 122
  initialization of formal arguments,
    106–109
  references, 112–115
incomplete declaration, 20–21
incomplete types
  casting, 100–101
  for decoupling, 20–21

increment operator, 264–268
index operator, predefined, 16–17
index operator ([ ]), 16–17
indexing
  array names, 16
  integers with pointers, 16–17
  pointers, 16
infix notation, 56–58, 258–259
inheritance
  access protection, 23
  hierarchy design, 281–285, 287–292
initialization
  vs. assignment, 125–129, 139–141
  bitwise copy of class objects, 136–138
  copy constructor base, 147–150
  copy operations, 132–136
  default
    vs. overloading, 8–9
    uses for, 7, 9
  direct argument, 156–158
  direct *vs.* copy, 153–156
  formal arguments, temporary, 106–109
  implicit copy operations
    bitwise copy of class objects, 136–138
    description, 132–136
  initializers, confused with arrays, 35–36
  member initialization list, ordering,
    141–142
  passing arguments, 126
  references, 112–115
  return value optimizations, 158–162
  runtime static, ordering, 150–153
  scoping variables, 129–132
  self-initialization, 53–55
  Singleton pattern, 7–8
  static members in constructors,
    163–165
  virtual base default, 142–147
initializers, confused with arrays, 35–36

integers, indexing, 16
interface classes, 145, 281, 284–285.
  See also mix-in classes.

J

Josuttis, Nicolai, xvi

K

Kernighan, Brian, xv

L

Lafferty, Debbie, xv
language (natural), 26
left angle brackets (<<<), Sergeant
  operator, 48–49
lexical analysis, 49
literals
  vs. const objects, 13–14
  vs. constants, 4–6
  defining, 61–63
local addresses
  disappearing stack frames, 185
  idiomatic problems, 186–187
  static interference, 186
local scope problems, 187
local variable lifetimes, 187
logical operators, 14–15, 40
lvalue
  binding references, 11, 112–115
  definition, 13–14
  function return, 11

initializing references. *See* binding,
   reference to lvalue.
nonmodifiable, 14, 62
result of conditional operator, 15–16

M

macros, side effects, 16, 64–66
magic numbers, 4–6
maintenance. *See also* comments;
      readability.
   and casts, 76, 84, 102, 103
   easing
      assertions, 73
      coding standards, 32, 40–41
      container ownership, 255
      container substitutability, 275
      declaration-specifier ordering, 51
      fallthrough, 17–18
      idioms, 27
      incomplete declarations, 20
      initializing static members, 164
      mnemonic names, 3
      naming conventions, 3
      precedence, 43–44
      scalar allocation *vs.* array, 170
      `for` statement, 45, 48
      type codes, 202
      typed-base control structures,
         293–294
   made difficult
      asking personal questions of
         objects, 299
      `auto_ptr`, 196
      code reuse, 281, 285
      comments, 1–4
      const and reference data
         members, 245

      `dynamic_cast`, 116
      global variables, 6–8
      implicit conversions, 92
      memory allocation failure, 171
      miscommunication of container
         ownership, 256
      naming conventions, 23
      overloading virtual functions, 215
      public inheritance, 281, 285
      resource acquisition is initialization,
         193–194
      switch on type codes, 200
      throwing/catching string literals, 178
      type-based control structures, 293
      unnecessary cleverness, 29–31, 115
   made impossible
      capability queries, 304
      cosmic hierarchies, 296–297
      `#if`, 69, 71
      initializing static members, 165
      local address abuse, 185
      platform dependence, 69
      static interference, 186
      varying class implementation, 71
   remote changes (bugs caused by), 77,
      101, 103, 105
`malloc` *vs.* `new`, 168–169
maximal munch
   description, 48–49
   examples, 30, 48–49
McKillen, Patrick, xv
meaningful names. *See* naming
      conventions.
member functions
   diction, 24
   template, 29
   virtual static, 205–206
member initialization list, ordering, 29,
      141–142

member *vs.* friend operators, 262–264
members
   pointers to, 9, 120–123
   requiring initialization, 139
memory and resource management
   allocation failure, 171–173
   `auto_ptr`, 195–197
   catch clauses, ordering, 184
   catching exceptions, 182–183
   catching string literals, 178–180
   exception handling, 177–184
   exception types, 178–180
   freeing
      arrays and scalars, 167–170
      resources of heap-allocated
        objects, 195
   local addresses
      disappearing stack frames, 185
      idiomatic problems, 186–187
      static interference, 186
   local scope problems, 187
   local variable lifetimes, 187
   memory leaks, 187, 253
   replacing global `new` and `delete`,
      173–176
   resource acquisition is initialization,
      190–195
   scalar *vs.* array allocation, 167–170
   scope and activation, `new` and `delete`,
      176–177
   static fix, 188–190
   throwing anonymous temporaries,
      181–182
   throwing pointers, 181
   throwing string literals, 177–180
memory leaks, 187, 253–258
methods, 24
Meyers, Scott, xvi, 105
migrating type-qualifiers, 52

mix-in classes, 281. *See also* interface
   classes.
mnemonic names, 3
Monostate pattern, 203–204
multiple inheritance, casting, 98–100

N

named return value optimization
   (NRV), 161
namespace
   anonymous, 55
   and `#define`, 62
naming conventions
   access protection, 23
   mnemonic names, 3
   self-documenting code, 3
   simplicity, 23
   specifying ownership, 254–255
   variable type in variable name, 23
`NDEBUG`, mysterious failures, 67
nonvirtual base class destructor
   addresses of base class subobjects,
      206–208
   exceptions, 208–209
   undefined behavior, 205
   virtual static member functions,
      205–206
NRV (named return value optimization), 161
null
   `dynamic_cast` result, 117
   pointers, 25
   references, 11
Null Object pattern, 282, 284, 294
numeric literals *vs.* constants, 4–6

O

object-oriented to non-object-oriented communication, 202
objects, temporary lifetime, 110–111
old-style casts, 102–103, 278
Oldham, Jeffrey, xv
operator delete, 206
operator new
  allocation failure, 172
  replacing, 173–176
  scalar allocation, 168–170
  scope and activation, 176–177
operator overloading, 258–264
operator precedence, 261–262
operators
  , (comma operator), 39–40
  ?: (conditional operator), 40
  -> (arrow operator), 58–60
  && (logical operator), 40
  || (logical operator), 40
  <<< (Sergeant operator), 48–49
  C++ base language, 14–17
  cast, 24–25
  cast *vs.* conversion, 24–25
  conversion, 24–25, 90–94
  evaluation order, 39–41
  function lookup, 56–58
  index operator, predefined, 16–17
  logical, 14–15
  lvalue, result of conditional operator, 15–16
  new [] operator, 39
  operator function lookup, 56–58
  overloading
    -> (arrow operator), 58–60
    evaluation order, 41
    operator function lookup, 56–58
    operators, 56–58
    precedence, 41

precedence, 17, 39–40
predefined index operator, 16–17
overloading
  -> (arrow operator), 58–60
  ambiguities, 5
  in class design, 258–262
  vs. default initialization, 8–9
  vs. hiding and overriding, 224–230
  increment/decrement operators, 264
  infix notation, 56–58
  operators, 56–58, 258–264
  virtual functions, 214–215
overriding
  definition, 232
  invisible functions, 228
  mechanisms, 230–236
  vs. overloading and hiding, 224–230
ownership. *See* aggregation *vs.* acquaintance.

P

parallel hierarchies, 274–275
parentheses (( )), allocating arrays, 35
passing arguments, 126
patterns
  Acyclic Visitor, 306
  Bridge, 21–22
  Command, 281–285
  Composite, 281, 283–284
  Decorator, 212, 281
  Factory Method, 229, 274–275
  Monostate, 203–204
  Null Object, 282, 284, 294
  Prototype, 223, 229, 282–283
  Proxy, 294
  Singleton, 7–8, 152, 204
  Strategy, 291–292

Template Method, 212–214
Visitor, 215, 227, 306
pencil cup, battleship in, 295
personal questions (about an object's
type), 116, 200, 275, 299–301
pimpl idiom. *See* Bridge pattern.
placement new
evaluation order of arguments, 39
invoking constructor, 127, 138, 155
replacing global new and delete, 174
platform dependence
conversions, 76
literals *vs.* constants, 5
POD (Plain Old Data) classes, 136
point of declaration of an enumerator, 54
pointer formal arguments, 49
pointer-to-const conversion, 81–82
pointer-to-multidimensional array, 87–88
pointer-to-pointer-to-base conversion,
86–87
pointer-to-pointer-to-const conversion,
82–86
pointers
containers of, 255–258
converting, 82–86
to functions, 13
to incomplete class types, 100–101
to local variables, 185
to members, 9
to members, converting, 120–123
ownership, 255–258
to pointers to derived classes, 86–87
precedence problems, 43–44
vs. references, 10–13
throwing, 181
polymorphism
algorithms, variant and invariant,
212–214

component coupling, 202
design firewalls, 202
dominance, 236–239
dynamic binding, 200
flexibility of template methods, 212–214
hiding
nonvirtual functions, 209–212
vs. overloading and overriding,
224–230
nonvirtual base class destructor
addresses of base class subobjects,
206–208
exceptions, 208–209
undefined behavior, 205
virtual static member functions,
205–206
object-oriented to non-object-oriented
communication, 202
overloading
vs. hiding and overriding, 224–230
virtual functions, 214–215. *See also*
default initialization.
overriding
definition, 232
mechanism, 230–236
vs. overloading and hiding, 224–230
switching on type codes, 200
type codes, 199–204
virtual assignment, 220–224
virtual copy construction, 223
virtual functions
calling in a nonvirtual manner, 211
calling in constructors and
destructors, 218–220
default argument initializers,
216–217. *See also* overloading,
virtual functions.
overloading, 214–215. *See also* default
initialization.

portability
  #if, 69–70
  null pointers, 25
precedence
  , (comma operator), 39–40
  ?: (conditional operator), 40
  && (logical operator), 40
  || (logical operator), 40
  and associativity, 42, 44–45
  fixing, 39–41
  index operators, 17
  levels of precedence, 42
  new [] operator, 39
  operator overloading, 41
  operators, 39–40, 261–262
  overview, 36–37
  pointers, 43–44
predefined index operator, 16–17
preprocessor
  assert macro, 72–74
  assertions, side effects, 72–74
  class implementation, varying with #if, 70–71
  constant-expressions, 67
  debug code, in executable modules, 67
  debugging, 66–69
  #define literals, 61–63
  #define pseudofunctions, 64–66
  #if
    debugging, 66–69
    platform independence, 69
    portability, 69–70
    in the real world, 71–72
    varying class implementation, 70–71
  literals, defining, 61–63
  NDEBUG, mysterious failures, 67
  pseudofunctions, defining, 64–66
  scope, #define literals, 61–63
preprocessor macros, side effects, 16

programmers
  adolescent behavior, 31–33
  ethical duties, 32–33
  unnecessary cleverness, 29–31
Programming in C++, 3
protected access, 277–280
protocol classes, 281. *See also* interface classes.
Prototype pattern, 223, 229, 282–283
Proxy pattern, 294
pseudofunctions, defining, 64–66
public inheritance, 281–285
pure virtual base classes, 24
pure virtual functions, calling, 212

Q

qualification conversions, 82–86
qualification of function typedef, 52
question mark colon (?:) conditional operator, 15–16, 40

R

readability. *See also* comments; maintenance.
  formatting code, 29–31
  unnecessary cleverness, 29–31
recompilation, avoiding, 21, 283
reference counting, 257
reference counting inclusions, 152–153. *See also* Schwarz counter.
reference data members, 245–247
reference type name, ignoring qualifiers, 10
references
  as aliases, 10–13, 112–115

to arrays, 12
binding to functions, 13
binding to lvalue, 11
casting objects, 12–13
`const` type-qualifier, 10–11
conversions, 112–115
to functions, 13
to incomplete class types, 100–101
initializing, 112–115
to local variables, 185
null, 11
vs. pointers, 10–13
return values for functions, 11–12
underusing, 10–13
`volatile` qualifiers, 10–11
`reinterpret_cast`, 76, 100–101, 146
remote changes (bugs caused by), 77, 101, 103, 105
resource acquisition is initialization, 28, 190–195
resource handle. *See* resource acquisition is initialization.
resource management. *See* memory and resource management.
resources, freeing heap-allocated objects, 195
return value optimization (RVO), 158–162
reuse
code, 281–285
global variables, 6
white-box. *See* inheritance.
runtime static initialization, ordering, 150–153
runtime type queries, 299–301
RVO (return value optimization), 158–162

S

Saks, Dan, xv, xvi
scalars, freeing, 167–170
Schwarz, Jerry, 152
Schwarz counter, 152–153. *See also* reference counting inclusions.
scope
#define literals, 61–63
local scope problems, 187
restriction, variables, 45–48
scoping variables, initialization, 129–132
self-documenting code
avoiding comments, 2
naming conventions, 3
self-initialization, 53–55
Semantics, xiv
Sergeant operator (<<<), 48–49
set/get interfaces, 241–245
Singleton pattern, 7–8, 152, 204
slicing
derived class objects, 79–81
hierarchy design, 286
smart pointer idiom, 59, 282
social commentary
adolescent behavior, 31–33
array/initializer confusion, 36
capability queries, 302
increment/decrement operators, 267
old-style casts, 102
operator overloading, 258
personal questions of an object, 299–300
unnecessary cleverness, 29
Software Engineering Code of Ethics..., 32
square brackets ([ ]), allocating arrays, 35

Stark, Kathy, 3
static casts, 103–105, 278
static members in constructors,
    initializing, 163–165
static types, 55
static variables, runtime static initializa-
    tion problems, 151
`static_cast`, 103–105, 278
Strategy pattern, 291–292
string literal temporary for `throw`
    expression, 181
string literals, throwing, 177–181
Stroustrup, Bjarne, 295
Strunk, William, 26
subexpressions, evaluation order, 37–39
Sutter, Herb, xvi
switch-statement structure, 18
switch-statements, 17
switching on type codes, 200, 292–295
syntax
  arrays
    confused with initializers, 35–36
    migrating type-qualifiers, 52
  associativity
    and precedence, 42
    problems, 44–45
  const member functions, 248
  const pointers, 50
  `const` type-qualifier, migrating, 52
  declaration-specifiers, ordering, 50–51
  evaluation order
    , (comma operator), 39–40
    ?: (conditional operator), 40
    && (logical operator), 40
    || (logical operator), 40
    fixing, 39–41
    `new` operator, 39
    operator overloading, 41

  overview, 36–37
  placement `new`, 39
  subexpressions, 37–39
extern types, 55
function/object ambiguity, 51
infix notation, 56–58
initialization
  initializers, confused with arrays,
    35–36
  self-initialization, 53–55
initializers, confused with arrays, 35–36
lexical analysis, 49
maximal munch, 48–49
migrating type-qualifiers, 52
`new [ ]` operator, 39
operator function lookup, 56–58
operator overloading
  evaluation order, 41
  operator function lookup, 56–58
overloading
  -> (arrow operator), 58–60
  infix notation, 56–58
  operators, 56–58
placement `new`, evaluation order, 39
pointer formal arguments, 49
pointers, precedence problems, 43–44
precedence problems
  and associativity, 42, 44–45
  levels of precedence, 42
  pointers, 43–44
scope restriction, variables, 45–48
self-initialization, 53–55
`for` statement
  variable scope restriction, 45–48
  vs. `while` statement, 47
static types, 55
subexpressions, evaluation order, 37–39
templates, instantiating, 49

token identification, 48–49
type-qualifiers, migrating, 52
types, linkage-specifiers, 55
variables, scope restriction, 45–48
`volatile` type-qualifiers,
    migrating, 52
`while` statement *vs.* `for` statement, 47

T

Template Method pattern, 212–214
template methods, flexibility, 212–214
templated copy operations, 268–270
templates, instantiating, 49
temporaries, conversions, 112–115
temporary objects, 110–111
terminology. *See* diction.
`throw` expression, 181
throwing
    anonymous temporaries, 181–182
    pointers, 181
    string literals, 177–180
thunks, 235
token identification, 48–49
type-based control structures, 292–295
type codes, 199–204, 292–295
type-qualifiers
    `const`
        migrating, 52
        references, 10–11
    `volatile`
        migrating, 52
        references, 10–11
types
    converting. *See* casting; `void *`.
    linkage-specifiers, 55

U

unnecessary cleverness, 29–31
uses. *See* acquaintance.

V

value semantics, 286
variables
    encoding type in name, 23
    scope restriction, 45–48
`vectors` *vs.* arrays, 36, 168, 196
vertical lines (||) logical operator, 40
virtual assignment, 220–224
virtual base default, initializing,
    142–147
virtual constructor idiom, 223. *See also*
    Prototype pattern.
virtual copy construction, 223
virtual functions
    calling in a nonvirtual manner, 211
    calling in constructors and destructors,
        218–220
    default argument initializers,
        216–217
    overloading, 214–215
    pure, calling, 212
virtual static member functions,
    205–206
visibility *vs.* access protection, 19–23
Visitor pattern, 215, 227, 306
`void *`, 75–78. *See also* casting.
`volatile` type-qualifier
    migrating, 52
    references, 10–11
vptr (pointer to a vtbl), 231
vtbl (virtual function table), 231–236

W

`while` statement *vs.* `for` statement, 47
White, E.B., 26
white-box reuse. *See* inheritance.
Wilson, Matthew, xv
word choice. *See* diction.
Writings from The New Yorker, 26

Z

Zolman, Leor, xv

informIT

YOUR GUIDE TO IT REFERENCE

Articles

Keep your edge with thousands of free articles, in-depth features, interviews, and IT reference recommendations – all written by experts you know and trust.

Online Books

Answers in an instant from **InformIT Online Book's** 600+ fully searchable on line books. For a limited time, you can get your first 14 days **free**.

POWERED BY
Safari
TECH BOOKS ONLINE

Catalog

Review online sample chapters, author biographies and customer rankings and choose exactly the right book from a selection of over 5,000 titles.

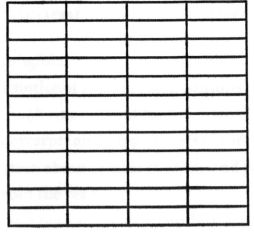

Register

Yo...

You ma...

- Adv... book
- Rel...
- Cha... ing titles
- Info... tions
  thr...
- Not... ces,
  trac... 's

Cont...

If you are...
manuscr...

Editorial...
Addison-...
75 Arling...
Boston, ...
Email: A...

DATE DUE

QA 76.73 .C153 D488 2003

Dewhurst, Stephen C.

C++ gotchas

DEMCO

Visit us on the Web: http://www.awprofessional.com